Fod...
Sin...

Fodor's Travel Publications, Inc.
New York • Toronto • London • Sydney • Auckland

ISBN 0–679–02340–2

Fodor's Singapore

Editor: Craig Seligman
Area Editor: Nigel Fisher
Contributors: Robin Dannhorn, Tan Lee Leng, Violet Oon, Marcy Pritchard, Linda K. Schmidt
Creative Director: Fabrizio La Rocca
Cartographer: David Lindroth
Illustrator: Karl Tanner
Cover Photograph: R. Ian Lloyd/Westlight

Design: Vignelli Associates

Special Sales

Fodor's Travel Publications are available at special discounts for bulk purchases (100 copies or more) for sales promotions or premiums. Special editions, including personalized covers, excerpts of existing guides, and corporate imprints, can be created in large quantities for special needs. For more information write to Special Marketing, Fodor's Travel Publications, 201 East 50th St., New York, NY 10022. Inquiries from Canada should be sent to Random House of Canada, Ltd., Marketing Dept., 1265 Aerowood Dr., Mississauga, Ontario L4W 1B9. Inquiries from the United Kingdom should be sent to Fodor's Travel Publications, 20 Vauxhall Bridge Rd., London, England SW1V 2SA.

Contents

Maps

Foreword

We wish to express our gratitude to United Airlines and Finnair for their help in producing this book.

While every care has been taken to assure the accuracy of the information in this guide, the passage of time will always bring change, and consequently, the publisher cannot accept responsibility for errors that may occur.

All prices and opening times quoted here are based on information supplied to us at press time. Hours and admission fees may change, however, and the prudent traveler will avoid inconvenience by calling ahead.

Fodor's wants to hear about your travel experiences, both pleasant and unpleasant. When a hotel or restaurant fails to live up to its billing, let us know; we will investigate the complaint and revise our entries where the facts warrant it.

Send your letters to the editors of Fodor's Travel Publications, 201 E. 50th Street, New York, NY 10022.

Highlights and Fodor's Choice

Highlights

More than 5 million visitors come to Singapore every year, generating an estimated S$6 billion. That is nearly two visitors for every resident. To promote tourism, the government imposes a 4% tax on restaurant and hotel bills to pay for Singapore Tourist Promotion Board's (STPB) advertising. Tourism is a big business for Singapore, and the republic has developed a highly efficient infrastructure to process visitors.

No other city in the world caters quite so diligently to the traveler. Consequently, the competition within the city for the traveler's patronage is fierce. Singapore is constantly building new hotels, renovating old properties, developing new recreation facilities, improving the transportation network, and trying to save or reconstruct the few monuments to its past that have managed to escape the bulldozer of urban renewal.

In the center of Singapore, off Orchard Road and behind the Hilton, the new 260-room **Four Seasons** hotel should open in 1993, but the most-talked-about new hotel development is the 102-year-old **Raffles.** In the scramble of the hotel-building boom of the past two decades, Raffles was forsaken— left as a nostalgic anomaly in the new republic and visited by tour groups searching for the romance of Joseph Conrad's Singapore. That Raffles is gone. After two years of renovation, a resurrection of the turn-of-the-century Raffles opened in 1991. Visiting tourists are directed to a new complex, designed to fit in context with the old hotel, where they can visit the Raffles museum, browse through a shopping arcade, and sip a Singapore sling in a reproduction of the Long Bar. Hotel guests stay in expensive suites furnished and decorated with period pieces from the 1920s. This new Raffles is sure to be a subject of criticism and acclaim until Singaporeans once again become accustomed to the sanitized reconstruction of their heritage.

In line with many of Singapore's redesigns of the old, the reconstituted **Haw Par Villa** (Tiger Balm Gardens), once a garden of eccentric statues portraying Chinese gods, is another plastic, Disney-like theme park, this time giving high-tech, multimedia renditions of Chinese mythology. Another theme park, the **Tang Dynasty Village** at Jurong Park, opened in 1992. The layout of the village follows the pattern of Chang-An (Xian), which was the capital of the Tang Dynasty some 1,300 years ago (AD 616–906). Like Haw Par Villa, it is a leisure and entertainment theme park that emphasizes ancient Chinese culture and history while blending with the modern leisure lifestyles of Singapore.

The restoration of shophouses in **Tanjong Pajar,** an integral part of Chinatown, is achieving some feeling of authenticity. The opening of two boutique hotels (the **Duxton** and the **Inn of the Sixth Happiness**), several superior restaurants, and a number of pubs and cafés has given the area new life. The government's current commitment is to revitalize the area with pedestrian streets and rebuild another 188 shop-7houses. A similar restoration project is under way along the Singapore River. By 1994, the warehouses and shophouses along the river's banks should be restored and converted to entertainment and leisure-related facilities, such as outdoor cafés and souvenir shops. The area's theme was inspired by the little-known fact that the Singapore cat is the smallest domestic cat in the world. Cat sculptures will be placed along the riverbank, cat stories will be created, and cat souvenirs will be on sale. Tourist commercialism is Singapore's forte.

Bugis Street, once a center of late-night risqué entertainment, is back in swing but a shadow of its former self. Lee Yuan Kew's government had closed down Bugis Street a decade ago—bars, clubs, and transvestites vying with the prettiest women for the attention of male carousers were not Lee's notion of a model society. The demise of Bugis Street symbolized for many a bland new Singapore, its heritage torn down and replaced. Concern that this image would deter tourists prompted the planned development of a re-created Bugis Street, but it lacks the old sparkle, and visitors look disappointed as they pass sanitized hawker food stands while searching in vain for the night performers and revelers.

Another re-creation is the **Telok Ayer Market.** The old covered Victorian market, which has been torn down to make way for office buildings, has been rebuilt off Boon Tat Street, near its original site, as a planned food court. It offers hawker stalls and, in the evening, performances by musicians and entertainers.

With the escalation of hotel rates and the costs of goods in stores, Singapore is no longer the bargain for luxury that it was five years ago, with one exception—dining out. For many people, dining in Singapore is a draw in itself. Singapore offers not only a wide range of cuisines, but also very reasonable prices at even the most elegant restaurants. An evening of gastronomy at the Oriental's Fourchettes restaurant or an Italian repast at the Sheraton Towers will be less than US$60 for two—meals that would cost four times as much in France or Italy, without the impeccable service. Until now, the top hotels have offered the finest dining, but new smaller, chef-owned restaurants catering to the growing middle class are appearing. Already there is a complex of small European restaurants in Marina Village, a new development area on reclaimed land south of the Shenton Way financial district. Hawker centers (complexes of food stalls), where a dinner of several dishes costs under S$20 for two, still offer the best value. One of the best hawker centers opened at Marina South.

Crime is still a rare occurrence in Singapore. Tough laws have prevented any increase in drug trafficking—the possession of 20 g of cocaine draws the death penalty. Though there is the occasional purse snatching, the visitor to Singapore enjoys a remarkable feeling of security.

Development continues for **Sentosa,** Singapore's resort island. In an attempt to lure more visitors to this pleasure park, a new 750-meter-long causeway will link the island to the main island of Singapore. The project, which will include a bridge for vehicles and an elevated track for a people-mover system, is set for completion by 1993. The island is being enlarged through a reclamation project to include the islet of Buran Durat.

In an attempt to make Sentosa a destination in its own right, the 215-room **Beaufort Resort Hotel** opened in 1992 on 25 acres of land. Another hotel, the **Shangri-La Sentosa Beach Resort,** built in the shape of a boomerang to fit in the side of a hill, also opened. Two more hotels are to be built before the end of the decade.

The new **Underwater World Sentosa** opened in 1991. This oceanarium has two tanks housing thousands of fish. A 100-meter-long curved acrylic tunnel with a moving walkway runs along the bottom of these tanks, minimizing the separation between the viewer and the underwater world. In addition, there are three new Disney-style theme parks. There will also be an **Asian Cultural and Entertainment Village,** which will feature each Asian country's culture in floating villages. However, even with these amusement parks and hotels, Sentosa is likely to remain an attraction for visitors from other Asian countries rather than from Europe or the Americas.

Lee Yuan Kew, who ruled as Singapore's prime minister for 31 years before stepping down, now serves as senior minister until he can be voted in as the republic's president. Though still treated with awe, Lee and his People's Action Party (PAP) face growing opposition to his Machiavellian tactics. Detention without trial still exists, and denial of free press continues. One recent dictate bans chewing gum in the republic; those convicted of selling it face hefty fines.

With its vast range of culinary delights, superb hotels, fashionable shops, and easy transportation system, Singapore will continue to be a very comfortable stop for tourists exploring the more exotic destinations of the republic's neighbors. With more exotic Southeast Asian destinations opening deluxe resorts, Singapore is looking to the convention business: By 1994 the new convention site at Marina Square should be open, and two adjacent hotels will be nearing completion.

Fodor's Choice

No two people will agree on what makes a perfect vacation, but it can be fun and helpful to know what others think. We hope you'll have a chance to experience some of Fodor's Choices yourself while visiting Singapore. For detailed information on individual entries, see the relevant sections of this guidebook.

Special Moments

Cricket on the Padang

Street *wayangs* (Chinese opera)

Sunday breakfast at a bird-singing café

Breakfast at the Jurong Bird Park

Breakfast at the zoo with Ah Meng, the star orangutan

Acrobatic *teppanyaki* at the Keyaki restaurant

The view from the Compass Rose restaurant

Sunsets from Mt. Faber

Taste Treats

Hairy crab in the autumn

Tea at Peranakan Place

High tea at Goodwood Park

Fiery-hot pepper crabs at the Long Beach Seafood Restaurant

Fish-head curry at Banana Leaf Apollo

Dim sum and Monk Jumps over the Wall at Hai Tien Lo

Dosai pancakes at Annalakshmi

Shark's fin at Tung Lok Shark's Fin Restaurant

Roast suckling pig at the Majestic Restaurant

Festivals and Seasonal Events

Thaipusam (mid-January–early February)

Festival of the Hungry Ghosts (August–September)

Sights and Museums

Botanic Gardens

Carved murals at The Dynasty hotel

Chinese exhibitions at Empress Place

Fuk Tak Chi Temple

Peranakan Place

Pioneers of Singapore Museum

Singapore Zoological Gardens

Sri Mariamman Temple

Sultan Mosque

Restaurants

Chiang Jian—Shanghainese (*Very Expensive*)

Latour—Continental (*Very Expensive*)

Li Bai—Cantonese (*Expensive–Very Expensive*)

Cherry Garden—Hunanese (*Expensive*)

Nadaman—Japanese (*Expensive*)

Tandoor—North Indian (*Expensive*)

Cairnhill Thai Seafood Restaurant—Thai (*Moderate–Expensive*)

Dragon City—Szechuan (*Moderate–Expensive*)

La Brasserie—French (*Moderate–Expensive*)

Long Beach Seafood Restaurant—Seafood (*Moderate–Expensive*)

Bombay Meadowlands—Indian Vegetarian (*Moderate*)

Pete's Place—Italian (*Moderate*)

Banana Leaf Apollo—South Indian (*Inexpensive*)

Hotels

Goodwood Park (*Very Expensive*)

The Oriental (*Very Expensive*)

Shangri-La (*Very Expensive*)

The Dynasty (*Expensive*)

Sheraton Towers (*Expensive*)

Duxton Hotel (*Moderate*)

Ladyhill Hotel (*Moderate*)

Cairnhill Hotel (*Inexpensive*)

Inn of the Sixth Happiness (*Inexpensive*)

RELC International House (*Inexpensive*)

Mitre Hotel (*Budget*)

Shopping

Tudor Court Gallery for fashion

Robinsons department store

Boutiques at the Hilton

Singapore Handicraft Centre

Holland Village for antiques and souvenirs

Zhu Jiao Market for Asian foods

Chinatown Centre's wet market

P. Govindasamy Pillai for Indian silks

China Silk House for Chinese silks

Islands

Kusu Island

Pulau Sakeng

Nightlife

Brannigans pub

Neptune nightclub

Saxophone jazz club

Night bazaar at Singapore Handicraft Centre

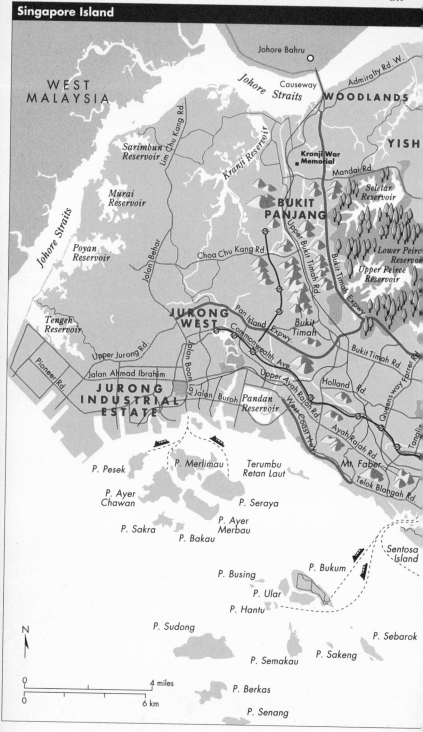

Singapore Island

WEST
MALAYSIA

Johore Bahru

Johore Straits

Causeway

Admiralty Rd. W.

WOODLANDS

Kranji War
Memorial

YISH

Sarimbun
Reservoir

Lim Chu Kang Rd.

Kranji Reservoir

Mandai Rd.

Murai
Reservoir

BUKIT
PANJANG

Seletar
Reservoir

Poyan
Reservoir

Johore Straits

Jalan Bahar

Choa Chu Kang Rd.

Upper Bukit Timah Rd.

Bukit Timah Expwy.

Lower Peirce
Reservoir

Upper Peirce
Reservoir

JURONG
WEST

Pan Island Expwy.

Bukit
Timah

Tengeh
Reservoir

Upper Jurong Rd.

Jalan Boon Lay

Commonwealth Ave.

Bukit Timah Rd.

Pioneer Rd.

Jalan Ahmad Ibrahim

Jalan Buroh

Upper Ayah Rajah Rd.

West Coast Hwy.

Holland Rd.

Queensway

Farrer Rd.

JURONG
INDUSTRIAL
ESTATE

Pandan
Reservoir

Ayah Rajah Rd.

Mt. Faber

Tanglin

P. Pesek

P. Merlimau

Terumbu
Retan Laut

Telok Blangah Rd.

P. Ayer
Chawan

P. Seraya

P. Sakra

P. Ayer
Merbau

P. Bakau

Sentosa
Island

P. Busing

P. Bukum

P. Ular

P. Hantu

N

P. Sudong

P. Sebarok

0 _____ 4 miles

P. Sakeng

0 _____ 6 km

P. Semakau

P. Berkas

P. Senang

TO DESARU,
MALAYSIA

WEST
MALAYSIA

Johore Straits

P.
Seletar

S. Seletar

Yishun Ave 2

P.
Serangoon

P. Ubin

TO P.
TEKONG

P. Ketam

Serangoon
Harbour

CHANGI

Yio Chu Kang Rd.

Punggol Rd.

Loyang Ave

PUNGGOL

S. Serangoon

Changi
Airport

SERANGOON

Upper Serangoon Rd.

U. Changi Rd.

Upper Thomson Rd.

Central Expwy.

Tampines Rd.

MacRitchie
Reservoir

Paya Lebar Rd.

Pan Island Expressway

BEDOK

Airport Blvd.

Changi Coast Rd.

New Upper Changi Rd.

Sims Ave.

Serangoon Rd.

Geylang Rd.

East Coast Rd.

Kallang Rd.

KATONG

Mountbatten Rd.

East Coast Parkway

Orchard Rd.

Nicoll Hwy.

National
Stadium

World Trade
Centre/Ferry
Terminal

P. Brani

Buran
Darat

Strait of Singapore

P. Tekukor

P. Renggit
Kusu Island

Lazarus Island

Sister's
Islands

St. John's
Island

Subway & Rail Lines
---- North-South MRT line
—— East-West MRT line
— Railroad lines
⊖ Subway stop

Southeast Asia

CHINA

Guangzho
Macao OO **HONG KO**

Mandalay   Hanoi
UNION OF   Luang
MYANMAR   Prabang   Haiphong
(BURMA)   **LAOS**
                Vientiane   *HAINAN*
Pegu   Chiang
        Mai
Yangon   Hue
(Rangoon)   Danang
        THAILAND

Bangkok   **VIETNAM**

Andaman   Angkor Wat
Sea   **CAMBODIA**
                (KAMPUCHEA)
Isthmus of   Phnom Penh   Ho Chi Minh City
Kra   *Gulf of*   (Saigon)
                Thailand
                                        PALAWAN

        Songkhla   *South China*
                        Sea
Georgetown   Bandar Seri
                PENINSULAR   Begawan
                MALAYSIA **MALAYSIA** **BRUNEI** *SABAI*
Medan   Kuala Lumpur
                                SARAWAK
                Johore Bahru   Kuching
                SINGAPORE   *BORNEO*
SUMATRA
                Karimata   KALIMANTAN
KEPULAUAN   Jambi
                        I N D O N E S I A
        Palembang   *Strait*
                                Banjarmasin
G R E A T E R   S U N D A   *I S L*
                Jakarta
                Bandung   *Java Sea*
                        Surabaya
                Yogyakarta *JAVA*
                        Malang   *LES*
                                BALI

0   500 miles   N
0   750 km   *LOMBOK*

INDIAN OCEAN

Taipei

TAIWAN

PACIFIC OCEAN

LUZON

Quezon City

Manila

PHILIPPINES

MINDORO

PALAU

PANAY

Ililo

Bacaloa

Cebu

SAMAR

NEGROS

Sulu Sea

MINDANAO

Davao

Celebes Sea

THE

HALMAHERA

Makassar Strait

SULUWESI
(The Celebes)

M O L U C C A S

BURU

SERAM

A N D S

Banda Sea

Ujung
Pandang

**PAPUA-
NEW GUINEA**

IRIAN JAYA

*KEPULAUAN
ARU*

Flores Sea

SER SUNDA ISLANDS

*KEPULAUAN
TANIMBAR*

FLORES

TIMOR

Timor Sea

SUMBA

World Time Zones

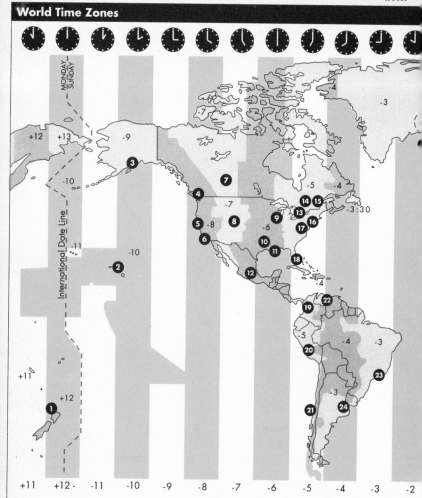

Numbers below vertical bands relate each zone to Greenwich Mean Time (0 hrs.).
Local times frequently differ from these general indications,
as indicated by light-face numbers on map.

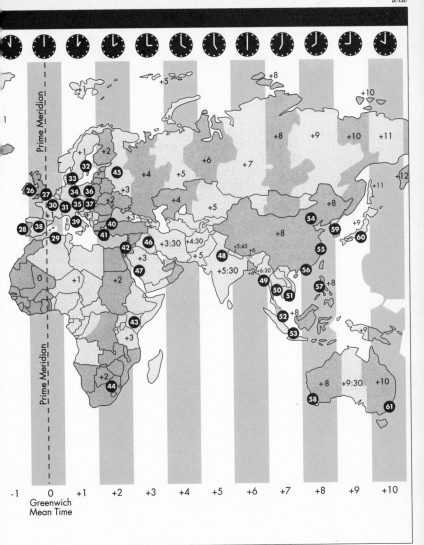

Introduction

By Nigel Fisher

Nigel Fisher is the editor of the monthly travel publication Voyager International. *He has traveled extensively throughout Asia and the world.*

As you are efficiently processed through Changi International Airport, then whisked away in a taxi or air-conditioned coach along a park-lined expressway to your high-rise hotel, don't let first impressions lead you to write Singapore off as just another modern international city. Though it may no longer be the richly exotic and romantic city so vividly documented by Conrad and Kipling, Singapore is yet a unique city where the flavor, spirituality, and gentle manners of the East peacefully coexist with the comforts, conveniences, and efficiency of the West.

Here you'll find some of the world's most luxurious hotels, offering incomparable service and all the amenities, from fitness centers with computer-monitored exercise equipment to thick terry-cloth bathrobes. On Orchard Road, smartly dressed shoppers browse among glittering shop windows before heading into the dozens of huge side-by-side shopping complexes, jam-packed with boutiques carrying the latest Paris fashions or Japanese electronics. And in elegant French restaurants, with gleaming silver and crystal and elaborate displays of orchids and roses, tuxedoed waiters serve some of the best cuisine this side of the Seine.

Here you'll also find ethnic neighborhoods, built up around mosques and temples, where Chinese or Indian or Malay merchants dressed in traditional garb hawk the herbal medicines or spices or batiks that spill out of their small shops onto the narrow streets. At the many food centers that dot the city, Teochew and Hokkien, Tamil and Malay cooks in adjacent open-front stalls whip up authentic and delicious dishes whose recipes have been handed down in their families for generations.

To arrive in Singapore is to step into a world where the muezzin call to prayer competes with the bustle of capitalism; where old men play mah-jongg in the streets and white-clad bowlers send the ball flying down well-tended cricket pitches; where Chinese fortune tellers and high-priced management consultants advise the same entrepreneur.

This great diversity of lifestyles, cultures, and religions thrives within the framework of a well-ordered society. Singapore is a spotlessly clean—some say sterile—modern metropolis, surrounded by green, groomed parks. It is populated by 2.7 million extremely polite, well-mannered people and efficiently run by an autocratic government that tolerates little dissent.

Singaporeans' standard of living and personal income are the highest in Asia, second only to Japan's. Hospitals and clinics are substantially subsidized. Public and private welfare agencies take care of the indigent, so there are virtually no beggars or homeless people. A compulsory savings scheme ensures that senior citizens are provided for when they retire. Housing is subsidized, and by the mid-1990s, 80% of the population will own their own apartment in 10- to 20-story concrete apartment blocks.

Singapore has little crime. Strict laws and education programs keep drugs from eating away at the fabric of society. The streets are well lit and litter-free, with clearly marked crosswalks, and there is an excellent and inexpensive public transport system. Education is free and compulsory. Every schoolchild must study English and either Mandarin, Malay, or Tamil (the four official languages).

All these benefits have been bought at a price. Critics see former prime minister Lee Kuan Yew, who steered the republic's evolution for three decades, as a benevolent dictator and accused him and the ruling party, the People's Action Party (PAP), of social programming, promoting a bland uniformity, and infringement of individual rights and freedoms.

Trial by jury has been replaced by a court where the accused's fate depends upon a single judge. In order to fight communism—a very real threat in the 1950s and 1960s—Singapore instituted the Internal Security Act, which allows the government to incarcerate indefinitely anyone it wishes, and without any trial at all. The death penalty is meted out to those caught in possession of drugs, and illegal workers currently are caned before being deported.

The policemen you see on the streets may be all smiles, but behind the scenes, highly specialized teams are ready to move in at a moment's notice. Where the police are not, video cameras may be—note the boxes suspended over busy intersections, poised to catch unsuspecting traffic violators.

There are fines for this and that. Littering can bring a fine of S$1,000 (about US$500); smoking or chewing gum in public places (including taxis and air-conditioned restaurants), S$500; jaywalking, S$50. Swampland and landfills are often turned into pleasant green parks, but with signs designating what behavior is permissible and what is not, along with the type of penalty imposed for infractions.

Freedom of the press has been curtailed. When the *Far Eastern Economic Review* (published in Hong Kong) printed an article on Singapore that the PAP did not like, the magazine was banned. The English-language newspaper, the *Straits Times*, and a spinoff, the *Business Times*, voice the ruling party's views. Several books are not permitted here, such as *The Last Temptation of Christ* by Nikos Kazantzakis and *Rock Star* by Jackie Collins.

In the name of progress, character-rich buildings and shop-houses that have been homes to generations have been torn down and replaced by modern, uniform concrete dwellings or glass office buildings. Singapore is architecturally sterile, with only isolated remains of its heritage. Only now are the voices of conservationists being heard—a little late, because the last Malay kampong was demolished in 1989.

Various "social engineering" campaigns are always in progress, such as for family planning, increased productivity, or greater courtesy. Since the family-planning campaign worked too well, there is now government pressure for the young to marry and start a family; various government departments arrange weekend "mixers" to help things along.

Singaporeans don't necessarily like the fact that Lee Kuan Yew has controlled their future, but they accept the sacrifices they must make, recognizing that it is largely as a result of his firm control and acumen that Singapore is a safe, clean, comfortable, prosperous nation. At the end of 1990 Lee resigned his prime ministership, though still remaining a senior minister in the government. Rumors suggest that he will accept the post as the republic's president and, at the same time, groom his son to take over the reins of the PAP leadership. In the meantime, Lee's designate, Goh Chok Tong, serves as Singapore's prime minister.

NOTE: Throughout this book, frequent and varied references to the country directly to the north of Singapore are made, and the nomenclature can be a bit confusing. *Malaysia* is the name given to the country in 1963, when it became an independent federation comprising *Peninsular Malaysia*, or *West Malaysia* (the southern part of the *Malay Peninsula*, which also includes part of Thailand), and *East Malaysia* (the northern portion of the island of Borneo, consisting of the states of Sabah and Sarawak). *Malaya* refers to pre-1963 Malaysia.

From Lion City to Asian Tiger: A Brief History

In a part of the world where histories tend to be ancient and rich, Singapore is unique in having almost no history at all. Modern Singapore tends to date its history from the early morning of January 29, 1819, when a representative of the British East India Company, Thomas Stamford Raffles, stepped ashore at the mouth of the Singapore River, beginning the process that would quickly turn a sleepy backwater into one of Asia's main commercial and financial centers. But let us go a bit farther back.

The Early Days

Though little is known of Singapore's early history, it is clear that by the 7th century AD Malays had a settlement here known as Temasek—"sea town." According to legend, a 13th-century prince of Palembang (Sumatra) landed on the island while seeking shelter from a storm and sighted a strange animal, which he believed to be a lion but was more likely a tiger. The prince subsequently fought and defeated the ruler of the settlement and proclaimed himself king, then renamed the island Singa Pura, Sanskrit for "lion city." (More appropriately, Singapore is today referred to as one of the Asian Tigers, in recognition of its economic success.)

The first recorded history of Singapore, from a Chinese chronicler who visited in 1330, tells of a thriving Malay settlement here. By the 14th century, Singa Pura had become an active trading city with wealth and importance enough to build a walled fortress—and enough to make others covet the island. Drawn into a battle between the Java-based Majapahit empire and the Siamese for control of the Malay Peninsula, Singa Pura was destroyed and the settlement was abandoned to the jungle.

In 1390 or so, Iskandar Shah (or Parameswara, as the Portuguese called him), another Palembang prince, broke from the Majapahit empire and was granted asylum on the island. After killing the chieftain, he installed himself as ruler but was driven out before long by the Javanese and fled north into the peninsula. Singa Pura became a Thai vassal state until it was claimed by the Malacca Sultanate, which Iskandar Shah had established and brought to great prominence a few years after fleeing the island.

When, in 1511, the Portuguese seized Malacca, the Malay admiral fled to Singa Pura and established a new capital at Johor Lama. Obscurity engulfed Singa Pura in 1613, when the Portuguese reported laying waste to a small Malay settlement at the mouth of the river.

Enter Raffles

With the development of shipping routes to the West around the Cape of Good Hope and the opening of China to trade, the Malay Peninsula became strategically and commercially important to the West. To protect its shipping interests, the British secured Penang in 1786 and threw the Dutch out of Malacca (who had thrown the Portuguese out earlier) in 1795. In 1818, to prevent any further northward expansion of the Dutch, who controlled the East Indies (now Indonesia), Lord Hastings, governor-general of India, gave tacit approval to Thomas Stamford Raffles, an employee of the British East India Company, to secure a British trading settlement and harbor on the southern part of the Malay Peninsula.

On January 29, 1819, Raffles made an exploratory visit to Singa Pura, which had come under the dominion of the Sultan of Johore. When Raffles arrived, the two sons of the previous sultan, who had died six years earlier, were in dispute over who would inherit the throne. Raffles backed the claim of the elder brother, Tunku Hussein Mohamed Shah, and proclaimed him sultan.

Offering to support the new sultanate with British military strength, Raffles persuaded him to grant the British a lease allowing them to establish a trading post on the island in return for an annual rent; within a week the negotiations were concluded. (A later treaty ceded the island outright to the British in return for increased pensions and cash payments for the sultan and his island representative.)

Thus began the continual rapid changing and adapting that characterizes Singapore to this day: Within three years, the small fishing village, surrounded by swamps and jungle and populated by only tigers and 200 or so Malays, had become a boomtown of 10,000 immigrants, administered by 74 British employees of the East India Company. In 1826 Singapore joined Penang and Malacca in Malaya to form the British India–controlled Straits Settlements (named for the Strait of Malacca, also called the Straits—the channel between Sumatra and the Malay Peninsula that connects the Indian Ocean with the South China Sea). In 1867 the Straits Settlements became a crown colony.

As colonial administrators and businessmen, the British led a segregated life, maintaining the British lifestyle and shielding themselves from the local population and the climate. In the humid tropical heat, they would promenade along the Padang (cricket green), men in high-collared, buttoned-up white linen suits and women in grand ensembles complete with corsets, petticoats, and long kid gloves. In part, they believed that maintaining a distance and the appearance of invulnerability would help them win the respect and fear of the locals. Indeed, the heavily outnumbered colonials needed all the respect they could muster.

But holding on to familiar ways also gave the colonials a sense of security in this foreign land where danger was never far away—in the mid-1850s, for example, five people a week were carried off by tigers.

As Singapore grew, the British erected splendid public buildings, churches (including St. Andrew's Cathedral, built to resemble Netley Abbey in Hampshire, England), and hotels, often using Indian convicts for labor. The Muslim, Hindu, Taoist, and Buddhist communities—swelling rapidly from the influx of fortune-seeking settlers from Malaya, India, and South China—built mosques, temples, and shrines. Magnificent houses for wealthy merchants sprang up, and the harbor became lined with *godowns* (warehouses) to hold all the goods passing through the port.

It was certainly an exotic trade that poured through Singapore. Chinese junks came loaded with tea, porcelain, silks, and artworks; Bugis (Indonesian) schooners carried in cargos of precious spices, rare tropical hardwoods, camphor, and produce from all parts of Indonesia. These goods, and more like them from Siam, the Philippines, and elsewhere in the region, were traded in Singapore for manufactured textiles, coal, iron, cement, weapons, and machinery and other fruits of Europe's industrial revolution. Another major product traded here by the British was opium, grown in India and sold to the Chinese.

Meanwhile, much of the island continued to be covered by thick jungle. As late as the 1850s, there were dozens of tigers still to be found here. Early experiments with agriculture (spices, cotton, coffee, etc.) were soon abandoned, as almost nothing except coconuts would grow successfully in the sandy and marshy soil. (Singapore does, however, have the distinction of having introduced the rubber plant to Malaya: In 1877 the first seedlings were successfully grown here by botanist H. N. Ridley, then director of Singapore's Botanic Gardens, from plants brought out of Brazil.)

With the advent of steamships (which found Singapore's deep-water harbor ideal) and the opening of the Suez Canal in 1869, the port thrived as the "Gateway to the East." Its position at the southern end of the Straits made it a vital link in the chain of ports and coaling stations for steamers. Shipyards were established to repair the oceangoing cargo carriers and to build the ever-increasing number of barges and lighters bringing cargo ashore to the godowns. With the development of the rubber industry in Malaya starting in the 1870s, Singapore became the world's top exporter of the commodity.

The 20th Century

By the turn of the century, Singapore had become the entrepôt of the East, a mixture of adventurers and "respectable middle classes." World War I hardly touched the island, although its defenses were strengthened to support the needs of the British navy, for which Singapore was an important base. Until 1921 the Japanese and the British were allies and no need was felt to maintain a large naval presence in the region, but then the United States, anxious about Japan's growing military strength, prevailed on Britain to cancel its treaty with the Japanese, and defense of Singapore became a priority. A massive military expansion took place: Barracks were created for up to 100,000 troops, and Sentosa Island was heavily fortified with huge naval guns.

As the likelihood of war in the Pacific grew, Singapore's garrison was further strengthened, and naval shipyards and airfields were constructed. The British were complacent about the impregnability of Singapore, expecting that any attack would come from the sea and that they were well prepared to meet such an attack. But the Japanese landed to the north, in Malaya. The two British battleships that had been posted to Singapore were sunk, and the Japanese land forces raced down the peninsula on bicycles.

When the Japanese made their first bombing runs on Singapore, all the city's lights were on. The key to turn off the switch was in the governor's pocket, and he was at the cinema. The big guns on Sentosa Island sat idle, trained vainly on the quiet sea; they were not designed to fire on land forces. In February 1942 the Japanese captured Singapore.

Huge numbers of Allied civilians and military were sent to Changi Prison; others were marched off to prison camps in Malaya or to work on the notorious "Death Railway" in Thailand. The 3½ years of occupation was a time of privation and fear for the civilian population; up to 100,000 deaths are estimated during this period. The Japanese surrendered on August 21, 1945, and the Allied military forces returned to Singapore. However, the security of the British Empire was never again to be felt, and independence for British Southeast Asia was only a matter of time.

Military control of Singapore ended in 1946. The former Straits Settlements crown colony was dissolved, and the island became a separate crown colony, with a partially elected legislative council representing various elements of the community. The first election was held in 1948. In the 1950s, the degree of autonomy allowed Singapore increased and various political parties were formed. One of these was the People's Action Party, established in 1954 under the leadership of a young Chinese lawyer, Lee Kuan Yew, who had recently graduated from Oxford.

In 1957 the British government agreed to the establishment of an elected 51-member legislative assembly. General elections in 1959 gave an overwhelming majority—43 of 51 seats—to the PAP, and Lee Kuan Yew became Singapore's first prime minister. In 1963 Singapore became part of the Federation of Malaysia, along with the newly independent state of Malaysia.

Mainly due to the Malays' anxiety over a possible takeover by the ethnic Chinese, the federation did not work. When it broke up two years later, Singapore became an independent sovereign state (its independence day—August 9, called National Day—is celebrated each year in grand style). In 1967 Singapore issued its own currency for the first time, and in the general election of 1968 the PAP won all 58 seats in Parliament.

In 1971 the last of the British military forces left the island. The economic future of the nation seemed unsure: How could it survive without the massive British military expenditure? But Singapore did more than survive—it boomed. The government engaged in programs for rapid modernization of the nation's infrastructure to attract foreign investment and to help its businesses compete in world markets.

The electorate stayed faithful to Lee Kuan Yew and the PAP, returning the party almost unchallenged in one election after another. It was something of a surprise when, at a by-election in 1981, a single opposition member, Indian lawyer J. B. Jeyaretnam, was elected to Parliament, followed by a second non-PAP member in the general election of 1984. Today the PAP's popular majority is the lowest it has ever been. Nevertheless, the party is still sufficiently entrenched to hold all but a few of the parliamentary seats. Lee has stepped down from the all-powerful post of prime minister, but as elder statesman he still acts as the guiding hand behind the PAP and, hence, the government. In recent years he has encouraged freer expression (to some extent, at least), and consequently more and more citizens have begun voicing their criticism of the government's sometimes heavy-handed dictates.

The Peoples of Singapore

The modern Singaporean is proud of his nation's multiracial heritage. In 1911 the census found 48 races speaking 54 languages, though some of these races have dwindled since then. Once 5,000 strong, the Armenian community, which built the Armenian Apostolic Church of St. Gregory in 1835, numbers fewer than 50 today. The Sephardic Jews, mostly from India and Persia, have moved out of Singapore to Israel, Australia, and elsewhere; just two synagogues, one on Waterloo Street and one on Oxley Rise, survive. The fortunes amassed by Bugis from the Celebes in Indonesia—pirates before Raffles arrived, later turned real-estate investors—have passed into the hands of the few Bugis families who remain.

Still, numerous ethnic communities exist: Filipinos, Japanese, and Thais, Germans, Swiss, and Italians. There are also about 20,000 Eurasians—half British, Dutch, or Portuguese; half Filipino, Chinese, Malay, Indian, Thai, Sri Lankan, Indonesian. An overwhelming 97% of the population, however, come from among just three ethnic groups: Chinese, Malay, and Indian. It had been Lee's wish to make Singapore multiracial, but increasingly in his later years Lee has spoken of Singapore as a Sinic society and sought immigrants from Hong Kong.

The Chinese

Raffles had one ambition for Singapore—to make it a thriving trading port that would secure British interests in the Orient and undermine the Dutch. To achieve these goals, he made the island a free port. Traders flocked to Singapore, and soon so did thousands of Chinese in search of work. Every year during the northeast monsoon, junks crammed to the gunnels with half-starved Chinese would ride the winds to Singapore. Many arrived intent only on saving money and then returning to their families on mainland China. However, most did not make the return journey.

These immigrants were from many different ethnic groups with different languages, different foods, different clothes, and often different religions. Each group carved out its own section of Chinatown, the part of Singapore that Raffles's master plan (drawn up with the intention of avoiding racial tensions) had allotted the Chinese, and there they lived basically separate lives.

The largest group was the Hokkien, traders and merchants from southern Fukien Province, who now make up 43% of the Chinese population and still work predominantly as merchants. The early arrivals settled in Amoy Street. One of Singapore's oldest temples, the Temple of Heavenly Happiness, was built in 1841 by Hokkien immigrants in honor of the goddess of the sea, and here they made offerings in thanks for their safe voyage.

On Philip Street in Chinatown is the Wak Hai Cheng Bio Temple, also dedicated to a goddess of the sea. It was built by the Teochews, the second-largest immigrant group (constituting 22% of Singapore's Chinese), who came from the Swatow region in Guangdong Province. The temple suggests one of their chosen professions—they dominate the port and maritime labor force—but they also make a strong showing as cooks, which will become clear as you sample your way through the food centers.

The Cantonese are the third-largest group, making up 16.5% of the Chinese population. They are often artisans and craftsmen. Their Fuk Tak Chi Temple on Telok Ayer Street is dedicated to Tua Pek Kong, who can bring prosperity and safety to a voyage. Southern neighbors of the

Teochews on the mainland, the Cantonese have food on their mind more than any other ethnic group. Some even say that the Cantonese live to eat. It is true that three-fourths of all the Chinese restaurants in Singapore serve Cantonese food.

The Hakka—who had lived a nomadic existence in Fukien, Guangdong, and Szechuan provinces—remember old times at the Ying He Hui Guan (Hakka Clan Association Hall), just off Telok Ayer Street, which served as a sort of foster home for immigrants stepping off the junks a century ago. The Hainanese, many of whom work in hotel or domestic service, were employed as cooks by the colonials (you'll often see "breaded pork cutlet" on the menus at Hainanese restaurants).

By the 1920s, the number of Straits Chinese—those born in Singapore or in Malaya—exceeded the number of mainland-born Chinese in Singapore. Though some continued to consider themselves "overseas Chinese," an increasing number began to recognize Singapore as their home. The Straits Chinese British Association (formed at the turn of the century) served as a forum for exchanging views on Singapore's future and, unofficially, worked alongside the colonial administration in the island's development. Chinese families that had made fortunes in the 19th century began sending their children to British universities. These graduates became businessmen, politicians, and statesmen. Today Chinese constitute 76% of Singapore's total population.

One of Singapore's most interesting aspects is the more than two dozen festivals celebrated so colorfully each year, and more than half of these are Chinese, based on traditions brought over from the mainland. Even the keenest Chinese businessman does not discount *joss*—fortune—and festivals are considered important in ensuring good joss, by appeasing ancestral spirits during the Festival of the Hungry Ghosts, celebrating the birthday of the mischievous Monkey God, or ushering in the Chinese New Year.

The Malays

When Raffles landed on the island in 1819, there were perhaps 100 Malay houses in a small fishing village on the banks of the Singapore River. Aside from the Malays, there were about 30 *orang laut* (sea gypsies) living farther upriver in houseboats. (The orang laut, aborigines from Johore, were later decimated by an epidemic of smallpox, but there were still families living in waterborne settlements until after the Second World War. Since then they have come ashore, intermarried with Malays, and become mainstream Singaporean.)

To help develop Singapore as a free port, the East India Company encouraged Malays to migrate from the peninsula. By 1824 their numbers had grown to more than 5,000, and today Malays account for 15% of Singapore's ethnic mix.

Malays, in contrast to the Chinese, did not adapt to the freewheeling entrepreneurial spirit that engulfed Singapore. Overwhelmingly Muslim, they sought fulfillment in serving the community and winning its respect rather than in profit making. Their lives traditionally centered on the *kampong*, or village, where the family houses are built around a central compound and food is grown for communal use. Kampongs have mostly disappeared from Singapore, but one does remain on the island of Pulau Sakeng. If you visit this island, you will immediately feel the pervasive community spirit and the warmth extended to visitors. With luck, you may even get to witness the traditional Malay sport called *sepak tatraw*—similar to badminton, except that the feet, arms, and body are used instead of racquets.

The early Malays chose to be fishermen, woodcutters, or carpenters rather than capitalists, and today they continue to concentrate on the community and their relationship with Allah. (No visitor to Singapore can fail to hear the plaintive call to prayer five times a day from the Sultan Mosque, whose gold-painted domes and minarets tower above the shophouses.) Hence, wealth and power have, for the most part, eluded the Malay community.

Still, the culture has infiltrated all aspects of Singapore life. Though there are four "official" languages—Malay, Mandarin, Tamil, and English—Malay is the national language, used, for example, in the national anthem, "Majulah Singapura" (May Singapore Prosper). Singaporeans have incorporated Malay food into their cooking as well. Nonya (Malay for "woman" or "wife"), or Peranakan, cuisine is one aspect of the blending of Chinese and Malay cultures, featuring Chinese ingredients prepared with local spices.

The Indians

At least seven centuries before Christ, Indian merchants were crossing the Bay of Bengal to trade in Malaya. Some settled in, and their success in trade made them respected members of the community. Hindu words were absorbed into the Malay language; Singapore's name, in fact, derives from the Sanskrit *singa pura* ("lion city").

With success stories floating back to the Indian subcontinent, little encouragement was needed to entice other Indians to seek their fortunes in the new Singapore. Some, however, had no choice. Seeing a way of both ridding Calcutta of its miscreants and building an infrastructure in Singapore, the East India Company sent Indian convicts to the island in chains and put them to work draining marshes and erecting bridges, churches, and other public buildings.

For themselves, the Indians built Sri Mariamman, Singapore's oldest and most important Hindu temple, in 1862 (it has since been expanded and repainted).

In fact, serving time in Singapore during the mid-19th century was not so bad. The convicts were encouraged to learn a trade, and often, after their term was served, they opted to stay. Many Tamils from South India went as indentured laborers to work Malaya's rubber plantations and, when their time was up, moved to Singapore.

The majority of Indians in Singapore are, in fact, Hindu Tamils from South India. There are also Muslims from South India and, in smaller numbers, Bengalis, Biharis, Gujeratis, Marathis, Kashmiris, and Punjabis, from the north, west, and east of India. From Sri Lanka come other Hindu Tamils, as well as the Sinhalese (often mistaken for Indians), who are neither Hindu nor Muslim but follow the gentle teachings of Hinayana Buddhism. The Sinhalese traditionally work in jewelry and precious gems; incidentally, they are among Singapore's finest cricket players—witness their domination of the teams playing at the prestigious Singapore Cricket Club.

During the colonial period, the Indians in Singapore regarded India, and more particularly their region, as their true home. They would send money back to their families and dream of returning. Of all the immigrant groups, they were the least committed to the future of Singapore. When the Japanese occupied the island in World War II, some 20,000 Singaporean Indians volunteered for the Japanese Indian National Army, led by Subhas Chandra Bose, which took advantage of local sentiment and Japanese expansionist goals in an attempt to evict the British from India. This collaboration left Singapore's Chinese and Malay communities—both of which had suffered greatly at the hands of the Japanese—distrustful of the Indians. However, India, after independence, actively discouraged expatriates from returning.

Today, Indians, who account for 7% of Singapore's population, increasingly see themselves as Singaporean. Their respect for education has taken them into the influential professions of law, medicine, and government. Nevertheless, the Tamil-language newspaper gives more space to events in South India than to local events, and the Indian remains deeply tied to his community and traditional customs. Hinduism remains a powerful force—Singapore has more than 20 major temples devoted to Hindu gods—and some of the Tamil Hindu festivals (such as Thaipusam) are expressed with more feverish ritualism than in India. Indian food, too, remains true to its roots; it has been said that one can eat better curries in Singapore than in India.

1 Essential Information

Before You Go

Government Tourist Offices

The **Singapore Tourist Promotion Board** (STPB) is a good source of general information. Call or write for free brochures with historical information; listings of hotels, restaurants, sights, and stores; and an up-to-date calendar of events.

In the U.S. 590 Fifth Ave., 12th floor, New York, NY 10036, tel. 212/302–4861; 333 N. Michigan Ave., Suite 818, Chicago, IL 60601, tel. 312/220–0099; 8484 Wilshire Blvd., Suite 510, Beverly Hills, CA 90211, tel. 213/852–1901.

In Canada 175 Bloor St. E, Suite 1112, North Tower, Toronto, Ont. N4W 3R8, tel. 416/323–9139.

In the U.K. 1st Floor, Carrington House, 126–130 Regent St., London W1R 5FE, tel. 071/437–0033.

In Australia Westpac Plaza, 60 Margaret St., Suite 1604, Level 16, Sydney, NSW 2000, Australia, tel. 02/241–3771; 8th Floor, St. George's Court, 16 St. George's Terr., Perth, WA 6000, tel. 09/325–8578.

Tour Groups

Package tours are a good idea if you are willing to trade independence for organization, a fairly solid guarantee that you will see at least the major highlights, and some savings on airfare, hotels, and ground transportation.

When considering a tour, be sure to find out (1) exactly what expenses are included—particularly tips, taxes, side trips, additional meals, and entertainment; (2) ratings of all hotels on the itinerary and the facilities they offer; (3) cancellation policies for both you and the tour operator; (4) the number of travelers in your group; and (5) if you are traveling alone, the cost of the single supplement. Note whether the tour operator reserves the right to change hotels, routes, or even prices after you've booked, and check out the operator's policy regarding cancellations, complaints, and trip-interruption insurance. Most tour operators request that bookings be made through a travel agent; in most cases there is no additional charge.

Package tours dealing with Singapore typically extend beyond it into Hong Kong, Thailand, and other destinations in the Orient; for additional Singapore-only deals, *see* Package Deals for Independent Travelers, below. The following is a sampling of tour operators with Singapore itineraries.

General-Interest Tours **Pacific Delight Tours** (132 Madison Ave., New York, NY 10016, tel. 800/221–7179 or in NY, 212/684–7707) offers the "Orient Escapade," tour, which includes a stop in Singapore. **Maupintour** (Box 807, Lawrence, KS 66046, tel. 800/255–4266 or in KS, 913/843–1211) tacks on Hong Kong and Bangkok in a popular Singapore itinerary. **InterPacific Tours International** (111 E. 15th St., New York, NY 10003, tel. 800/221–3594 or in NY, 212/953–6010) has a base of operations in Hong Kong and a particularly wide range of Orient packages (and prices) as a result. **American Express Vacations** (Box 5014, Atlanta, GA 30302, tel. 800/241–1700 or, in GA, 800/282–0800) is another veritable supermarket of mixed Orient packages. At the poshest, priciest end of the market, **Abercrombie & Kent International** (1520 Kensington Rd., Oak Brook, IL 60521, tel. 800/323–7308 or in IL, 708/954–2944) treks through Singapore and the Orient in high style.

Special-Interest Tours

Art

InnerAsia Expeditions (2627 Lombard St., San Francisco, CA 94123, tel. 800/777–8183 or in CA, 415/922–0448) offers an in-depth look at the art of Singapore, Thailand, Hong Kong, and China.

Bird-Watching

King Bird Tours (Box 196, Planetarium Station, New York, NY 10024, tel. 212/866–7923) arranges small group tours focusing specifically on birdlife.

Culinary

InnerAsia *(see* Art, *above)*, in conjunction with the California Culinary Academy, opens the doors to cooking schools in Singapore and Bangkok. Led by a noted authority on Oriental cooking, the group goes behind the scenes at restaurants and into the markets to learn about shopping for native ingredients.

British Tour Operators

Kuoni Travel (Kuoni House, Dorking, Surrey RH5 4AZ, tel. 0306/744–444) has a variety of five-night packages at luxury hotels, starting at around £650.

Thomas Cook Holidays (Thorpe Wood, Box 36, Peterborough, Cambridgeshire PE3 6SB, tel. 0733/330300) offers packages for seven nights (£800–£1,025) and up. Or opt for "2 Centre" holidays, which allow you to combine a stay in Singapore with one in Penang (Malaysia) or Bali.

Cruises

Abercrombie & Kent *(see* General-Interest Tours, *above)* offers five two- to three-week cruises to and from Singapore, to destinations including Bali, Borneo, Vietnam, Thailand, and the Seychelles, between May and June. The line is noted for high-caliber onboard lectures and programs by experts in the history, culture, animal life, and other facets of the area. Make reservations *at least* six months before you want to travel; a year would be an even better idea.

Pearl Cruises (1510 S.E. 17th St., Fort Lauderdale, FL 33316, tel. 305/728–8800 or 800/556–8850), whose 480-passenger *Ocean Pearl* is the only luxury ship to cruise the Far East year-round, offers a number of Southeast Asia programs that begin and/or end in Singapore.

Package Deals for Independent Travelers

Japan & Orient Tours (3131 Camino del Rio N, Suite 1080, San Diego, CA 92108, tel. 800/377–1080 or 619/282–3131) includes Singapore on several of its Orient itineraries, as do **Globus-Gateway** (95–25 Queens Blvd., 3rd Floor, Rego Park, NY 11374, tel. 718/268–1700 or 800/556–5454) and **Olson-Travelworld** (1334 Parkview Ave., Suite 210, Manhattan Beach, CA 90266, tel. 800/421–2255 or 310/546–8400). The "TravPaks" packages offered by **InterPacific Tours International** *(see* General-Interest Tours, *above)* are three-day affairs with a half-day of sightseeing and tour guides available to answer questions and offer advice. **Delta Dream Vacations** (tel. 800/221–6666) arranges a deluxe, 12-night "city spree," combining Tokyo, Bangkok, and Singapore. Other good sources of independent packages are **American Express** *(see* General-Interest Tours, *above)* and **United Airlines Vacations** (tel. 800/328–6877).

When to Go

Singapore has neither peak nor off-peak tourist seasons. Hotel prices remain the same throughout the year, though during quiet spells many properties will discount room rates upon request (either in person or by mail). The busiest tourist months are December and July.

Climate With the equator only 129 kilometers (80 miles) to the south, Singapore is usually either hot or very hot. The average daily temperature is 80°F (or 26.6°C); it usually reaches 87°F (30.7°C) in the afternoon and drops to a cool 75°F (23.8°C) just before dawn. The months from November through January, during the northeast monsoon, are generally the coolest. The average daily relative humidity is 84.5%, though it drops to 65%–70% on dry afternoons.

Rain falls year-round, but the wettest months are November through January. February is usually the sunniest month; December, the most inclement. Though Singapore has been known to have as much as 20 inches (512.2 millimeters) of rainfall in one 24-hour period, brief, frequent rainstorms are the norm, and the washed streets soon dry in the sun that follows.

The climate may sound daunting, but don't let it put you off. All the hotels, except those in the budget range, are centrally air-conditioned. So are the shopping malls and restaurants and most sightseeing coaches and taxis. Try to do most of your walking in the morning or late afternoon. The heat grows really sticky in the early afternoon—that's the time to seek out air-conditioning or a cool sea breeze.

The following are average daily maximum and minimum temperatures for Singapore.

Jan.	86F	30C	May	89F	32C	Sept.	88F	31C
	74	23		75	24		75	24
Feb.	88F	31C	June	88F	31C	Oct.	88F	31C
	74	23		75	24		74	23
Mar.	88F	31C	July	88F	31C	Nov.	88F	31C
	75	24		75	24		74	23
Apr.	88F	31C	Aug.	88F	31C	Dec.	88F	31C
	75	24		75	24		74	23

Weather Information Current weather information for foreign and domestic cities may be obtained by calling the Weather Channel Connection at 900/WEATHER from a touch-tone phone. In addition to offering the weather report, the Weather Channel Connection offers local time and travel tips as well as hurricane, foliage, and ski reports. Calls cost 95¢ per minute.

Festivals and Seasonal Events

Singapore has 11 **public holidays:** New Year's Day (January 1), Chinese New Year (two days, February or March), Good Friday (March or April), Hari Raya Puasa (March through June, according to the year), Labor Day (May 1), Vesak Day (May), Hari Raya Haji (July), National Day (August 9), Deepvali (November), and Christmas Day (December 25).

Singapore is a city of festivals, from the truly exotic (Thaipusam, Festival of the Nine Emperor Gods) to the strictly-for-tourists (International Shopping Festival, Miss Tourism Pageant). Timing your visit to coincide with one of the more colorful celebrations can greatly increase the pleasure of your stay. This should be fairly easy to do: With so many different cultural and religious groups, you'll find festivals going on almost all the time. If the Indian or Chinese Hindus are not celebrating something, the Malay Muslims are. There are numerous national holidays and celebrations as well.

Except for the family-oriented festivals and the month-long fast of Ramadan, these events are as much fun for visitors as they are for the native celebrants. The following is a chronological listing of the major festivals. The exact dates vary from year to year according to the lunar or Islamic calendar. For a complete listing with current dates, contact the Singapore Tourist Promotion Board.

Mid-Jan. During **Ponggal**, the four-day harvest festival, Tamil Indians from South India offer rice, curries, vegetables, sugarcane, and spices in thanksgiving to the Hindu gods. In the morning, rice is cooked at home in a new pot and allowed to boil over, symbolizing prosperity. In the evening, the celebration moves to the temples, where more rice is cooked while prayers are chanted to the music of bells, drums, clarinets, and conch shells. The devotees then eat the offerings, which they believe will cleanse them of sin. The Perumal Temple on Serangoon Road is the best place to view these rites. During this holiday, the Tamils give presents and send greeting cards depicting a girl carrying an earthenware vessel overflowing with rice. The cards are sold in most Indian shops and stalls along Serangoon Road.

Mid-Jan.–Feb. **Thaipusam,** probably the most spectacular—and certainly the most gruesome—festival in Asia, celebrates the victory of the Hindu god Subramaniam over the demon Idumban, who, according to legend, tried to run off with two sacred mountains. On a night with a full moon and during the next day, followers of Lord Subramaniam do penance and demonstrate their devotion. The day before the festival's spectacular procession, the image of Lord Subramaniam leaves its home at the Chettiar Temple on Tank Road to visit the Sri Mariamman Temple in Chinatown before continuing on to the Vinayakar Temple (dedicated to Ganesh, the god's brother) on Keong Saik Road. In the evening, the image is returned to the Chettiar Temple.

After night-long ritual purification and chanting, penitents enter a trance and pierce their flesh—including their tongues and cheeks—with knives, steel rods, and fish hooks, which they wear during the procession. Mysteriously, the wounds do not bleed or leave scars. The devotees carry *kavadi* (half hoops adorned with peacock feathers) to symbolize the mountains that caused the epic battle. The 8-kilometer (5-mile) procession begins at the Perumal Temple on Serangoon Road, passes the Sri Mariamman Temple on South Bridge Road, and ends at the Chettiar Temple. Crowds line the procession route to cheer and sing religious songs as the devotees pass. At the Chettiar Temple, women pour pots of milk over the image of Lord Subramaniam.

Visitors have access to all the temples, and picture-taking is not restricted. However, remember to remove your shoes before entering temple grounds, and expect huge crowds at

Perumal and Chettiar. Thaipusam is not for the squeamish, but it is an extraordinary demonstration of faith.

Chinese New Year is the only time the Chinese stop working. The lunar New Year celebration lasts for 15 days, and most shops and businesses close for about a week. Employees and children are given *hong bao* (small red envelopes containing money), and hawkers and vendors do brisk business selling such delicacies as flattened waxed ducks, white mushrooms, red sausages, melon seeds, and other treats.

Like many Chinese festivals, the New Year celebration is family-oriented: People clean their houses, settle debts, and buy new clothes. Calligraphers brush messages to hang above doorways, and bright red banners frame the entrances of homes and shops. Mandarin oranges, which symbolize gold and the wish for prosperity, are given in even numbers (odd numbers bring bad luck) to friends, relatives, and business associates.

Because Chinese New Year is a family affair, there is not a lot for the visitor to see (except for the Chingay Procession at the end of the New Year festival, *see below*). If you are in Singapore at this time, be sure to try the special salad, *yu sang*, that is traditionally served for the first two days of the New Year (especially good at the Capital restaurant, at 207 Cantonment Road). It is made from slivers of sliced raw fish and as many as 17 different vegetables and seasonings. Anyone who eats it must first help toss the ingredients, for good luck.

Feb. The end of the Chinese New Year is marked by the **Chingay Procession.** Chinese, Malays, and Indians all get into the act for this event. Clashing gongs and beating drums, lion dancers lead a procession of Chinese stilt-walkers, swordsmen, warriors, acrobats, and characters from Chinese myth and legend. A giant dragon weaves through the dancers in its eternal pursuit of a flaming pearl. There are bands of every type, groups of flag-wavers, Indian dancers, a Malay bridal entourage in a tableau staged on a truck, and modern floats featuring Oriental and Western motifs. The parade route varies from year to year, but all the details are described in local newspapers. This procession is not to be missed if you are in town.

Feb. or Mar. The **Birthday of the Monkey God** celebrates this character greatly loved by the Chinese (many ask him to be godfather to their children). Among other things, he is believed to cure the sick and absolve sins. The amusing stories of his life—the tricky way he achieved immortality, his bold attempt at overthrowing the Jade Emperor of Heaven, and the way his mischief was finally controlled—are popular themes in Chinese opera. His birth is marked with a festival twice a year in Chinese temples—once in the spring and again around September. Mediums, with skewers piercing their cheeks and tongues, go into trances during the festival and cut themselves. Then they write out special charms with their own blood and dispense them to devotees. Chinese street operas and puppet shows are usually performed in temple courtyards, and processions are held at the temples along Eng Hoon and Cumming streets. Visitors are welcome to take photographs, but stand back: When the medium dressed as the Monkey God leaps from the throne, burning incense flies in all directions.

Mar. or Apr. On the **Birthday of the Saint of the Poor,** the image of Guang Ze Zun Wang is carried from the White Cloud Temple on Ganges

Avenue, around the neighborhood, and back to the temple through streets thronged with devotees. Spirit mediums— their cheeks, arms, and tongues again pierced with metal skewers—join the procession.

Respect, even worship, of one's ancestors is an important Chinese custom. During the **Qing Ming Festival,** families honor their ancestors by visiting their graves, cleaning the cemeteries, and making offerings of food and incense. This is not a sad event; it is a celebration. Its origins stem from the Han Dynasty (206 BC to AD 220), when tombs were accorded the same veneration as temples. The cemeteries where the festival is most often celebrated are along Upper Thomson Road, Lim Chu Kang, and Lornie Road. However, photographers and spectators are not welcome—the Chinese consider Qing Ming a private affair.

Good Friday is a national holiday in Singapore, and Christians celebrate it by attending church services and observing family ceremonies. There is a candlelight procession on the grounds of St. Joseph's Catholic Church on Victoria Street, during which a wax figure of Christ is carried among the congregation.

Songkran is a traditional Thai water festival that marks the beginning of the year's solar cycle. In Singapore's Thai Buddhist temples, images of Buddha are bathed with perfumed holy water, caged birds are set free, and blessings of water are splashed on worshipers and visitors. The liveliest (and wettest) celebrations are at the Ananda Metyrama Thai temple on Silat Road and the Sapthapuchaniyaram Temple on Holland Road. Visitors are welcome. Keep your camera in a waterproof bag— everyone tries to throw as much water as possible on everyone else.

Apr.–May   **Ramadan** is the month of daytime fasting among the city's Muslim population. Attendance at prayers during the day is required, and the mosques are packed with worshipers. Special stalls in Bussorah Street and around the Sultan Mosque sell a variety of dishes, including Malay rice cakes wrapped in banana leaves, fragrant puddings flavored with pandanus and coated in coconut syrup, and mutton cubes topped with sweet, roasted coconut. The best time to visit the food stalls is between 5 and 7:30 PM, when the Muslim community emerges from the day's fast with a binge of snacking. The end of Ramadan is marked with another festival, **Hari Raya Puasa.** A major feast is undertaken, as celebrating Muslims, dressed in traditional garb, visit friends and relatives; nighttime concerts and fairs are held in Geylang.

May or June   The **Birthday of the Third Prince** celebrates this child god, who carries a magic bracelet in one hand, a spear in the other, and rides on the wheels of wind and fire. The Chinese worship him as a hero and a miracle-worker. A temple in his honor is located at the junction of Clarke Street and North Boat Quay, near Chinatown; on his birthday, it is crowded with noisy worshipers who come to watch the flashy Chinese operas, which begin around noon. Offerings of paper cars and houses and imitation money are burned, and in the evening, there is a colorful procession. Again, the priests are active with skewers, and the resulting blood is used to write good-luck charms. When blood is in short supply, red ink is substituted without diminishing the charms' effectiveness.

Vesak Day commemorates the Buddha's birth, Enlightenment, and death. It is the most sacred annual festival in the Buddhist calendar. Throughout the day, starting before dawn, saffron-robed monks chant holy sutras in all the major Buddhist temples. Captive birds are set free. Many temples offer vegetarian feasts, conduct special exhibitions, and offer lectures on the Buddha's teachings. Visitors are permitted at any temple; particularly recommended are the Kong Meng San Phor Kark See temple complex on Bright Hill Drive and the Temple of 1,000 Lights on Race Course Road. Candlelight processions are held around some of the temples in the evening.

June The **Arts Festival** is a new biannual international event that features both Asian and Western attractions—musical recitals, concerts, plays, Chinese opera—with local and visiting performers. Cleo Laine, Marcel Marceau, the orchestra of St. Martin-in-the-Field, and a Balinese dance troupe have appeared. Performances take place throughout the city; the STPB will have the schedule.

The **Dragon Boat Festival** commemorates the martyrdom of Qu Yuan, a Chinese poet and minister of state during the Chou dynasty (4th century BC). Exiled by the court for his protests against their injustice and corruption, he wandered from place to place writing poems on his love for his country. Persecuted by the officials wherever he went, he finally threw himself into the river. On seeing Qu Yuan's final and desperate act, local fishermen thrashed the water with their oars and beat drums to prevent fish from devouring their drowning hero. Every year after that, the fishermen threw rice dumplings into the water to succor Qu Yuan's spirit. Today, the anniversary of his death is celebrated with a regatta of boats decorated with dragon heads and painted in brilliant colors. The 11.6-meter-long (38-foot-long) boats—each manned by up to 24 rowers and a drummer—compete in the sea off East Coast Park. In recent years, the race has attracted crews from Australia, Europe, New Zealand, and the United States.

As part of the celebration, steamed dumplings are exchanged among friends and family members. Known as *chang* or *zong zi*, the dumplings consist of spiced-meat filling surrounded by glutinous rice and wrapped in bamboo leaves. Each is shaped to form a pyramid. Many hawker stalls begin offering this special food about two weeks before the festival.

July During the **Birdsong Festival,** owners of tuneful birds hold competitions to see whose chirps best. This is serious business for the bird owners and interesting entertainment for visitors. Places and times vary; contact the STPB.

Hari Raya Haji is a holy day for Muslims, commemorating the Haj, or pilgrimage, to Mecca. Prayers are said in the mornings at the mosques. Later in the day, in remembrance of the Prophet Ibrahim's willingness to sacrifice his son, animals are ritually slaughtered and their meat distributed among the poor.

Aug. 9 **National Day,** the anniversary of the nation's independence, is a day of processions, fireworks, folk and dragon dances, and national pride. It's a highly organized and colorful event, with floats, bands, military and school groups, acrobats, and masses of flag-wavers parading through the city. The finest view is from the Padang, where the main participants put on their best show. Tickets for special seating areas are available through the STPB.

Aug.–Sept. For a month each year, during the Chinese **Festival of the Hungry Ghosts,** the Gates of Hell are opened and ghosts are free to wander the earth. It's a busy time. The happy ghosts visit their families, where they are entertained with sumptuous feasts. The unhappy ghosts, those who died without descendants, may cause trouble and must therefore be placated with offerings. Imitation money ("Hell money") and joss sticks are burned, and prayers are said at all Chinese temples and in front of Chinese shops and homes. Noisy auctions are also held, to raise money for the next year's festivities. This is the time to watch Chinese-opera (*wayang*) performances on open-air stages set up in the streets (though, sadly, some of these are being replaced by pop concerts). Performances of the street operas begin in the late afternoon and continue until late evening. The STPB has details.

Sept. The **Mooncake Festival,** a traditional Chinese celebration, is named for special cakes—found for the most part only during this festival—that are the subject of legend. In one version, Chinese patriots are said to have hidden secret messages inside these pastries to gather support for a revolt they were planning against the occupying Mongols. Lanterns signaled the start of the revolution, which ended Mongol rule in China. Another legend tells of a cruel king of the Hsia dynasty who discovered an elixir for immortality. His good-hearted wife tried to destroy the elixir to save his subjects from eternal tyranny, but the king caught her. Desperate to stop him from drinking it, she swallowed every drop and escaped by leaping up to the moon, where she has lived ever since. The mooncakes are eaten in memory of this heroine.

The festival is held on the night of the year when the full moon is thought to be at its brightest. The Chinese have nighttime picnics and carry lanterns through the streets. There are lantern-making competitions and special entertainments, including fancy-dress shows with children in historical costumes, and lion and dragon dances. (Locations are published in local newspapers.) Mooncakes—sweet pastries filled with red-bean paste, lotus seeds, nuts, and egg yolks—are eaten in abundance.

Sept.–Oct. During the nine-day **Navarathri Festival,** Hindus pay homage to three goddesses. The first three days are devoted to Parvati, consort of Shiva the Destroyer. The next three are for Lakshmi, goddess of wealth and consort of Vishnu the Protector. The final three are for Sarawathi, goddess of education and consort of Brahma the Creator. On all nights, at the Chettiar Temple on Tank Road, there are performances of classical Indian music, drama, and dancing from 7 to 10 PM. In Indian homes, lavish shrines to the goddesses are set up and gifts are exchanged. Hindu temples are packed with devotees, all dressed in their finest, and on the last evening the image of a silver horse is taken from its home in the Chettiar Temple and paraded around the streets. Thousands take part in the procession, including women in glittering saris, and the air is heavy with perfumes and incense. The festival is best seen at the Sri Mariamman Temple.

Oct. The Chinese believe that the deities celebrated in the **Festival of the Nine Emperor Gods** can cure illness, bring good luck and

wealth, and encourage longevity. Understandably, these deities are very popular! They are honored in most Chinese temples on the ninth day of the ninth lunar month; the celebrations
are at their most spectacular in the temples on Upper
Serangoon Road (8 kilometers, or 5 miles, from the city) and at
Lorong Tai Seng. Mediums chant, inhale incense, go into
trances, and pierce themselves with knives and barbed thongs
while images of the nine emperor gods pass by in sedan chairs.
The gods are believed to visit Earth during this festival.

Oct.–Nov. During the **Pilgrimage to Kusu Island,** more than 100,000 Taoist believers travel to Kusu Island and the temple of Da Bo
Gong, the god of prosperity. They bring offerings of exotic
foods, flowers, joss sticks, and candles, and pray for good
health, prosperity, and obedient children. If you want to join
in, take one of the many ferries that leave from Clifford Pier.
Be prepared to deal with immense crowds.

In the **Thimithi Festival,** Indian Hindus honor the goddess
Duropadai by walking on fire. According to myth, Duropadai
proved her chastity by walking over flaming coals. Today worshipers repeat her feat by walking barefoot over a bed of red-
hot embers. The bed is 1 meter (3 feet) deep and burns for five
hours before the head priest leads the way across it. Only the
"pure of heart and soul" are said to be able to accomplish this
feat—some *do* walk more quickly than others! See the specta-
cle at the Sri Mariamman Temple on South Bridge Road. The
fire-walking ceremony begins at 4 PM.

Deepavali celebrates the triumph of Krishna over the demon
king Nasakasura. Some also say it is the day when Lakshmi,
goddess of wealth, returns to Earth. All Indian homes and temples are decorated with oil lamps and garlands for the Hindu
festival, which marks a time for cleaning house and wearing
new clothes. Little India is where the festival is best seen. The
streets are brilliantly illuminated, and Indians throng the markets, which do a roaring business selling special greeting
cards, gifts, clothes, and food.

Nov. **Merlion Week** is Singapore's version of Carnival, with food
fairs, fashion shows, masquerade balls, and fireworks displays.
The events start with the crowning of Miss Tourism Singapore
and end with the international Singapore Powerboat Grand
Prix. Brochures of the activities are available in every hotel.

Nov.–Dec. Being a multiracial society, Singapore has taken **Christmas** to
heart—and a very commercial heart it is. All the shops are
deep in artificial snow, and a Chinese Santa Claus appears every so often to encourage everyone to buy and give presents,
which they do with enthusiasm. The hotels make a big performance of Christmas, turning up the air-conditioning against
the extra heat of all the candles, and spending thousands on exterior decorations. A lighting ceremony takes place on Orchard
Road, the fashionable shopping street, sometime during the
last 10 days of November.

What to Pack

Pack lightly: Baggage carts are scarce at airports, and luggage
restrictions on international flights are tight. Singapore is one
of the best shopping centers in Asia, so there is no need to wor-
ry should you forget anything.

Clothing   Take casual, loose-fitting clothes made of natural fabrics to see you through days of heat and high humidity. Walking shorts, T-shirts, slacks, and sundresses are acceptable everywhere. Immodest clothing is frowned upon. You'll need a sweater or jacket to cope with air-conditioning in hotels and restaurants that sometimes borders on the glacial. Evening wear is casual; few restaurants require jacket and tie. For business meetings, bring standard business attire. Same-day laundry service is available at most hotels, but it can be expensive.

Miscellaneous   It's advisable to wear a hat, sunglasses, sunblock, and of course comfortable shoes while sightseeing. Bring a spare pair of eyeglasses and sunglasses and an adequate supply of any prescription drugs you may need. You can probably find what you need in the pharmacies, but you may need a local doctor's prescription. Although you'll need an umbrella during the rainy season, you can pick up inexpensive ones locally. Leave the plastic or nylon raincoats at home—the high humidity makes them extremely uncomfortable.

Luggage   Passengers on U.S. airlines are limited to two carry-on bags.
Carry-on   For a bag you wish to store under the seat, the maximum dimensions are $9 \times 14 \times 22$ inches. For bags that can be hung in a closet or on a luggage rack, the maximum dimensions are $4 \times 23 \times 45$ inches. For bags you wish to store in an overhead bin, the maximum dimensions are $10 \times 14 \times 36$ inches. Any item that exceeds the specified dimensions may be rejected as a carryon and taken as checked baggage. Keep in mind that an airline can adapt the rules to circumstances, so on an especially crowded flight don't be surprised if you are allowed only *one* carry-on bag.

In addition to the two carryons, you may bring aboard a handbag (pocketbook or purse); an overcoat or wrap; an umbrella; a camera; a reasonable amount of reading material; crutches, a cane, braces, or other prosthetic device; an infant bag; and an infant/child safety seat, provided that the parents have purchased a ticket for the child or that there is enough space in the cabin.

Foreign airlines have slightly different policies. They generally allow only one piece of carry-on luggage in tourist class, in addition to handbags and bags filled with duty-free goods. Passengers in first and business class are also allowed to carry on one garment bag. It is best to call your airline to find out its current policy.

Checked   U.S. airlines generally allow passengers to check in two suitcases. The total dimensions (length + width + height) of each bag should not exceed 62 inches, and the weight per bag should not be more than 70 pounds.

Rules governing foreign carriers vary, so check with your travel agent or the airline itself before you go. All airlines allow passengers to check in two bags. In general, the weight restriction on the bags is not more than 70 pounds each; the size restriction is usually 62 inches total dimensions per bag.

Taking Money Abroad

Traveler's checks and all major U.S. credit cards are widely accepted in Singapore. The large hotels, restaurants, and department stores accept cards readily. Some of the smaller restaurants and shops, however, operate on a cash-only basis. You can expect a 3% to 5% discount in most shops if you pay with cash. Always check on this, as the savings can be substantial.

Although you won't get as good an exchange rate at home as abroad, many U.S. banks will change your money into Singapore dollars. If your local bank can't provide this service, you can exchange money through **Thomas Cook Currency Services.** To find the office nearest you, contact them at 630 Fifth Avenue, New York, NY 10011, tel. 212/757–6915.

For safety, it's always wise to carry traveler's checks. The most widely recognized are **American Express, Barclay's, Thomas Cook,** and those issued through major commercial banks such as **Citibank** and **Bank of America.** American Express now issues **Traveler's Cheques for Two**—a system that allows both you and your traveling companion to sign and use the same checks. Some banks will issue the checks free to established customers, but most charge a 1% commission fee. Buy some checks in small denominations to cash toward the end of your trip; this will prevent your having to cash a large check and ending up with more foreign currency than you need. You can also buy traveler's checks in Singapore dollars, a good idea if the dollar is falling and you want to lock in the current rate. Remember to take the addresses of offices in Singapore where you can get refunds for lost or stolen traveler's checks.

The best places to change money are at money-exchange counters at Changi airport and money-changing booths in shopping centers. Money changers give slightly better rates than banks, and both offer considerably better rates than those you can expect from hotels and shops. For most currencies, traveler's checks get a better rate of exchange than cash.

Getting Money from Home

Cash Machines   Where possible, use automated-teller machines (ATMs) to withdraw money from your checking account with a bank card, or, though it's more expensive, advance cash with your credit card. Before leaving home, ask your local bank for a Personal Identification Number (PIN) for your bank and credit cards. Also request a list of affiliated cash-machine networks (e.g., Cirrus and Plus), their ATM locations, the fees for withdrawals or cash advances made overseas, and limits on these transactions within given time periods. Cash advances can also be made through bank tellers. Either way, you pay interest from the day of posting, and some banks tack on an extra service charge.

Bank Transfers   Just have your bank send money to a bank in Singapore. It's easiest to transfer money between like branches; otherwise, the process takes a couple days longer and costs more.

American Express   The company's Express Cash system links your U.S. checking
Cardholder   account to your Amex card. Overseas you can withdraw up to
Services $1,000 in a 21-day period (more if your card is Gold or Platinum). For each transaction there's a 2% fee (minimum $2, maximum $6). Call 800/227–4669 for information.

Cardholders can also cash personal or counter checks at any American Express office for up to $1,000, of which $500 may be claimed in cash and the balance in traveler's checks carrying a 1% commission.

Wiring Money You don't have to be a cardholder to have an American Express MoneyGram sent to you overseas. Just have a friend at home fill out a MoneyGram for up to $10,000 at an American Express MoneyGram agent (call 800/543–4080 for locations). Payment of up to $1,000 may be made with a credit card (AE, D, MC, and V); the balance must be in cash. Your friend then telephones you with a reference number and the MoneyGram agent authorizes a funds transfer to the participating office nearest you. Present proper I.D. and the reference number for payment. Fees are roughly 5% to 10%, depending upon the amount and method of payment.

Alternatively, you can use Western Union (tel. 800/325–6000). A friend at home can bring cash or a check to the nearest Western Union office or pay over the phone with a credit card. Delivery usually takes two business days, and fees are roughly 5% to 10%.

Currency

The local currency is the Singapore dollar (S$), which is divided into 100 cents. At press time, the following exchange rates applied: US$1 = S$1.65, UK£ = S$2.80, A$1 = S$2.16. Notes in circulation are S$1, S$5, S$10, S$20, S$50, S$100, S$500, S$1,000, and S$10,000. Coins: S$.01, S$.05, S$.20, S$.50, and S$1.

What It Will Cost

Compared with other world capitals, Singapore is still inexpensive. However, prices have risen consistently over the last five years, and while a gastronomical delight will still cost half what you would pay in Paris, hotel rooms are in the New York range. Prices continue to rise, and we expect that all hotels will again increase their tariffs by 10%–15% in 1993. You can keep costs down by eating at the inexpensive but hygienic hawker food centers and using the efficient, clean public transportation system, which provides easy access around the city of Singapore and the island very inexpensively.

Taxes There is no sales tax in Singapore. A 4% government tax is added to restaurant and hotel bills; sometimes a 10% service charge is added as well. There is a S$12 airport departure tax (for travelers to Malaysia, the tax is S$5). It is payable at the airport. To save time and avoid standing in line, you can buy a tax voucher at your hotel or any airline office.

Sample Costs Cup of coffee, 70¢; large bottle of beer, $3; lunch at a hawker stand, $7; dinner at an elegant restaurant, $40; full breakfast at a luxury hotel, $12. The cost of a standard double room: moderate, $125–$150; very expensive, over $240.

Passports and Visas

Americans All U.S. citizens entering Singapore must have a valid passport and a return ticket. Visas are not required for a stay of up to 14 days. Applications for a new passport must be made in person; renewals can be obtained in person or by mail. First-time applicants should apply at least five weeks in advance of their departure date to one of the 13 U.S. Passport Agency offices. In addition, local county courthouses, many state and probate courts, and some post offices accept passport applications. Necessary documents include (1) a completed passport application (Form DSP-11); (2) proof of citizenship (certified birth certificate issued by the Hall of Records of your state of birth, or naturalization papers); (3) proof of identity (valid driver's license, or state, military, or student ID card with your photograph and signature); (4) two recent, identical, 2-inch-square photographs (black-and-white or color head shot with a white or off-white background); (5) a $65 application fee for a 10-year passport (those under 18 pay $40 for a five-year passport). You may pay with a check, money order, or exact cash amount; no exact change is given. Passports are mailed to you in about 10 to 15 working days.

To renew your passport by mail, send a completed Form DSP-82; two recent, identical passport photographs; your current passport (if less than 12 years old and issued after your 16th birthday); and a check or money order for $55.

For further information, contact the Embasy of Singapore, 1842 R St. NW, Washington, DC 20009, tel. 202/667–7555.

Canadians   All Canadians need a passport and a return ticket to enter Singapore. Visas are not required for a stay of up to 14 days. To acquire a passport, send a completed application, available at any post office or passport office, to the Bureau of Passports (Suite 215, West Tower, Guy Favreau Complex, 200 René Lévesque Blvd. W, Montréal, Québec H2Z 1X4). Include $25, two photographs, a guarantor, and proof of Canadian citizenship. Applications can be made in person at the regional passport offices in several locations, including Edmonton, Halifax, Montréal, Toronto, Vancouver, and Winnipeg. Passports are valid for five years and are nonrenewable.

Britons   British citizens require a valid 10-year passport; a visa is required only if you are staying more than 14 days. Passport applications are available from travel agencies or a main post office. Send the completed form to a regional Passport Office. The application must be countersigned by your bank manager or by a solicitor, barrister, doctor, clergyman, or Justice of the Peace who knows you personally. In addition, you'll need two photographs and the £15 fee.

Australians   A valid passport, but no visa, is required for a stay of up to 14 days.

Customs and Duties

On Arrival   Duty-free customs allowances in Singapore are in line with those of other countries in the region: Visitors over 18 are allowed to bring in up to one liter of spirits, wine, or beer. Singapore does not permit importing any duty-free cigarettes. Chewing gum is now banned; a stick or two may not cause problems, but more than that will be deemed contraband. Special import permits are required for animals, live plants, meats, arms, and controlled drugs. Penalties for drug abuse are very severe in Singapore and rigidly enforced. Customs also restricts any form of pornography, which in the past has been interpreted to include *Playboy* magazine. Customs is also extremely strict regarding the import of any form of arms, including such items as ceremonial daggers purchased as souvenirs in other countries. These are held in bond and returned to you on your departure.

There are no restrictions or limitations on the amount of cash, foreign currencies, checks, and drafts imported or exported by visitors.

On Departure   If you are bringing any foreign-made equipment from home, such as cameras, it's wise to carry the original receipt with you or register it with U.S. Customs before you leave (Form 4457). Otherwise you may end up paying duty on your return.

U.S. Residents   You may bring home duty free up to $400 in foreign goods, as long as you have been out of the country for at least 48 hours and you haven't made an international trip in the past 30 days. Each member of the family is entitled to the same exemption, regardless of age, and exemptions may be pooled. For the next $1,000 worth of goods, a flat 10% rate is assessed; above $1,400, duties vary with the merchandise. Included for travelers 21 or older are one liter of alcohol, 100 cigars (non-Cuban), and 200 cigarettes. Only one bottle of perfume trademarked in the United States may be brought in. However, there is no duty on antiques or works of art over 100 years old. Anything exceeding these limits will be taxed at the port of entry, and may be taxed additionally in the traveler's home state. Gifts valued at under $50 may be mailed to friends or relatives at home duty free, but you may not send more than one package per day to any one addressee, and packages may not include perfumes costing more than $5, tobacco, or liquor. The free brochure *Know Before You Go*, which outlines what returning residents may and may not bring back, and at what cost, is available from the U.S. Customs Service (1301 Constitution Ave., Washington, DC 20229).

Canadian Residents   Exemptions range from C$20 to C$300, depending on length of stay out of the country. For the C$300 exemption, you must have been out of the country for at least one week. In any given year, you are allowed only one C$300 exemption. You may bring in duty free up to 50 cigars, 200 cigarettes, 2.2 pounds of tobacco, and 40 ounces of liquor, provided these are declared in writing to Customs on arrival and accompany you in hand or checked baggage. Personal gifts should be mailed as "Unsolicited Gift—Value under C$40." Obtain a copy of the Canadian Customs brochure *I Declare* for further details.

British and Australian Residents   Returning to the United Kingdom or Australia, persons 17 or over may bring home: (1) 200 cigarettes or 100 cigarillos or 50 cigars or 250 grams of tobacco; (2) two liters of table wine and (a) one liter of alcohol over 22% by volume (most spirits) or (b) two liters of alcohol under 22% by volume (fortified or sparkling wine), or (c) two more liters of table wine; (3) 60 milliliters of perfume and 250 milliliters of toilet water; and (4) other goods up to a value of £32, but no more than 50 liters of beer or 25 lighters.

Traveling with Film

If your camera is new, shoot and develop a few rolls before leaving home. Pack some lens tissue and an extra battery for your built-in light meter. Film doesn't like hot weather, so if you're driving in summer or a hot place, don't store film in the glove compartment or on the shelf under the rear window. Put it behind the front seat on the floor, on the side opposite the exhaust pipe.

On a plane trip, never pack unprocessed film in checked luggage; if your bags get X-rayed, you could lose your pictures. Always carry undeveloped film with you through security, and ask to have it inspected by hand. (It helps to isolate your film in a plastic bag, ready for quick inspection.) Inspectors at American airports are required by law to honor requests for hand inspection; abroad, you'll have to depend on the kindness of strangers. The old airport scanning machines—still in use in some countries—use heavy doses of radiation that can turn a family portrait into an early morning fog. The newer models—used in all U.S. airports—are safe for five to 500 scans, depending on the speed of your film.

Language

Singapore is a multiracial society with four official languages: Malay, Mandarin, Tamil, and English. The national language is Malay; the lingua franca is English. English is also the language of administration, is a required course for every school-child, and is used in the entrance examinations for universities. Hence, virtually all Singaporeans speak English with varying degrees of fluency. Mandarin is increasingly replacing the other Chinese dialects. However, many older Chinese do not speak Mandarin and communicate in SinEnglish, a Singaporean version of English that has its own grammar.

Staying Healthy

There are no serious health risks associated with travel to Singapore. Proof of vaccination against yellow fever is required if you are entering from an infected area (e.g., often, Africa or South America). If you have a health problem that might require purchasing prescription drugs while in Singapore, have your doctor write a prescription using the drug's generic name; brand names vary widely from country to country.

Many hotels have physicians on call 24 hours a day. Also, the **International Association for Medical Assistance to Travelers (IAMAT)** offers a list of approved English-speaking doctors whose training meets British and American standards. Membership is free. For a list of physicians in Singapore who are part of this network, contact IAMAT (417 Center St., Lewiston, NY 14092, tel. 716/754–4883; in Canada: 40 Regal Rd., Guelph, Ont. N1K 1B5; in Europe: 57 Voirets, 1212 Grand-Lancy, Geneva, Switzerland).

Precautions Tap water is safe to drink, and every eating establishment—from the most elegant hotel dining room to the smallest sidewalk stall—is regularly inspected by the very strict health authorities.

Insurance

Travelers may seek insurance coverage in areas such as health and accident, lost luggage, trip cancellation, and flight. Your first step is to review your existing health and home-owner policies; some health insurance plans cover health expenses incurred while traveling, some home-owner policies cover luggage theft, and some major-medical plans cover emergency transportation.

Companies offering comprehensive travel insurance packages that cover personal accident, trip cancellation, lost luggage, and sometimes default and bankruptcy include **Access America, Inc.**, a subsidiary of Blue Cross/Blue Shield (Box 11188, Richmond, VA 23230, tel. 800/334–7525); **Carefree Travel Insurance** (Box 310, 120 Mineola Blvd., Mineola, NY 11501, tel. 516/294–0220 or 800/323–3149); **Near Services** (450 Prairie Ave., Suite 101, Calumet City, IL 60409, tel. 708/868–6700 or 800/654–6700); and **Travel Guard International,** underwritten by Transamerica Occidental Life Companies (1145 Clark St., Stevens Point, WI 54481, tel. 715/345–0505 or 800/782–5151).

Health and Accident Several companies offer coverage designed to supplement existing health insurance for travelers, including the following:

The **Association of British Insurers** (51 Gresham St., London EC2V 7HQ, tel. 071/600–3333) gives free general advice on holiday insurance.

Carefree Travel Insurance (*see above*) provides coverage for emergency medical evacuation and accidental death and dismemberment. It also offers 24-hour medical advice by phone.

Europ Assistance (252 Hight St., Croyden, Surrey CR0 1NF, tel. 081/680–1234) is a proven leader in the holiday-insurance field.

International SOS Assistance (Box 11568, Philadelphia, PA 19116, tel. 215/244–1500 or 800/523–8930), a medical-assistance company, provides emergency evacuation services, worldwide medical referrals, and optional medical insurance.

Travel Guard International (*see above*) offers reimbursement for medical expenses with no deductibles or daily limits and emergency evacuation services.

Wallach and Company, Inc. (Box 480, Middleburg, VA 22117, tel. 703/687–3166 or 800/237–6615) offers comprehensive medical coverage, including emergency evacuation for international trips of 10–90 days.

Luggage Luggage loss is usually covered as part of a comprehensive travel-insurance package that includes personal accident, trip cancellation, and, sometimes, default and bankruptcy insurance. **Access America, Inc., Carefree Travel Insurance, Near Services,** and **Travel Guard International** (*see above*) all offer comprehensive policies.

On international flights, airlines are responsible for lost or damaged property only up to $9.07 per pound ($20 per kilo) for checked baggage and up to $400 per passenger for unchecked baggage. If you're carrying valuables, either take them with you on the airplane or purchase additional insurance.

Two companies that issue luggage insurance are **Tele-Trip** (Box 31685, 3201 Farnam St., Omaha, NE 68131, tel. 800/228–9792), a subsidiary of Mutual of Omaha, and **The Traveler** (Ticket and Travel Dept., 1 Tower Sq., Hartford, CT 06183, tel. 203/277–0111 or 800/243–3174). Tele-Trip operates sales booths at airports and also issues insurance through travel agents. Tele-Trip will insure checked or hand luggage through its travel insurance packages. Rates vary according to the length of the trip. The Traveler will insure checked or hand luggage for $500–$2,000 valuation per person, for a maximum of 180 days.

Rates for up to five days for $500 valuation are $10; for 180 days, $85.

Before you go, itemize the contents of each bag in case you need to file an insurance claim. Be certain to put your home address on each piece of luggage, including carry-on bags. If your luggage is stolen and later recovered, the airline must deliver the luggage to your home free of charge.

Trip-Cancellation and Flight Insurance Consider purchasing trip-cancellation insurance if you are traveling on a promotional or discounted ticket that does not allow changes or cancellations; you are then covered if an emergency causes you to cancel or postpone your trip. It is usually included in combination travel-insurance packages available from most tour operators, travel agents, and insurance agents.

Flight insurance, which covers passengers in the case of death or dismemberment, is often included in the price of a ticket when paid for with American Express, MasterCard, or other major credit cards.

Car Rentals

Driver's licenses issued in the United States are valid in Singapore. To rent a car, you must be at least 23 years old and have a major credit card.

You'll have to weigh the added expense of renting from a major company with an airport office against the savings on a car from a budget company with offices in town.

If you're arriving and departing from different airports, look for a one-way car rental with no return fees. Rental rates vary widely, depending on size and model, number of days you use the car, insurance coverage, and whether drop-off fees are imposed. In most cases, rates quoted include unlimited free mileage and standard liability protection. Not included are the Collision Damage Waiver (CDW), which eliminates your deductible payment should you have an accident; personal accident insurance; and gasoline.

It's best to arrange a rental before you leave home. You won't save money by waiting until you arrive, and you may find that the type of car you want is not available at the last minute. Rental companies usually charge according to the exchange rate of the U.S. dollar at the time the car is returned or when the credit-card payment is processed. Companies that serve Singapore include **Avis** (tel. 800/331–1212), **Hertz** (tel. 800/223–6472, in NY 800/522–5568), and **National** (tel. 800/CAR–EURO). (For more on renting a car in Singapore, and for local telephone numbers of car-rental companies, *see* Getting Around Singapore By Car, in Staying in Singapore, *below*.)

Student and Youth Travel

The **International Student Identity Card** (ISIC) entitles students to youth rail passes, special fares on local transportation, and discounts at museums, theaters, sports events, and many other attractions. If purchased in the United States, the $14 ISIC also includes $3,000 in emergency medical insurance, $100 a day for up to 60 days of hospital coverage, and a collect phone number to call in case of emergencies. Apply to the **Council on International Educational Exchange** (CIEE; 205 E. 42nd St.,

New York, NY 10017, tel. 212/661–1414). In Canada, the ISIC is available for C$13 from **Travel Cuts** (187 College St., Toronto, Ont. M5T 1P7, tel. 416/979–2406).

Council Travel, a CIEE subsidiary, is the foremost U.S. student travel agency, specializing in low-cost charters and serving as the exclusive U.S. agent for many student airfare bargains and student tours. (CIEE's 72-page *Student Travel Catalog* and "Council Charter" brochure are available free from any Council Travel office in the United States; enclose $1 postage if ordering by mail.) In addition to the CIEE headquarters at 205 East 42nd Street and a branch office at 35 West 8th Street in New York City (tel. 212/254–2525), there are offices throughout the United States; check with the New York City office for the one nearest you.

Students who would like to work abroad should contact **CIEE's Work Abroad Department** (205 E. 42nd St., New York, NY 10017, tel. 212/661–1414, ext. 1130). The council arranges various types of paid and voluntary work experiences overseas for periods of up to six months. CIEE also sponsors study programs in Latin America and Asia and publishes many books of interest to the student traveler, including *Work, Study, Travel Abroad: The Whole World Handbook* ($12.95 plus $1.50 book-rate postage or $3 first-class postage) and *Volunteer! The Comprehensive Guide to Voluntary Service in the U.S. and Abroad* ($8.95 plus $1.50 book-rate postage or $3 first-class postage).

The Information Center at the **Institute of International Education (IIE;** 809 UN Plaza, New York, NY 10017, tel. 212/883–8200) has reference books, foreign-university catalogues, study-abroad brochures, and other materials that may be consulted by students and nonstudents alike, free of charge. The Information Center is open weekdays 10–4.

IIE administers a variety of grant and study programs offered by U.S. and foreign organizations and publishes a well-known annual series of study-abroad guides, including *Academic Year Abroad, Vacation Study Abroad, Study in the United Kingdom and Ireland,* and *Management Study Abroad.* The institute also publishes *Teaching Abroad,* listing employment and study opportunities overseas for U.S. teachers. For a current list of IIE publications, prices, and ordering information, write to the Institute of International Education Books (809 UN Plaza, New York, NY 10017). Books must be purchased by mail or in person; telephone orders are not accepted. General information on IIE programs and services is available from its regional offices in Atlanta, Chicago, Denver, Houston, San Francisco, and Washington, DC.

Traveling with Children

Publications   *Family Travel Times* is an eight- to 12-page newsletter published 10 times a year by TWYCH (Travel with Your Children, 45 W. 18th St., 7th Floor Tower, New York, NY 10011, tel. 212/206–0688). Subscription costs $35 and includes access to back issues and twice-weekly opportunities to call in for specific information. Send $1 for a sample issue.

Great Vacations with Your Kids, by Dorothy Jordan (founder of TWYCH) and Marjorie Cohen, offers complete advice on planning a trip with children, toddlers to teens ($12.95 paperback,

E.P. Dutton, 375 Hudson St., New York, NY 10014, tel. 212/366–2000).

Kids and Teens in Flight is a brochure developed by the U.S. Department of Transportation on children traveling alone. To order a free copy, call 202/366–2220.

Traveling with Children—and Enjoying It ($11.95 plus $2 shipping and handling from the Globe Pequot Press, Box 833, Old Saybrook, CT 06475, tel. 800/243–0495 or, in CT, 800/962–0973) offers tips on cutting costs, keeping kids busy, eating out, reducing jet lag, and packing properly when traveling in the United States and abroad.

Family Travel Guides (Carousel Press, Box 6061, Albany, CA 94706, tel. 415/527–5849) is a catalog of guidebooks, games, and magazine articles geared to traveling with children. Send $1 for postage and handling.

Getting There All children, including infants, must have a passport for foreign travel; family passports are no longer issued. (For more information, *see* Passports and Visas, *above*.)

On international flights, children under two not occupying a seat pay 10% of adult fare. Various discounts apply to children 2–12 years of age. Regulations about infant travel on airplanes are in the process of changing. Until they do, if you want to be sure your infant is secure and traveling in his or her own safety seat, you must buy a separate ticket for your baby and bring your own infant car seat. (Check with the airline in advance; certain seats are not allowed.) Some airlines allow babies to travel in their own car seats at no charge if there's a spare seat available, otherwise safety seats will be stored and the child will have to be held by a parent. (For the booklet "Child/Infant Safety Seats Acceptable for Use in Aircraft," write to the Federal Aviation Administration, APA-200, 800 Independence Ave., SW, Washington, DC 20591, tel. 202/267–3479.) If you opt to hold your baby on your lap, do so with the infant outside the seat belt so he or she won't be crushed in case of a sudden stop.

Also inquire about special children's meals or snacks. The February 1992 and 1994 issues of *Family Travel Times* are scheduled to include "TWYCH's Airline Guide," which contains a rundown of the children's services offered by 46 airlines.

Hints for Disabled Travelers

Organizations The **Information Center for Individuals with Disabilities** (Fort Point Place, 1st floor, 27–43 Wormwood St., Boston, MA 02210, tel. 617/727–5540) offers problem-solving assistance, including lists of travel agents who specialize in tours for the disabled.

Mobility International USA (Box 3551, Eugene, OR 97403, tel. 503/343–1284) is an internationally affiliated organization with 500 members. For a $20 annual fee, it coordinates exchange programs for disabled people around the world and offers information on accommodations and organized study programs.

The **Society for the Advancement of Travel for the Handicapped** (347 Fifth Ave., Suite 610, New York, NY 10016, tel. 212/447–7284) offers access information. Annual membership costs $45, $25 for senior travelers and students. Send $1 and a stamped, addressed envelope.

Travel Industry and Disabled Exchange (TIDE, 5435 Donna Ave., Tarzana, CA 91356, tel. 818/368–5648) is an industry-based organization with a $15-per-person annual membership fee. Members receive a quarterly newsletter and information on travel agencies and tours.

Evergreen Travel Service (19505-L 44th Ave. W., Lunnwood, WA 98036, tel. 206/776–1184 or 800/435–2288) has been specializing in unique tours for the disabled for 34 years.

Publications **The Itinerary** (Box 2012, Bayonne, NJ 07002, tel. 201/858–3400) is a bimonthly travel magazine for the disabled. Call for a subscription ($10 for one year, $20 for two); it's not available in stores.

Twin Peaks Press (Box 129, Vancouver, WA 98666, tel. 206/694–2462 or 800/637–2256 for orders only) specializes in books for the disabled. *Travel for the Disabled* offers helpful hints as well as a comprehensive list of guidebooks and facilities geared to the disabled. The *Directory of Travel Agencies for the Disabled* lists more than 350 agencies throughout the world. They also offer a "Traveling Nurses Network," which provides registered nurses trained in all medical areas to accompany and assist disabled travelers. Add $2 shipping per book, $1 for each additional book.

Hints for Older Travelers

Organizations The **American Association of Retired Persons (AARP;** 601 E St. NW, Washington, DC 20049, tel. 202/434–2277) has a program for independent travelers called the Purchase Privilege Program, which offers discounts on hotels, airfare, car rentals, and sightseeing. **AARP Travel Experience from American Express** (400 Pinnacle Way, Suite 450, Norcross, GA 30071, tel. 800/927–0111) arranges group tours and cruises for AARP members. AARP members must be at least 50 years old. Annual dues are $5 per person or per couple.

If you're planning to use an AARP or other senior-citizen identification card to obtain a reduced hotel rate, mention it at the time you make your reservation rather than when you check out. At participating restaurants, show your card to the maître d' before you're seated; discounts may be limited to certain set menus, days, or hours. Your AARP card will identify you as a retired person but will not ensure a discount in all hotels and restaurants. For a free list of hotels and restaurants that offer discounts, call or write the AARP and ask for the "Purchase Privilege" brochure or call the AARP Travel Service. When renting a car, be sure to ask about special promotional rates which may offer greater savings than the available discount.

National Council of Senior Citizens (1331 F St. NW, Washington, DC 20004, tel. 202/347–8800) is a nonprofit advocacy group with some 5,000 local clubs across the country. Annual membership is $12 per person or per couple. Members receive a monthly newspaper with travel information and an ID for reduced rates on hotels and car rentals.

Mature Outlook (6001 N. Clark St., Chicago, IL 60660, tel. 800/336–6330), a subsidiary of Sears, Roebuck & Co., is a travel club for people over 50 years of age, offering Holiday Inn discounts and a bimonthly newsletter. Annual membership is $9.95 per person or couple.

Vantage Travel Service (111 Cypress St., Brookline, MA 02146, tel. 800/322–6677) offers land/cruise tours geared toward senior citizens. Nonsenior adult companions are welcome.

Publications   *The International Health Guide for Senior Citizen Travelers,* by W. Robert Lange, MD, is available for $4.95 plus $1.50 for shipping from Pilot Books (103 Cooper St., Babylon, NY 11702, tel. 516/422–2225).

Further Reading

A great book to take home with you is *Singapore*, with wonderful photographs by Ian Lloyd and text by Betty Rabb Schafer (Times Editions, 1988). It is available in most Singapore bookstores. Other books on Singapore include the following: *A History of Singapore, 1819–1975,* by Constance M. Turnbull (Oxford University Press, 1977); *The Worst Disaster: The Fall of Singapore,* by Raymond A. Callahan (University of Delaware Press, 1977); *Raffles of the Eastern Isles,* by Charles Wurtzburg (Oxford University Press, 1984); and *Saint Jack,* a novel set in Singapore, by Paul Theroux (Houghton Mifflin, 1984).

Arriving and Departing

From the United States by Plane

Singapore is the transport hub of the Orient. Fifty-two airlines link the republic with 111 cities in 54 countries. The distance between Singapore and North America is too great for planes to fly without refueling and changing crews. There are, however, "direct" flights with no change of airplane, but one or two stops in major cities.

Airport   Your first experience of Singapore's modern efficiency is likely to be in **Changi International Airport,** 20 kilometers (12 miles) north of the city. When it opened in 1981, it met with immediate praise and was ranked the best airport in the Orient. Eager to keep this distinction, which has recently been challenged by Bangkok's airport, Changi opened a second terminal (Terminal 2) in 1991 and now has facilities to handle 24 million passengers a year. A "Skytrain" every five minutes speeds passengers in five minutes between the two terminals.

Planes taxi up to nose-in docks that lead to centrally air-conditioned terminals. Moving walkways bring you close to Immigration and Customs. En route, you can stop at the duty-free shops, though only for alcohol. (Importing duty-free cigarettes and tobacco is not permitted.)

In the arrival hall are a hotel reservations desk, a money-changing bureau, and a desk where you can pick up a Singapore map. Outside are taxis and public buses that will take you into the city. There are no hotel buses or limousines, though some properties will have VIP guests met if they know the flight numbers and arrival times. The Mandarin Oriental, for example, will have a Mercedes (S$50) or a Jaguar (S$80) meet and take you to their hotel in style.

If you're just changing flights in Singapore and have at least four hours between planes, you can take advantage of

Singapore's new **City Tour,** departing from the airport daily at
2:30 and 4:30. It's free.

Airlines   **Singapore Airlines** (tel. 800/742–3333) is the national carrier,
with direct flights from Los Angeles (stop in Tokyo) and San
Francisco (stop in Hong Kong). **United Airlines** (tel. 800/241–
6522) has direct flights from Los Angeles (stop in Tokyo) and
San Francisco (stop in Hong Kong) that connect with many
flights from other U.S. cities. United also flies direct from Chicago and New York to Tokyo, where one can make a United connection to Singapore—thus making it a mere two-hop trip from
the eastern United States. United Airlines has upgraded its
Business Class to "Connoisseur Class" to promote its Pacific
Rim flights.

The east coast of the United States is practically on the opposite side of the world from Singapore, but flying time is four to
five hours shorter if you make the trip across the Atlantic rather than the Pacific Ocean. **Finnair** (tel. 800/950–5000), in particular, promotes this route from New York with a change of
planes in Helsinki. Moreover, the fare is slightly cheaper than
the Pacific route, and the service is excellent. The Helsinki–
Singapore Finnair flight makes a stop in Bangkok, so you can
easily include a visit to Thailand on your Singapore trip without paying additional airfare. You may stop over in Helsinki at
no additional cost, thus breaking the 18-hour flight into two
segments and adding a visit to Scandinavia or Russia.

Flying Time   Flying east to west, including stopovers: from Los Angeles, 16
hours; from San Francisco, 15 hours; from Chicago, 23 hours;
from New York, 23 hours. Flying eastward from the North
American east coast, subtract five hours.

Enjoying   Drinking lots of nonalcoholic liquids can help one survive the
the Flight   usually dry air on planes; booze usually adds to jet lag, as do
heavy meals. Since feet swell at high altitudes, it can be more
comfortable to remove your shoes (but be prepared to struggle
to get them back on). If you are the wandering type, be sure to
ask for an aisle seat; if you like to sleep—and not be disturbed
by wanderers—then book a window seat. Aisle seats are also
good for people who like a bit more room.

Bulkhead seats (located in the front row of each cabin) have
more legroom, but they have no place in front to store bags or
briefcases, and trays do not fold down from the seats in front.
Furthermore, in some planes the last row in the first-class section is for smokers, and the residue of their pleasure tends to
drift straight back to those nonsmokers who sit in the bulkhead
seats behind them.

Dietary Needs   It's always good to remember that all airlines offer a wide variety of food services. Vegetarians, lacto-vegetarians, diabetics,
and Jews and Muslims with special dietary needs all should remember to ask for their own particular foods at the time they
book their flights. Be sure to call again two or three days before
the flight to make sure your request was properly entered in
the master computer.

Smoking   If smoking bothers you, request a nonsmoking seat during
check-in or when you book your ticket. If the airline tells you
there are no seats available in the nonsmoking section, insist on
one: Department of Transportation regulations require U.S.

carriers to find seats for all nonsmokers, on the day of the flight, provided they meet check-in time restrictions.

Discount Flights The major airlines offer a range of tickets that can increase the price of any given seat by more than 300%, depending on the day of purchase. As a rule, the farther in advance you buy the ticket, the less expensive it is and the greater the penalty (up to 100%) for canceling. Check with airlines for details.

It's important to distinguish between companies that sell seats on charter flights and companies that sell one of a block of tickets on scheduled airlines. Charter flights are the least expensive and the least reliable—with chronically late departures and not infrequent cancellations. They also tend to depart less frequently (usually once a week) than regularly scheduled flights. A wise alternative is a ticket broker. It's an unbeatable deal: a scheduled flight at up to 50% off the APEX fare. Tickets can usually be purchased up to three days before departure (but in high season expect to wait in line an hour or so). Brokers offering flights to Singapore all charge an annual fee of about $35–$50. These include **Travelers Advantage** (CUC Travel Service, 49 Music Square W, Nashville, TN 37203, tel. 800/548–1116) and **Worldwide Discount Travel Club** (1674 Meridian Ave., Miami Beach, FL 33139, tel. 305/534–2082).

Between the Airport and Center City
By Taxi Under normal traffic conditions, the trip by taxi takes 20 to 30 minutes, depending on the location of your hotel. The fare ranges from S$13 to S$16, plus a S$3 airport surcharge (not applicable for trips *to* the airport, but be wary of taxi drivers who try imposing this charge anyway). Other surcharges apply when baggage is stored in the trunk or when more than two adults travel in the same cab.

By Bus Public buses leave at frequent intervals from the basement level of both terminals. The fare is S$1.20 to Orchard Road, where, if necessary, you can catch a taxi or change buses to get to your hotel. Bus No. 390 returns to the airport from downtown Singapore via Orchard Road. Fare: S$1.20.

By Car Should you wish to rent a car, major agencies are represented at the airport's car-rental counter (*see* Getting Around Singapore By Car, *below*).

From the United Kingdom by Plane

Singapore Airlines (tel. 081/747–0007) has daily nonstop flights to Singapore from Heathrow Airport (flight time: 13 hours). **British Airways** (tel. 081/897–4000) also has daily nonstops from Heathrow. **Thai International Airways'** (tel. 071/499–9113) flights to Singapore via Bangkok, Tuesday through Thursday, allow you to include a visit to Thailand. Flight time is approximately 16 hours through to Singapore. PEX fares, which allow travelers to reserve up to a day before, are actually cheaper (at around £650 return) than APEX fares (which run about £378 each way). Check the small ads in the *Times*, the *Guardian*, the *Evening Standard*, and the travel sections of the Sunday newspapers for budget-flight offers.

From Canada by Plane

Singapore Airlines (tel. 604/689–1223 or 800/663–0513) has two flights a week from Vancouver to Singapore. There is a stopover in Seoul (flight time: approximately 17½ hours). **Air Canada** (tel. 514/393–3333 or check with your local operator for the 800 number for your area) has four flights a week from Toronto with stopovers in London and Bombay (flight time: approximately 24 hours, 40 minutes).

From Malaysia

By Car Kuala Lumpur is approximately 400 kilometers (250 miles) from Singapore and a good six-hour drive, most of it on a traffic-congested two-lane highway. Navigation is easy, though. The only way into Singapore by car is over the causeway from Johore Bahru, the city at the southern tip of the Malay Peninsula. Malay and Singapore checkpoints are on either side of the causeway. During rush hours there can be lines, but the formalities are as straightforward as those required at the airport. Make sure that your car has the necessary insurance to be driven into Singapore. Once in Singapore, pick up the expressway, which will lead you into the center of the city.

By Train Six trains a day operated by Malay Railways arrive from Kuala Lumpur and points north, such as Ipoh and Butterworth (Penang), at Singapore's **Keppel Road station** (tel. 222–5165). Immigration and Customs are at the station. Keppel Road is at the southern end of the city's business district, a good 15 to 20 minutes by taxi from Orchard Road. But there is an MRT subway station at Tanjong Pagar, six minutes away by foot, that will whisk you to Orchard Road in about 10 minutes for S$.80.

The same company that operates the *Venice Simplon–Orient Express* now runs the ***Eastern & Oriental Express*** deluxe train once a week between Singapore and Bangkok, with a stop in Butterworth (Malaysia) permitting an excursion to Penang. The 1,943-kilometer (1,200-mile) journey takes 41 hours and includes two nights and one full day on board. The cabin decor is modeled on the Josef von Sternberg–Marlene Dietrich movie *Shanghai Express*. Fares, which vary according to cabin type and include meals, start at US$860 per person one-way. For information in the United States, tel. 800/524–2420.

By Bus You can board a public bus at the Johore bus station or after the Malaysia checkpoint, at the causeway. You get off the bus on the other side of the causeway at the Singapore checkpoint, then reboard the bus for the ride into the city's center. Since you may not be reboarding the same bus—depending on the line at Immigration—do not leave your belongings behind when you get off. You do not pay the fare (S$.80) until after the Singapore checkpoint.

Staying in Singapore

Important Addresses and Numbers

Tourist Information The most useful address in Singapore is that of the **Singapore Tourist Promotion Board** (Raffles City Tower, 250 North Bridge Rd., tel. 330–0431 or 339–6622 for the main switchboard). The staff here will answer any question that you may have on Singapore and will attend to legitimate complaints. Open weekdays 8–5, Saturday 8–1. A branch of the tourist board is at #02–02 Scotts Shopping Centre (tel. 738–3778), on the second floor of a large shopping complex close to the busy intersection of Orchard and Scotts roads. Open daily 9:30–9:30. To verify departure and arrival times for air travel, phone **Changi Airport, Flight Information** (tel. 542–5680).

Should you have questions about your visitor's permit or wish to extend your stay beyond the time stamped in your passport, contact the **Immigration Department** (95 South Bridge Rd., #08-26 South Bridge Centre, tel. 532–2877).

Taxis Taxis are available 24 hours a day through the **Taxi Service** (tel. 452–5555 or 250–0700).

Embassies and Diplomatic Missions Most countries maintain embassies, consulates, or high commissions in Singapore. It is advisable to telephone ahead to confirm their hours. If you decide to travel to other countries in the area but did not obtain the appropriate visas before leaving home, be aware that the visa-application process at one of these Singapore consular offices may take several days.

Australia High Commission, 25 Napier Rd., tel. 737–9311. Open weekdays 8:30–noon and 2–4.
British High Commission, Tanglin Rd., tel. 473–9333. Open weekdays 9–noon and 2–4.
Brunei Darussalem High Commission, 7A Tanglin Hill, tel. 474–3393. Open weekdays 8:30–12:30 and 1:30–4:30.
Canadian High Commission, 80 Anson Rd., #14-00, tel. 225–6363. Open weekdays 8–12:30 and 1:30–4:30.
India, 31 Grange Rd., tel. 737–6809. Open weekdays 9–5.
Indonesia, 7 Chatsworth Rd., tel. 737–7422. Open weekdays 8:30–12:30 and 2–4:30.
Japan, 16 Nassim Rd., tel. 235–8855. Open Monday, Tuesday, Thursday, Friday 8:30–12:30 and 2–4:30; Wednesday and Saturday 8:30–12:30.
Malaysia, 301 Jervois Rd., tel. 235–0111. Open weekdays 8:30–3:15.
New Zealand, 13 Nassim Rd., tel. 235–9966. Open weekdays 9–noon and 2–4.
Philippines, 20B Nassim Rd., tel. 737–3977. Open weekdays 9–noon and 2–4:30.
Sri Lanka, 51 Newton Rd., #13-07 Goldhill Plaza, tel. 254–4595. Open weekdays 8:45–1 and 2–5.
Thailand, 370 Orchard Rd., tel. 235–4175 or 737–2644. Open weekdays 9–12:30 and 2–5.
Union of Myanmar, 15 St. Martin Dr., tel. 235–8704. Open weekdays 9:30–1 and 2–5.
United States of America, 30 Hill St., tel. 338–0251. Open weekdays 8:30–noon.

Emergencies **Police,** tel. 999; **ambulance and fire,** tel. 995.

Doctors and Hospitals Singapore's medical facilities are among the best in the world, and most hotels have their own doctors on 24-hour call. **Paul's Clinic** (435 Orchard Rd., #11-01 Wisma Atria, tel. 235–2511), a centrally located clinic with several doctors, is open weekdays 9–5. The following are some of the government hospitals accustomed to treating overseas visitors: **Alexandra Hospital** (Alexandra Rd., tel. 473–5222), **Kadang Kerbau Hospital** (Maternity–Hampshire Rd., tel. 293–4044), and **Singapore General Hospital** (Outram Rd., tel. 222–3322).

Pharmacies Pharmaceuticals are available at supermarkets, department stores, hotels, and shopping centers. Registered pharmacists work 9–6. Some pharmacies in the major shopping centers stay open until 10 PM. Prescriptions must be written by locally registered doctors. Hospitals can fill prescriptions 24 hours a day.

Credit Cards For assistance with lost or stolen cards: **American Express** (tel. 235–8133), **Diners Club** (tel. 294–4222), **MasterCard** (tel. 244–0444), and **Visa** (tel. 522–9032).

English-Language Bookstores Since English is the lingua franca, all regular bookstores carry English-language books, and there are bookstores in most of the larger shopping centers. Most major hotels also have a bookstore/newsstand, though selections are often limited. Should you have trouble finding a book, try the head office of the **Times Bookstore** (tel. 284–8844), which will tell you whether any of its branches carries the title. Its main shops are at the Centrepoint, Plaza Singapura, Lucky Plaza, Specialists Centre, Raffles City, and Marina Square shopping complexes.

Singapore has a policy of censorship. Certain books are banned from being sold or even owned. The law also applies to news magazines, such as the *Far Eastern Economic Review*. Only one serious English-language newspaper, the *Straits Times*, is published in Singapore. It concentrates on local news but has international coverage as well. Editorially, it speaks for the ruling Political Action Party. The same publisher prints the *Business Times*. A popular newcomer, *The New Paper*, is a daily tabloid with a focus on local news and sports. For more international news coverage, seek out the *International Herald Tribune* or the *Asian Wall Street Journal*. Usually, both are available at the newsstands of leading hotels, though it is wise to reserve your copy ahead of time. (At press time, the *Asian Wall Street Journal* was banned for "suggesting that a judge was biased" in finding the *Far Eastern Economic Review* guilty of wrongly impugning Lee Kuan Yew.)

Travel Agencies It is convenient to have your hotel's concierge handle airplane reservations and ticket confirmations, but airline tickets are less expensive if you buy them from a travel agent. Agencies abound in Singapore and will arrange tours, transportation, and hotels in Indonesia, Malaysia, and Thailand—or anywhere else, for that matter.

Two of the better-known international travel agencies are **American Express Travel Services** (#02-02/04 UDL Bldg., 96 Somerset Rd., tel. 235–8133) and **Thomas Cook Travel Services** (#03-05 Sanford Bldg., 15 Hoe Chiang Rd., tel. 221–0222; #02-04 Far East Plaza, 14 Scotts Rd., tel. 737–0366). Significant cost savings (up to 25%) are possible if you shop around for airline tickets. Try **Dragon Tour** (109 N. Bridge Rd., #05-04 Funan Centre, Singapore 0617, tel. 338–5454).

Telephones

Local Calls From a pay phone, the cost is S$.10; insert a coin and dial the seven-digit number. Hotels charge anywhere from S$.10 to S$.50 a call. There are free public phones at Changi Airport, just past Immigration.

International Calls Direct dialing is available to most overseas countries. The top hotels provide direct-dial phones in guest rooms; smaller hotels have switchboards that will place your calls. In either case, check the service charge: It can be substantial. You can avoid the hotel charge by making international calls from the General

Post Office (*see* Mail, *below*), by using the international telephone services at Changi Airport, or by using your Singapore Telecoms phone card (*see below*) from a public phone. (Phone cards offer considerable savings over the use of hotel telephones, which add an 80% mark-up on overseas calls.) International cables may also be sent from the GPO or the airport. (*See* also Operators and Information, *below*.)

The direct-dial prefix for Malaysia is 106. For other international calls, dial 104 and the country code. The country code for Singapore (for calls from outside the republic) is 65.

Phone Cards The Telecoms phone card can be useful if you'll be making several long-distance calls during your stay in Singapore. The cards, similar to the Foncards in Great Britain, can be purchased in denominations of S$10, S$20, and S$50 and permit you to make local and overseas calls. The price of each call is deducted from the card total, and your balance is roughly indicated by the punched hole in the card. Phone cards are available from post offices, Telecoms Customer Services outlets, and many drugstores. Telephones that accept the phone card are most frequently found in shopping centers, post offices, subway stations, and at the airport. For inquiries, call 288-6633. Several public phones at the airport and many at city post offices accept Diners Club, MasterCard, and Visa.

Operators and Information For directory inquiries, dial 103. An economical way to call North America or the United Kingdom is to use international Home Countries Direct phones—USA Direct or UK Direct—which put you immediately in touch with either an American or a British telephone operator. The operator will place your call, either charging your telephone credit card or making the call collect. These phones may be found at the GPO and at many of the post offices around the city center, such as the one in the Raffles City shopping complex. You can also use pay phones by first depositing S$.10 and then dialing 800-0011 to reach the U.S. operator.

Mail

Most hotels sell stamps and mail guests' letters. In addition, there are 87 post offices on the island, most of them open weekdays 8:30–6 (Wednesday until 8) and Saturday 8:30–1. The airport post office and the Orchard Point post office are open daily 8–8. For postal inquiries, contact the **General Post Office (GPO)** in Fullerton Square, off Collyer Quay (tel. 533–6234).

Postal Rates Postage on **local** letters up to 20 grams (0.8 ounces) is S$.10. **Airmail** takes about five business days to reach North America and Great Britain. An airmail postcard costs S$.30 to most overseas destinations. A letter up to 10 grams (0.4 ounces) is S$.35 within Asia, S$.50 to Australia, S$.75 to Great Britain, and S$1 to North America. Printed **aerogramme** letters (available at most post offices) are S$.35.

Shops are normally trustworthy in shipping major purchases, but if you prefer to make arrangements yourself, you will find post office staff helpful and efficient. All branches sell "Postpac" packing cartons, which come in different sizes.

Receiving Mail If you know which hotel you'll be staying at, have mail sent there marked "Hold for Arrival." If you are not sure where you will be staying, you can pick up mail addressed to you c/o General Delivery, General Post Office, Fullerton Sq., Singapore. American Express cardholders or traveler's-check users can have mail sent c/o American Express International, #14-00 UDL Bldg., Singapore 0923. Envelopes should be marked "Client Mail."

Electronic Mail Telex, fax, and Datel services are available at most of the top hotels. Nonguests are usually allowed access to the machines. Cables can be sent from the GPO or the airport.

Tipping

Tipping is not customary in Singapore, and the government actively discourages it. It is prohibited at the airport and not encouraged in hotels that levy a 10% service charge or in restaurants. Hotel **bellboys** are usually tipped S$1 per bag for handling luggage. **Taxi drivers** are not tipped by Singaporeans, who become upset when they see tourists tip; of course, the drivers don't mind!

Opening and Closing Times

Businesses are generally open weekdays 9 or 9:30 to 5 or 5:30; some, not many, are also open on Saturday mornings.

Banks Banking hours are weekdays 10–3, Saturday 9:30–11:30 AM. Branches of the Development Bank of Singapore stay open until 3 PM on Saturdays. The bank at Changi Airport is open whenever there are flights. Money-changers operate whenever there are customers in the shopping centers they serve.

Museums Many museums close on Monday; otherwise, they are generally open 9–5.

Shops Shop opening times vary. Department stores and many shops in big shopping centers are generally open seven days a week from around 10 AM to 9 PM (later some evenings). Smaller shops tend to close on Sunday, although there is no firm rule now that competition is so intense.

Getting Around Singapore

The government tries to discourage the use of private transport by imposing heavy import taxes on automobiles. It also applies a diesel fuel tax that affects taxis. The other side of the coin is that Singapore has one of the best public transport systems in the world: It's cheap, convenient, and easy to use.

By Subway The most recent addition to Singapore's public transport system is a superb subway, known as the MRT, consisting of two lines that run north–south and east–west and cross at the City Hall and Raffles Place interchanges. The system includes a total of 42 stations along 67 kilometers (42 miles). All cars and underground stations are air-conditioned, and the trains operate between 5:45 AM and midnight daily.

Tickets may be purchased in the stations from vending machines (which give change) or at a booth. Large maps showing the stations and the fares between them hang above each vending machine. There's a S$2 fine for underpaying, so make sure you buy the right ticket for your destination. The magnetic tickets are inserted in turnstiles to let you on and off the platform. Fares start at S$.60 for about two stations; the maximum fare is S$1.10. The fare between Orchard Road Station and Raffles Place Station (in the business district) is S$.70. For information, call 732–4411.

By Bus Buses are much cheaper than taxis and—with a little practice—easy to use. During rush hours, they can be quicker than cabs, since there are special bus lanes along the main roads. Some buses are air-conditioned, and service is frequent—usually every five to 10 minutes on most routes. Even without the excellent *Bus Guide,* available for S$.75 at any bookstore, finding your way around is relatively easy. Bus stops close to sightseeing attractions have signs pointing out the attractions.

The minimum fare is S$.40, the maximum S$.80 for non-air-conditioned buses, S$.50–S$1.00 for air-conditioned ones. Exact change is necessary (conductors cannot give change) and should be deposited in the box as you enter the bus. Remember to collect your ticket. Bus numbers are clearly marked, and most stops have a list of destinations with the numbers of the buses that service them. Buses run from 5:30 or 6 AM until around 11:30 PM.

The **Singapore Explorer Bus Ticket,** which may be purchased at most major hotels, lets you travel anywhere on the island on any bus operated by Singapore Bus Service (SBS—the red-and-white buses) or Trans Island Bus Service (TIBS—the orange-and-yellow buses). You may embark and disembark as frequently as you like, flashing your pass as you board. A one-day pass costs S$5 and a three-day pass costs S$12. With this ticket you also receive an **Explorer Bus Map** with color-coded routes showing bus stops and all major points of interest. Most major hotels and tour agents sell Explorer tickets; they are also available at the SBS Travelcentres at bus interchanges. For further details, call the Singapore Bus Service Passenger Relations Center (tel. 287–2727).

The recently introduced **Farecard** functions as a pre-paid mass-transit ticket. You can purchase one for S$12 or S$22 (including a S$2 deposit), from Transitlink sales offices at MRT stations and at bus interchanges. The card lets you travel on the trains and on many buses; the fare for each trip is deducted from the balance on the card. Any unused fare and the deposit can be refunded at Transitlink offices. (Since this is a new system, not all buses have been equipped with validators yet.)

By Taxi There are more than 10,000 taxis in Singapore, strictly regulated and metered. Many are air-conditioned. The starting fare is S$2.20 for the first 1.5 kilometers (0.9 miles) and S$.10 for each subsequent 275 meters (900 feet). After 10 kilometers (6 miles) the rate increases to S$.10 for every 250 meters (820 feet). Every 45 seconds of waiting time carries a S$.10 charge. Drivers do not expect tips.

Several surcharges also apply: There is a charge of S$.50 for each additional person (the maximum is four passengers); S$1 is added for every piece of luggage stored in the trunk; trips made between midnight and 6 AM have a 50% surcharge; rides from, *not to*, the airport carry a S$3 surcharge; and there are "entrance and exit fees" on taxis and private cars going into and out of the central business district, or CBD. Unless a taxi displays a yellow permit, a S$1 surcharge is added to fares from the CBD between 4 and 7 PM on weekdays, and noon and 3 PM on Saturdays. To the CBD, a S$3 fee applies to rides between 7:30 and 10:15 AM Monday through Saturday.

Taxis may be found at stands or hailed from any curb not marked with a double yellow line. Radio cab services are available 24 hours (tel. 452–5555, 474–7707, or 250–0700); a S$2 surcharge is imposed, and the meter should not be switched on until after you have entered the taxi. A driver showing a red disk in the window is returning to his garage and may pick up passengers going only in his direction.

Drivers carry tariff cards, which you may see if you want clarification of your tab. Complaints should be registered with the STPB. Just threatening to complain usually resolves any difficulty, since drivers can lose their licenses if they break the law.

By Cycle-Rickshaw Once the major method of getting around the city, rickshaws are now driven mostly by elderly Chinese, and there are only a few dozen left. The best place to get a rickshaw is in the square before the National Museum. Bargain for the fare; you should not pay more than S$15 for a 45-minute ride. The best time to take a rickshaw ride is early evening, after rush hour.

By Ferry One of the pleasures of visiting Singapore is touring the harbor and visiting the islands, the three most popular of which are Sentosa, Kusu, and St. John's. Most of the regularly scheduled ferries leave from the World Trade Centre. On weekdays, departures are at 10 AM and 1:30 PM (cost: S$5 round-trip); but on Sunday and public holidays, there are eight scheduled departures. Check the return schedule before leaving.

By Bumboat Bumboats are motorized launches that serve as water taxis. Sailors use these to shuttle between Singapore and their ships. You can hire bumboats to the islands from Clifford Pier or Jardine Steps. The charge is approximately S$30 an hour for a boat that can comfortably accommodate six passengers.

By Car Hiring a chauffeur-driven or self-drive car is not at all necessary in Singapore. Distances are short, and parking, especially in the central business district, is very difficult. Taxis and public transportation are far more convenient and less expensive. Even to visit attractions out of the downtown area, buses or taxis are nearly as convenient and much more economical. And almost everything worth seeing is accessible by tour bus (*see* Guided Tours, *below*).

Should you want to look up firms in the Singapore Yellow Pages, check under "Motorcar Renting and Leasing." (For toll-free numbers of rental companies to contact in the United States before leaving for Singapore, *see* Car Rentals in Before You Go, *above*.) The following are some local branches of international agencies: **Avis:** Changi Airport, tel. 542–8833; Shangri-La Hotel, tel. 734–4169; Liat Towers, Orchard Road, tel. 737–1668. **Hertz:** Changi Airport, tel. 545–8181; Marina Square, tel. 336–5200; Tanglin Shopping Centre, Tanglin Road, tel. 734–4646; Westin Stamford Hotel, tel. 339–5656. **National:** 200 Orchard Blvd., tel. 737–1668. **Sintat/Thrifty:** Changi Airport, tel. 542–7288; Dynasty Hotel, tel. 235–5855.

Rates start at S$90 a day, or S$475 a week, with unlimited mileage. A collision/damage waiver (CDW) insurance premium of S$90 per week will cover you for the initial S$2,000 not covered by the insurance included in the basic charge. There is a surcharge for taking the car into Malaysia: Avis, for example, adds S$50 a day, or S$300 per week, to its base charge for compact cars. The CDW is also higher for cars driven into Malaysia.

If you plan to do an overland drive through Malaysia, you can rent a car from a Singapore agency, but it is significantly less expensive to do so in Malaysia. Take the bus for S$.80 to Johore Bahru and you can save approximately S$50 a day on your car rental. Furthermore, you can make reservations with a rental agency in Johore (for example, Sintat/Thrifty, tel. 03/248–2388) from Singapore, and even be picked up from your Singapore hotel by private car at no extra charge.

Singapore's **speed limits** are 80 km/hour (50 mi/hour) on expressways unless otherwise posted, and 50 km/hour (31 mi/hour) on other roads. One rule to keep in mind: Yield right of way at rotaries. Drive on the left-hand side of the road in both Malaysia and Singapore. Gas costs S$1.40 per liter in Singapore, significantly less in Malaysia. A new government ruling requires any car passing the causeway out of Singapore to have at least half a tank of gas or be fined; the republic's huge losses in revenue as a result of Singaporeans' driving to Malaysia to gas up cheaply led to the understandably unpopular ruling.

Guided Tours

A wide range of sightseeing tours cover the highlights of Singapore. They are a good introduction to the island and are especially convenient for business travelers or others on a tight schedule. There is no need to book these tours in advance of your visit; they can be easily arranged through the tour desks in hotels. The following are a few of the tour operators providing services through major hotels, but there are many others as well. **RMG Tours** (5001 Beach Rd., #08-12 Golden Mile Complex, tel. 337–7626) organizes nightlife and food tours. **Siakson Coach Tours** (3 Miller St., Siakson Bldg., tel. 336–0288) has daily tours to the zoo and Mandai Gardens, plus excursions to Malaysia. **Tour East International** (163 Tanglin Rd., tel. 235–5709) offers a variety of tours in Singapore and excursions to Malaysia and Indonesia.

Water Tours (3-A, 1st floor, Clifford Pier, tel. 914–4519) operates motorized junks for cruises in the harbor and to Kusu Island. **Elpin Tours and Limousine Services** (317 Outram Rd., #02-23 Glass Hotel, tel. 235–3111) arranges tours of Sentosa Island. **J & N Cruise** (24 Raffles Pl., #26-02 Clifford Centre, tel. 533–2733) operates the *Equator Dream*, a catamaran that offers lunch, high tea, and dinner cruises (with disco) around the harbor and to the islands. **Island Cruises** (50 Collyer Quay, #01-27 Overseas Union House, tel. 221–8333) offers breakfast, lunch, teatime, and starlight cruises (with strolling musicians) on the sleek new *Singapore Princess*.

Tours can take two hours or the whole day, and prices range from S$16 to S$70. Most are operated in comfortable, air-conditioned coaches with guides and include pickup and return at your hotel. Tour agencies can also arrange private-car tours with guides; these are considerably more expensive.

Prices quoted are only a rough guide; they include admission charges, transportation, etc. All tours are available daily except as noted.

Orientation Tours
City Highlights
These are 3½-hour tours, given in the morning or the afternoon. Itineraries vary slightly, but generally you will be shown some of the major sightseeing and shopping areas, including

Orchard Road, the high-rise business district along Shenton Way, and the historic buildings along the Padang. You will also see Chinatown and probably the Thian Hock Keng Temple. A visit to the Sri Mariamman Temple, a stroll through the beautiful Botanical Gardens, a drive up Mount Faber for a panoramic view of the city, and a visit to a handicraft factory are also likely to be included. A morning city tour usually features the "Instant Asia" cultural show (*see* The Arts in Chapter 7). An afternoon tour would, instead, probably include a stroll through the Haw Par Villa (Tiger Balm Gardens). These tours give a good feeling for Singapore's general layout and should suggest ideas for more in-depth exploration on your own. Cost: S$24.

City and East or West Coast The morning version of this tour usually includes elements of the above, with both the "Instant Asia" show and the Tiger Balm Gardens. If the tour covers the east coast, you'll see the city highlights and visit some rural sights, such as a Malay village and/or the Kuan Yin Temple. You may also visit the infamous Changi Prison, used as a World War II prison camp (you will need your passport for this), and drive through the green coastal area. This tour takes 4½ hours and costs S$21. The west-coast tour includes the Chinese and Japanese gardens and the Jurong Bird Park. It may also include the Haw Par Villa.

Special-Interest Tours
Jurong Bird Park A morning or afternoon drive takes you through the city and east to the industrial town of Jurong, where a 5-acre bird park has been created with more than 100 species of birds. It has the world's largest walk-in aviaries and a huge man-made waterfall. The 3½-hour tour includes a show of performing birds and, sometimes, a visit to a reconstruction of a Ming Dynasty Chinese village with a handicrafts display. Cost: S$23.

Sentosa Island This 3½-hour morning or afternoon tour takes you by bus to Jardine Steps for the 10-minute ferry crossing to the island. There you ride around on the monorail or in an open-top bus to visit the Coralarium, Handicraft Centre, Maritime Museum, and the old fortifications. You'll also see the Surrender Chambers—a wax reconstruction of the Allied and Japanese surrender ceremonies of World War II. The return to Singapore is by cable car, with superb views of the harbor and the city. A bus returns you to your hotel. Note, however, that this tour is not operated on Sundays. Cost: S$32.

Hawker Center Dinner For those who are not sure how to sample Singapore's famous outdoor eating stalls (*see* Chapter 5)—a great experience!—this two-hour tour gives a taste of the best. You will visit several stalls in a hawker center, each specializing in a particular Chinese, Malay, Indonesian, or Indian dish. The guide will select a wide range of dishes for you to sample. Cost: S$25.

Singapore by Night As a variation on the hawker-center tours, a number of operators add activities to the stall-dinner program. These may include a trip to a night market, a stroll through Chinatown, or a trip to a nightclub. Tours take 3½ hours and cost S$39–S$45.

Boat Trips
Harbor Cruise Morning or afternoon cruises begin at Clifford Pier, where you board an old, converted Chinese junk for a two- to three-hour trip around the harbor. The spectacular modern skyline of the downtown business district serves as a backdrop as the junk glides by the barges and lighters used to unload the big freighters. Visits to some of the islands are included, but itineraries vary depending on the time of day. Among the likely stops and sights are Kusu Island, with its Tua Pek Kong Temple; Pulau

Terkukor, once a base for pirates; and the resort of Sentosa Island. Best of all is the cruise through the outer harbor, with its packed ships, tankers, and freighters from all over the world. Light refreshments are usually included on this tour. (*See* Getting Around Singapore, *above*, for information on ferry services, which will provide harbor views without the narration.) Cost: S$20.

Dinner Cruise This three-hour cruise is a variation on the above. You set out at dusk to watch the sunset, then enjoy a buffet dinner of Oriental and Western food, returning to Clifford Pier by 9 PM. Bus transfers between the dock and your hotel are generally not provided. Cost: S$34 and up.

Personal Guides Some 500 tourist guides, speaking a total of 26 languages and dialects, are licensed by the STPB. Call the **Registered Tourist Guides Association** (tel. 734–6425 or 734–6472) to make arrangements. These guides are knowledgeable, and if they are unable to answer a question, they will seek out the information and satisfy your curiosity later.

Excursions A number of tour operators arrange trips into Malaysia and Indonesia. These run the gamut: a half-day trip to Johore Bahru for S$19, a full-day trip to Malacca for S$68, a two-day visit to the Riau Islands of Indonesia for S$180, a three-day trip to Tioman Island (off the east coast of Malaysia) for S$370. There are also longer tours, which include Kuala Lumpur and Penang in Malaysia, and Lake Toba on the Indonesian island of Sumatra. Several cruises stopping in at Southeast Asian ports in the area begin and/or end in Singapore (*see* Tour Groups in Before You Go, *above*).

Credit Cards

The following credit card abbreviations have been used: AE, American Express: DC, Diners Club; MC, MasterCard; V, Visa.

Itineraries

You can do as much or as little as you like in Singapore. If you took all nine tours in the Exploring chapter of this guide without stopping for breath, you would see virtually all of Singapore in five days—and you have not even begun to shop! So there's plenty to see if you have the time. Another delight of Singapore is its comfort. The hotels are excellent; the food is delicious and safe; and everything works efficiently. In short, Singapore is a good home away from home. Fodor's recommendation, therefore, is that you think of Singapore as a base for exploring not only the city but the neighboring countries. With that thought, we offer the following itineraries, based on one- and two-week stays.

One Week

Day 1 Spend your first couple of days in Singapore covering the central city. On the first morning, you might visit the Colonial and Chinatown districts, then spend the afternoon shopping and exploring on Orchard Street. In the evening, dine at one of the city's many excellent restaurants.

Day 2 Have breakfast at the zoo, then return to the city to explore Little India and the Arab District. In the afternoon, you may want to go over to Sentosa Island to see the Pioneers of Singapore Museum. In the evening, try dining at a food center, such as Newton Circus.

Day 3 Take a trip out to Kusu or one of the other islands and spend a few hours exploring the shops or sights, or just sunbathing.

Days 4–6 Having made arrangements beforehand, travel to Johore Bahru to pick up a rental car and follow all or part of the itinerary described in the Malaysia excursion (*see* Chapter 8). This will take at least three days. Then return to Singapore.

Day 7 Do your final shopping, see any attractions you have missed, and enjoy again some of Singapore's superb cuisines.

Two Weeks

Capital Cities This itinerary allows three days in Singapore, followed by a quick tour of some of the old capitals of Southeast Asia.

Days 1–3 Arrive in and explore Singapore.

Day 4 Travel to Malacca (Malaysia) for lunch and a bit of sightseeing, then on to Kuala Lumpur.

Day 5 Explore Kuala Lumpur; in the evening, fly to Bangkok (Thailand).

Day 6 Explore Bangkok.

Day 7 Visit the Damnoen Saduak floating market outside Bangkok; in the evening, fly to Chiang Mai.

Day 8 Explore Chiang Mai.

Day 9 Travel by bus or train to Sukhothai, the old Thai capital, then take a one-hour bus ride to Phitsanulok and spend the night.

Day 10 Train to Ayutthaya, another old capital. After a visit, train to Bangkok's Don Muang Airport, then fly to Rangoon (at press time, travel to Burma was possible only through a group tour).

Day 11 Explore Rangoon.

Day 12 Explore Pagan and Mandalay.

Days 13–14 Fly to and finish exploring Singapore.

Going South This itinerary hits the hot spots of Indonesia and finishes with a day in Kuala Lumpur.

Days 1–3 Arrive in and explore Singapore.

Days 4–6 Fly to and explore Bali.

Days 7–8 Fly to and explore Yogyakarta.

Days 9–10 Fly to and explore Jakarta.

Days 11–12 Fly to Medan, Sumatra, then travel to and explore Lake Toba.

Day 13 Fly to and explore Kuala Lumpur.

Day 14 Fly or train to Singapore; spend a last evening before the flight home.

Hitting the Beaches This itinerary allows three days in Singapore and a taste of some of the beaches of Southeast Asia, plus a day and a half in Bangkok.

Days 1–3 Arrive in and explore Singapore.

Days 4–5 Fly to and explore Penang (Malaysia).

Days 6–9 Fly to and explore Phuket (Thailand), with excursions to the nearby Phi Phi Islands.

Days 10–11 Fly to and explore Bangkok.

Days 12–13 Take bus/limo or car to and explore Pattaya or Hua Hin.

Day 14 Fly to Singapore and spend a last evening.

2 Exploring Singapore

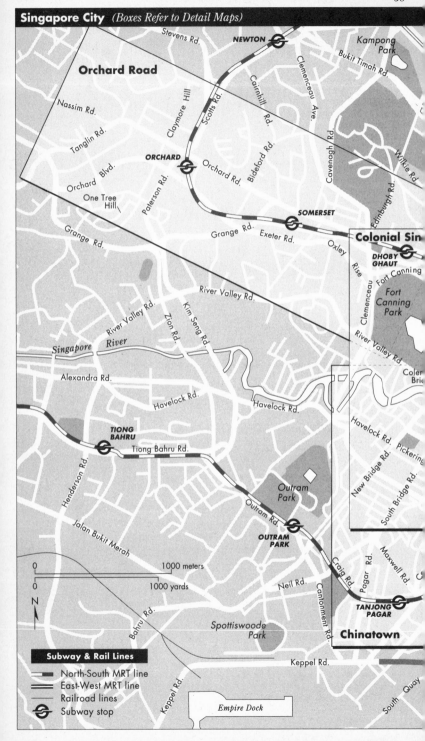

38

Singapore City *(Boxes Refer to Detail Maps)*

Stevens Rd.

NEWTON

Kampong Park

Bukit Timah Rd.

Orchard Road

Claymore Hill

Scots Rd.

Cairnhill Rd.

Clemenceau Ave.

Cavenagh Rd.

Wilkie Rd.

Nassim Rd.

Tanglin Rd.

ORCHARD

Orchard Rd.

Bideford Rd.

Edinburgh Rd.

Orchard Blvd.

One Tree Hill

Paterson Rd.

SOMERSET

Colonial Sin

Grange Rd.

Grange Rd.

Exeter Rd.

Oxley

DHOBY GHAUT

Fort Canning

Rise

Clemenceau

Fort Canning Park

River Valley Rd.

River Valley Rd.

River Valley Rd.

Zion Rd.

Kim Seng Rd.

River Valley Rd.

Coler Brid

Singapore River

Alexandra Rd.

Havelock Rd.

Havelock Rd.

Havelock Rd.

Pickering

TIONG BAHRU

Tiong Bahru Rd.

New Bridge Rd.

South Bridge Rd.

Henderson Rd.

Outram Park

Jalan Bukit Merah

Outram Rd.

OUTRAM PARK

Craig Rd.

Pagar Rd.

Maxwell Rd.

0 — 1000 meters

0 — 1000 yards

N

Bahru Rd.

Neil Rd.

Cantonment Rd.

TANJONG PAGAR

Spottiswoode Park

Chinatown

Keppel Rd.

Keppel Rd.

South Quay

Subway & Rail Lines

━━ North-South MRT line

═══ East-West MRT line

── Railroad lines

⊖ Subway stop

Empire Dock

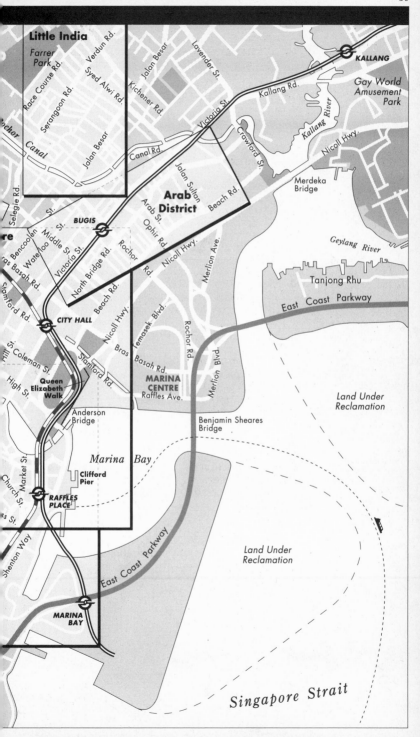

Little India

Farrer
Park

Race Course Rd.

Verdun Rd.

Syed Alwi Rd.

Serangoon Rd.

Jalan Besar

Kichener Rd.

Jalan Besar

Lavender St.

Canal Rd.

chor Canal

Kallang Rd.

KALLANG

Gay World
Amusement
Park

Kallang River

Victoria St.

Crawford St.

Nicoll Hwy.

Selegie Rd.

St.

BUGIS

Jalan Sultan

Beach Rd.

Arab St.

Ophir Rd.

Merdeka
Bridge

Kallang River

Geylang River

**Arab
District**

re

Bencoolen

Middle St.

Waterloo

Victoria St.

North Bridge Rd.

Rochor Rd.

Beach Rd.

Nicoll Hwy.

Rochor Rd.

Merlion Ave.

Tanjong Rhu

ras Basah Rd.

CITY HALL

Stamford Rd.

Bras Basah Rd.

Temasek Blvd.

Merlion Blvd.

East Coast Parkway

Hill St.

Coleman St.

Stamford Rd.

Nicoll Hwy.

**Queen
Elizabeth
Walk**

High St.

Anderson
Bridge

**MARINA
CENTRE**
Raffles Ave.

Land Under
Reclamation

Benjamin Sheares
Bridge

Marina Bay

Market St.

Church St.

**Clifford
Pier**

**RAFFLES
PLACE**

ss St.

Shenton Way

East Coast Parkway

Land Under
Reclamation

**MARINA
BAY**

Singapore Strait

Orientation

The main island of Singapore is shaped like a flattened diamond, 42 kilometers (26 miles) east to west and 23 kilometers (14 miles) north to south. At the top is the causeway leading to peninsular Malaysia (Kuala Lumpur is under six hours away by car). At the bottom is Singapore city, the docks, and, offshore, Sentosa and 57 smaller islands—most of them uninhabited—that serve as bases for oil refining or as playground or beach escape from the city. To the east is Changi International Airport and, between it and the city, a parkway lined for miles with amusement centers of one sort or another. To the west is the industrial city of Jurong and several decidedly unindustrial attractions, including gardens and a bird park. At the center of the diamond is Singapore island's "clean and green" heart, with a splendid zoo, an orchid garden, and reservoirs surrounded by some very luxuriant tropical forest. Of the island's total land area, less than half is built up, with the balance made up of farmland, plantations, swamp areas, and forest. Besides the cities of Singapore and Jurong, there are several suburbs, such as Kallang, an old colonial residential district; Katong, a stronghold of Peranakan culture, with pastel terrace houses and Nonya restaurants; Bedok, once an area of Malay kampongs and now a modern suburb of high rises; and Ponggal, a fishing village on the northeast shore that is a popular destination with seekers of water sports and seafood restaurants. Well-paved roads connect all parts of the island, and Singapore city is served with excellent public transportation.

No other capital city in Southeast Asia is as easy to explore independently as is Singapore. The best way is by foot, wandering the streets to discover small shops, a special house, or a temple, or just watch the daily scene. When leaving the city to explore the rest of the island, you might consider taking an organized tour, since they are relatively inexpensive and transport is provided, but with public transportation so cheap and easy to use, such tours are not at all necessary.

It is very difficult to get lost in Singapore. Visitors can orient themselves in a general way by such landmarks as the financial district's skyscrapers, the new buildings of the Marina Square complex, and Fort Canning Rise, a small hill in the center of town. Also, every street is signposted in English, and most Singaporeans speak English. Getting around is easy, thanks to the efficient and convenient bus and subway service and the numerous (except in heavy rain) taxis waiting to be flagged.

Highlights for First-time Visitors

Chettiar Temple (*see* Tour 5)
Empress Place (*see* Tour 1)
Haw Par Villa (*see* Tour 7)
Kuan Yin Temple (*see* Tour 4)
Pioneers of Singapore/Surrender Chambers (*see* Tour 9)
Raffles Hotel (*see* Tour 1)
Singapore Zoological Gardens (*see* Tour 8)
Sri Mariamman Temple (*see* Tour 2)
Sultan Mosque (*see* Tour 4)
Temple of 1,000 Lights (*see* Tour 3)
Thian Hock Keng Temple (*see* Tour 2)

Tour 1: Colonial Singapore

Numbers in the margin correspond to points of interest on the Tour 1: Colonial Singapore map.

A convenient place to start exploring colonial Singapore is at
❶ Clifford Pier and **Collyer Quay,** where most Europeans alighted from their ships to set foot on the island. Don't let the truth spoil your moments here: Forget that land reclamation in 1933 pushed the seafront back and that Collyer Quay, which now fronts Telok Ayer Street, is three blocks from its original site. In the 19th century, the view from the quay would have included a virtual wall of ships lying at anchor. Today, one looks out upon a graceful bridge carrying the East Coast Parkway from one landfill headland to another, enclosing what is now called Marina Bay.

A stroll around Clifford Pier, a covered jetty with high vaulted ceilings, still reveals some of the excitement of the days when European traders arrived by steamship and Chinese immigrants by wind-dependent junks. Now Indonesian sailors sit around smoking scented cigarettes, and seamen from every seafaring nation come ashore to stock up on liquor and duty-free electronics.

Passengers from the ocean liners no longer come ashore here— those whose trade the jet aircraft and Changi Airport have not stolen now arrive at the new cruise terminal at the World Trade Centre—but tourists set sail from Collyer Quay for day cruises around Singapore's harbor and to the outlying islands. Bumboats (small launches) wallow in the bay, waiting to take sailors back to their ships or carry tourists wherever they want to go for about S$30 an hour.

Leaving Clifford Pier, walk up Collyer Quay toward the Singapore River; **Change Alley**—once the site of a popular old bazaar and row of money changers—would have been on your left. In 1989 the area was closed down to make way for a modern busi-
❷ ness complex. Beyond what was Change Alley is the **General Post Office** (GPO), a proud Victorian building of gray stone with huge pillars. It's hopelessly outdated, an anachronism in an area of glass-and-steel high rises, but if you step inside, you will be surprised at how smartly the old place has been dressed up and adapted to its new role as a modern post office.

To the left as you face the GPO is Fullerton Square, a rest stop for snoozing cycle-rickshaw drivers, who don't seem too eager to find passengers. Walk down the short, narrow, tree-lined street alongside the GPO and past the riverbank mini–food
❸ center to cross the gracious old iron-link **Cavenagh Bridge,** named after Major General Orfeur Cavenagh, governor of the Straits Settlements from 1859 to 1867. The bridge, built in 1868 from iron girders imported from Scotland, once carried the main road across the river; now the Anderson Bridge bears the main burden of traffic.

Once over the Cavenagh Bridge, take a left onto North Boat Quay. Slightly back from the river is Empress Place, a huge white Victorian building that has been meticulously restored as an exhibition hall. We shall return here shortly, but for now
❹ let us proceed a bit farther along the quay to a **statue of Sir Thomas Stamford Raffles,** who is believed to have landed on

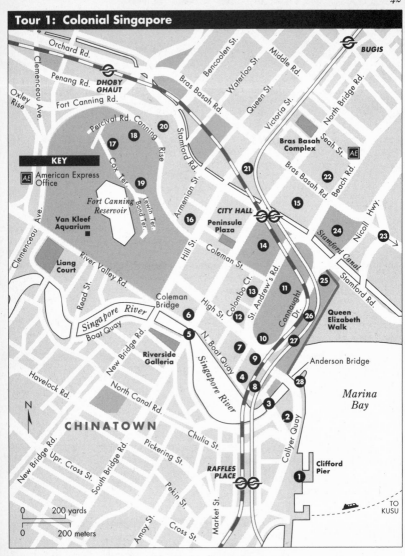

Tour 1: Colonial Singapore

this spot early on the morning of January 29, 1819. Pause here a moment to observe the contrast between the old and the new. Once this river was the organ of bustling commercial life, packed with barges and lighters that ferried goods from the cargo ships to the docks. There were no cranes—the unloading was done by teams of coolies. Swarms of them would totter under heavy loads, back and forth from the lighters to the riverside godowns, amid yells and screams from the *compradores* (factotums).

Now all that seeming mayhem is gone, and the river is close to being the sleepy waterway it was when Raffles first arrived. Cargo vessels are banned from entering the river, and the riverfront shops and two-story godowns are empty. Slated for the wrecker's ball not long ago, these buildings now await the finalization of a government plan to restore the area—one of many recent attempts to reclaim previously undervalued pieces of Singapore's history. Bumboats offer 30-minute **cruises** along the river and into Marina Bay; you can see as much from the shore as from the water, but it's a pleasant ride, and a respite for tired feet. *Dock kiosk, North Boat Quay (behind Parliament House), tel. 227–9228. Cost: S$6 adults, S$3 children under 12. Operating times: daily 9–7.*

⑤ Head west along the quay to **Elgin Bridge,** named after Lord Elgin, a governor-general of India. Built to link Chinatown to the colonial quarter, the original rickety wooden bridge was replaced in 1863 with an iron bridge imported from Calcutta; the current ferroconcrete structure was installed in 1926. At the bridge, turn right onto North Bridge Road and you'll see **⑥** the **High Street Centre.** Take the elevator to the top floor of this office-and-shopping complex for one of the best panoramic views of downtown and colonial Singapore—and it's free.

Back at street level, continue on to High Street and turn right to pass under a sheltered, colonnaded walkway lined with mostly open-front shops of Indian merchants. Though many have closed their doors and moved to the new shopping plazas, a few remain, selling a garish assortment of goods from silks to cheap jewelry. Farther down High Street are graceful old **⑦** buildings housing the attorney general's chambers and **Parliament House.** Irishman George Coleman, the architect of many of Singapore's early buildings, designed the Parliament House building in 1827 for a wealthy merchant, but it went unoccupied until the government purchased it for S$15,600 in 1841 as a courthouse. It is considered the oldest government building in Singapore. Additions were built, and in the 1870s it became the meeting place for Parliament. Out front the bronze statue of an elephant was a gift presented by King Chulalongkorn of Siam during his state visit in 1871.

⑧ Across from Parliament House stands the neoclassical **Empress Place** building we saw earlier. Constructed in the 1860s as the new courthouse, it has had four major additions and housed nearly every government body, including the Registry of Births and Deaths and the Immigration Department. Virtually every adult Singaporean has been inside this building at one time or another. Now, after a S$22 million renovation, Empress Place has a new lease on life as a cultural exhibition center. Its vast halls, high ceilings, and many columns give a majestic drama to exhibitions from around the world. Through 1994, the major exhibit will be a series of art collections from

China. *1 Empress Place, tel. 336–7633. Admission: S$6 adults, S$3 children. Open daily 9:30–9:30.*

⑨ On your right as you leave Empress Place are the adjacent **Victoria Memorial Hall,** built in 1905 as a tribute to Queen Victoria, and the **Victoria Theatre,** built in 1862 as the town hall. These buildings are the city's main cultural centers, offering regular exhibitions, concerts, and theatrical performances of all types (*see* Chapter 7). In front of the clock tower is a 2.4-meter-high (8-foot-high) **bronze statue of Raffles** by Thomas Woolner. (The Raffles statue by the river is a copy of this.) Originally on the Padang (*see below*), it was unveiled as part of the celebrations for Queen Victoria's Golden Jubilee in 1887.

⑩ Across the road from the theater is the old **Singapore Cricket Club.** Founded during the 1850s, it became the main center for the social and sporting life of the British community. It now has a multiracial membership of over 4,000 and offers facilities for various sports, in addition to bars and restaurants. If you are going to be in Singapore for more than a couple of weeks, you may apply, with the support of a member, for a visiting membership. The club is not open to passing sightseers, but you can sneak a quick look at the deep, shaded verandas around back, from which members still watch cricket, rugby, and tennis matches.

⑪ The **Padang** (Malay for "field" or "plain")—the playing field on which these matches take place—was originally only half its present size; it was extended through land reclamation in the 1890s. From the beginning, the Padang has been a center for Singapore's political and social events. Once called the Esplanade, it was where the colonial gentry strolled, exchanging pleasantries and gossip. It was also where, in World War II, 2,000 British civilians gathered, a ragged bunch of prisoners, to be marched off by the Japanese to Changi Prison and, in many cases, to their deaths.

Looking out over the Padang are two splendidly pretentious, imperial-looking gray-white buildings: the **Supreme Court** and
⑫
⑬ **City Hall.** In the neoclassical style so beloved by Victorian colonials, they boast Corinthian pillars and the look of arrogant certainty. However, they are not as old as they seem. The Supreme Court was completed in 1939, replacing the famous Hôtel de l'Europe, where Conrad used to prop up the bar eavesdropping on sailors' tales that he would later use in his novels. The pedimental sculptures of the Grecian templelike facade portray Justice and other allegorical figures. Inside, the echoing hall and staircase are on a grand scale and, high above, the vast paneled ceiling is an exercise in showmanship. All of this was completed just in time for the Japanese to use the building as their headquarters.

City Hall, completed in 1929, now houses a number of government ministries, including the Ministry of Foreign Affairs. It was here that the British surrender took place in 1942, followed by the surrender of the Japanese in 1945. Each year on August 9, the building's steps serve as a reviewing stand for the National Day Parade, celebrating Singapore's independence from Great Britain and the birth of the republic.

Continuing north on St. Andrew's Road, which runs along the Padang, cross Coleman Street (named after the architect)
⑭ toward the green lawns that surround the Anglican **St. An-**

drew's Cathedral. The first church was built on this site in 1834; after being struck twice by lightning, it was demolished in 1852. Locals took the bolts from the heavens as a sure sign that the site was bedeviled. It was suggested that before another place of worship be built here, the spirits should be appeased with the blood from 30 heads; fortunately, the suggestion was ignored.

Indian convicts were brought in to construct a new cathedral in the 12th-century English Gothic style. The structure, completed in 1862, with bells cast by the firm that made Big Ben's, resembles Netley Abbey in Hampshire, England. So impressed by the cathedral were the British overlords that freedom was granted to the Indian convict who supplied the working drawings.

The cathedral's lofty interior is white and simple, with stained-glass windows coloring the sunlight as it enters. Around the walls are marble and brass memorial plaques, including one remembering the British who died in the 1915 Mutiny of Native Light Infantry, and another in memory of 41 Australian army nurses killed in the 1942 Japanese invasion of Singapore.

To the northeast of the cathedral, within easy walking distance, is the huge **Raffles City** complex, easily recognized by the towers of the two Westin hotels. Beyond them is the venerable Raffles Hotel. However, let's delay our visit there awhile. From the cathedral, return to Coleman Street and turn right (away from the Padang). Cross Hill Street, and on the right-hand corner is the **Armenian Church** or, more correctly, the Church of St. Gregory the Illuminator, one of the most endearing buildings in Singapore. It was built in 1835, which makes it the oldest surviving church in the republic, and it is still used for regular services.

The Armenians were but one of many minority groups who came to Singapore in search of fortune. A dozen wealthy Armenian families supplied the funds for the ubiquitous Coleman to design this church. It is, perhaps, his finest work. The main internal circular structure is imposed on a square plan with four projecting porticoes. In the churchyard is the weathered tombstone of Agnes Joaquim, who bred the parent plants of Singapore's national flower. The orchid, with a purplish-pink center, was discovered in her garden in the 1890s and still carries her name.

Behind the Armenian Church is **Fort Canning Rise.** Seven centuries ago this hill was home to the royal palaces of the Majapahit rulers, who no doubt chose it for the cool breezes and commanding view of the river. The last five kings of Singa Pura, including the legendary Iskandar Shah, are said to be buried on the hill. Some dispute this, claiming that Iskandar Shah escaped from Singa Pura before its destruction in 1391.

For several hundred years the site was abandoned to the jungle. It was referred to by the Malays as Bukit Larangan, the Forbidden Hill, a place where the spirits of bygone kings roamed on sacred ground. Then Raffles came and, defying the legends, established government house (headquarters for the colonial governor) on the Rise. Later, in 1859, a fort was constructed; its guns were fired to mark dawn, noon, and night for the colony.

(17) Little remains of these grand constructions, but **Fort Canning Park** offers a green and peaceful retreat from the city center. Since public display of affection is frowned upon in Singapore, young romantics come here to be alone. On the slope, beneath

(18) the ruins of the fort, is an old **European cemetery.** Originally, one side of the cemetery was for Protestants and the other for Catholics. A wall was later built to divide the two sects. Now the tombstones have been moved to form a wall around an open field. The plaques are weathered, and it is difficult to read the inscriptions, but their brevity suggests the loneliness of the expatriates who had sought fortune far from home.

(19) Farther up the slope and to the left is the sacred **tomb of Iskandar Shah.** The government once decided to have the grave opened to determine whether the ruler was actually buried here, but no one would dig it up. Though there are plans to turn the area into a historic attraction—with a museum and restored colonial buildings and underground bunkers—by 1993, at present Fort Canning remains hallowed ground, a green sanctuary from the surrounding city's mass of concrete commercialism.

Exit the park from the north end, via Percival Road, to reach

(20) the **National Museum and Art Gallery.** Both the museum and the gallery have recently reopened. Housed in a grand colonial building topped by a giant silver dome, the museum originally opened as the Raffles Museum in 1887. Included in its collection are 20 dioramas depicting the republic's past; the Revere Bell, donated to the original St. Andrew's Church in 1843 by the daughter of American patriot Paul Revere; the 380-piece Haw Par Jade Collection, one of the largest of its kind; ethnographic collections from Southeast Asia; and many historical documents. The Art Gallery displays contemporary works by local artists, and is often a disappointment after the permanent exhibits. *Stamford Rd., tel. 330–9562. Admission: S$1. Open Tues.–Sun. 9–4:30. Closed Mon.*

Leaving the museum, walk east on Stamford Road for three blocks, then turn left onto Victoria Street. On the right, you'll

(21) pass the **Convent of the Holy Infant Jesus,** one of Singapore's most charming Victorian buildings. The convent church has been slated for renovations, but financial commitment has yet to be made. The arcaded buildings around the church, with their lovely old tiled roofs and thick pillars, are also sorely in need of repair.

Turn right onto Bras Basah Road and walk toward the sea. On your left, opposite Singapore's tallest hotel and largest conven-

(22) tion center, is the **Raffles Hotel.** Once a "tiffin house," or tearoom, the Raffles Hotel started life as the home of a British sea captain. In 1896 the Armenian Sarkies brothers took over the building and greatly expanded it, making it into one of the grandest hotels in Asia. The Raffles has had many ups and downs, especially during World War II, when it was first a center for British refugees, then quarters for Japanese officers, then a center for released Allied prisoners of war.

There is a certain delicious irony to Raffles: Viewed as a bastion of colonialism, it was not only the creation of Armenians, but in its 130 years of hosting expatriates, it only once had a British manager. Even so, service by the hotel's staff has been unfailingly loyal to the colonial heritage. In the nick of time before the Japanese arrived, the Chinese waiters took the silverware from the dining rooms and buried it in the Palm Court garden, where it remained safely hidden until the occupiers departed.

After the war the hotel deteriorated. It survived mostly as a tourist site, trading on its heritage rather than its facilities. However, in late 1991, after two years of renovating and rebuilding some of the original structures and adding new buildings, Raffles reopened as the republic's most expensive hotel. The casual tourist is no longer welcome to roam around, but instead is channeled through new buildings in the colonial style— to visit the museum of Raffles memorabilia (open daily 9–7); attend the multimedia show on the history of the hotel at the Victorian-style Jubilee Hall playhouse; and take refreshment in a reproduction of the Long Bar, where the famous Singapore sling was created in 1903 by the bartender Ngiam Tong Boon. The sling here is still regarded as the best in Singapore, slightly drier than the one, for example, at the Westin Stamford's Compass Rose lounge. The S$14.65 tab includes service and tax, but not the glass—that's another S$7.05. If you're hungry there's the new Empress Café; if you want to browse, there are 60 shops in the new arcade. However, if you are persistent and walk to the end of the constructed tourist attractions and then turn left, you can reach the original Tiffin Room and the Bar and Billiard Room. Casual visitors are discouraged from entering the original part of the hotel, but you may want to brazen it out just to see how unlikely it would be to find a Conrad at the tiny and stiff new Writers Bar.

㉓ Across Nicoll Highway is **Marina Square,** a minicity of its own, with its 200 shops and three smart atrium hotels—the Pan Pacific, the Marina Mandarin, and the estimable Oriental. The whole area is built on reclaimed land. A convention center, now under construction, should be completed in 1994, with two more hotels following soon after.

To return to Collyer Quay and Clifford Pier, recross Nicoll Highway. In a park below Bras Basah Road you'll notice the four 70-meter (230-foot) tapering white columns (known locally **㉔** as "The Four Chopsticks") of the **War Memorial,** which commemorates the thousands of civilians from the four main ethnic groups (Chinese, Malay, Indian, and European) who lost their lives during the Japanese occupation of Singapore. The highest of the "chopsticks" represents the Chinese, who were the most persecuted—some 25,000 were immediately executed for being too Western, and others were sent to help build the bridge over the River Kwai. Another tribute to the war dead of all Allied nations is the **Kranji War Memorial,** a meticulously maintained cemetery in the north of the island (*see* Museums, Monuments, and Memorials in Sightseeing Checklists, *below*).

Farther south on Connaught Drive, across Stamford Road, is **㉕** an ornate **Victorian fountain,** sculpted with Greek-inspired figures wearing Empire dress. In 1882, the colonial government commissioned Andrew Handyside and Company in England to build it as a memorial to Tan King Seng, a wealthy Chinese who helped provide Singapore with a fresh-water supply.

Time Out Just behind the fountain is a delightful alfresco eating place. It is known as the **Satay Club,** but the open-air stalls offer other local dishes besides satay (*see* Glossary of Food Terms in Chapter 5). The recent expansion has made it a convenient refreshment hawker center any time that you are near the Padang.

26 As you continue south, the imposing structure you'll see on the left is the **Cenotaph War Memorial** to the dead of the two world wars. From here, you can cross over the grass to join **Queen Elizabeth Walk,** running alongside Marina Bay. It was opened in 1953 to mark the queen's coronation and remains a popular place to take the evening air.

27 A few yards farther on is the **memorial to Major General Lim Bo Seng,** a well-loved freedom fighter of World War II who was tortured and died in a Japanese prison camp in 1944. At the end of Queen Elizabeth Walk is Anderson Bridge. On the other side, 28 in **Merlion Park,** stands a statue of Singapore's tourism symbol, the Merlion—half lion, half fish. In the evening, the statue—on a point of land looking out over the harbor—is floodlit, its eyes are lighted, and its mouth spews water. Once over the bridge, you are on Fullerton Road, which eventually becomes Collyer Quay.

Tour 2: Chinatown

In a country where 76% of the people are Chinese, it may seem strange to name a small urban area Chinatown. But Chinatown was born some 170 years ago, when the Chinese were a minority (if only for half a century) in the newly formed British settlement. In the belief that it would minimize racial tension, Raffles allotted sections of the settlement to different ethnic groups. The Chinese immigrants were given the area to the south of the Singapore River. Today, the river is still the northern boundary of old Chinatown, while Maxwell Road marks its southern perimeter and New Bridge Road its western. Before the 1933 land reclamation, the western perimeter was the sea. The reclaimed area between Telok Ayer Street and Collyer Quay–Shenton Way has become the business district, often referred to as Singapore's Wall Street.

Within the relatively small rectangle apportioned to the Chinese, immigrants from mainland China—many of them penniless and half starved—were crammed. Within three years of the formation of the Straits Settlement, 3,000 Chinese had moved in; this number increased tenfold over the next decade. The most numerous of these immigrants were the Hokkien people, traders from Fukien Province. They made up about a quarter of Chinatown's immigrant community. Other leading groups were the Teochews, from the Swatow region of Guangdong Province, and their mainland neighbors, the Cantonese. In smaller groups, the Hainanese, the nomadic Hakkas, and peoples from Guangxi arrived in tightly packed junks, riding on the northeast monsoon winds.

Most immigrants arrived with the sole intention of exchanging their rags for riches, then returning to China. They had no allegiance to Singapore or to Chinatown, which was no melting pot but, rather, consisted of separate pockets of ethnically diverse groups, each with a different dialect, a different cuisine, and different cultural, social, and religious attitudes.

In the shophouses—two-story buildings with shops or small factories on the ground floor and living quarters upstairs—

as many as 30 lodgers would live together in a single room. Life was a fight for space and survival. Crime was rampant. What order existed was maintained not by the colonial powers but by Chinese guilds, clan associations, and secret societies, which fought—sometimes savagely—for control of various lucrative aspects of community life.

Until recently, all of Chinatown was slated for the bulldozer, to be wiped clean of its past and replaced by uniform concrete structures. The traditional ways of the individual Chinese groups were to melt away into the modern Singaporean lifestyle. In the name of "progressive social engineering," much of the original community was disassembled and entire blocks were cleared of shophouses. However, the government finally recognized not only the people's desire to maintain Chinese customs and strong family ties, but also the important role these play in modern society. Chinatown received a stay of execution, and an ambitious plan to restore a large area of shophouses is partially completed. Fortunately, enough of the old remains to permit the imaginative visitor to experience a traditional Chinese community.

Numbers in the margin correspond to points of interest on the Tour 2: Chinatown map.

The only way to appreciate Chinatown is to walk its streets, letting sights and smells guide your feet. The following excursion covers many of the highlights, but let your curiosity lead you down any street that takes your fancy.

One starting point is as good as another. We'll begin at Elgin Bridge, built to link Chinatown with the colonial administrative center. At the south end of the bridge, logically enough, South Bridge Road begins. Off to the right is Upper Circular ❶ Road, on the left-hand side of which is **Yeo Swee Huat,** at No. 13 (tel. 533–4288). If you peep inside, you'll see a cottage industry designed to help Chinese take care of one obligation to their ancestors: making sure they have everything they need in the afterlife. Here, paper models of the necessities of life—horses, cars, boats, planes, even fake money—are made, to be purchased by relatives of the deceased (you can buy them, too) and ritually burned so that their essence passes through to the spirit world in flames and smoke.

Time Out At the corner of Upper Circular Road and New Bridge Road is the **Hong Eng Hong** coffee shop (11 New Bridge Rd., tel. 532–4198), a popular place where locals gather in the morning for a dim sum breakfast.

Back on South Bridge Road, at the corner of Circular Road, is ❷ the **Sam Yew Shop** (21 South Bridge Rd., tel. 534–4638). Here you can have your name—translated into Chinese characters—carved onto an ivory chop, or seal, for about S$60. (If your name requires many strokes and characters, the price could be more than twice that amount.)

Circular Road is the cloth wholesalers' street, and shops on either side are crammed with rolls of textiles. Architecturally ❸ the most interesting buildings are at the junction of **Lopong Telok Street,** where, on the left-hand side, at Nos. 27, 28, and 29, there are intricately carved panels above the shops' doorways. Across the street are old clan houses whose stonework

50

Tour 2: Chinatown

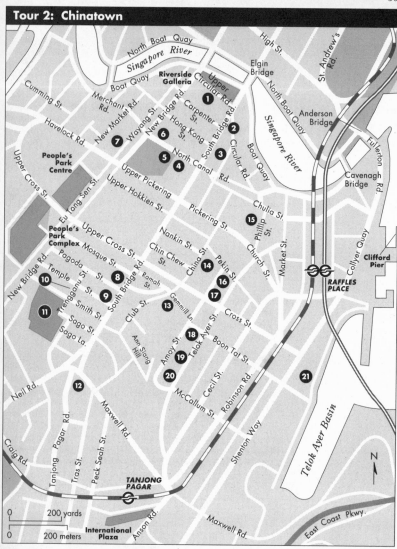

Al Abrar Mosque, **20**

Brothel, **10**

Chinatown Centre, **11**

Fuk Tak Chi Temple, **16**

Guan Chay Foodstuffs, **4**

Hakka Clan Hall, **17**

Jamae Mosque, **8**

Jen Foh Medical Hall, **14**

Jinriksha Station, **12**

Lopong Telok Street, **3**

Nagore Durghe Shrine, **18**

Poh Heng, **6**

Sam Yew Shop, **2**

Say Tian Hong Buddha Shop, **13**

Sri Mariamman Temple, **9**

Telok Ayer Market, **21**

Thian Hock Keng Temple, **19**

Thong Chai Medical Institute, **7**

Wak Hai Cheng Bio Temple, **15**

Wing Joo Long, **5**

Yeo Swee Huat, **1**

facades appear to have a Portuguese influence—possibly by way of Malacca, a Portuguese trading post in the 17th century until the Dutch, and then the British, took possession.

Walk down Lopong Telok and take a right onto North Canal Road. Here are stores selling dried foods, turtles for soup, and, at **Guan Chay Foodstuffs (No. 7)**, fine preparations of birds' nests (a small box of these can cost S$200). At Nos. 44 and 45 you'll see stacks of sharks' fins, sea cucumbers, black fungi, and other types of mushrooms. **Wing Joo Long**, at No. 31, has ginseng and other Chinese herbs. You'll easily spot **Poh Heng**, on the right-hand side at No. 27, by the gold chariot studded with jade and precious stones in the window, but don't let this opulent window display prevent you from entering. Inside you'll find quite reasonably priced gold necklaces.

Cross New Bridge Road and take a right onto Merchant Road. On the left you'll notice a store displaying marvelous lion-head costumes and drums, to be used for festivals. Then, past the herbalist pounding secret ingredients, turn left onto New Market Road. The crumbling building on your left, built in 1921 and currently the site of a biscuit-tin company, was once the Chinese Opera House.

Next door is the back entrance to the **Thong Chai Medical Institute,** a national monument dating from 1892. Once home to a free clinic, today the building is leased out as an arts-and-crafts emporium, where you can shop for bonsai trees, porcelain, scroll paintings, and jade and ivory carvings. Be aware that the appealingly displayed "antiques" are in fact replicas, not the real thing. Leave by the main entrance, on Wayang Street, noticing as you go the intricately carved roof decorations. The beams supporting the roof are held together not by nails but by perfectly fitting dovetail joints. *3 Wayang St. Open Mon.–Sat. 9:30–5:30.*

Leaving Wayang Street, walk south down New Bridge Road past the Furama Singapore Hotel (you may want to ask at the lobby desk for a free map with six walking tours of Chinatown) and the **People's Park Centre,** one of Singapore's most competitive shopping centers (*see* Chapter 3). Cross Upper Cross Street and take a left onto **Mosque Street.** The old shophouses here—mercifully spared by the demolition squad—were originally built as stables. Now they house Hakka families selling second- or, more likely, third-hand wares, from clothes to old medicine bottles.

Time Out If you are hungry and it's before 11 AM, you might try one of the coffee houses on the right-hand side of the street. They serve fine dim sum. The restaurants on the opposite side serve Teochew food and especially good roast-pork dishes.

Turn right onto South Bridge Road. Just past a shoe shop selling beaded slippers is the arched entrance to the **Jamae Mosque,** popularly called Masjid Chulia. The simple, almost austere mosque was built in the 1830s by Chulia Muslims from India's Coromandel Coast. So long as it is not prayer time and the doors are open, you are welcome to step inside for a look (you must be dressed conservatively and take your shoes off before entering).

9 On the next block is the **Sri Mariamman Temple,** the oldest Hindu temple in Singapore. Its pagodalike entrance is topped by one of the most ornate *gopurams* (pyramidal gateway towers) you are ever likely to see. Hundreds of brightly colored statues of deities and mythical animals line the tiers of this towering porch; glazed cement cows sit, seemingly in great contentment, atop the surrounding walls.

The story of this Hindu temple smack in the heart of Chinatown begins with Naraina Pillay, who came to Singapore on the same ship as Raffles in 1819 and started work as a clerk. Within a short time, he had set up his own construction business, often using convicts sent over to Singapore from India, and quickly made a fortune. He obtained this site to build a temple on, so that devotees could pray on the way to and from work at the harbor. This first temple, built in 1827 of wood and *atap* (wattle and daub), was replaced in 1843 by the current brick structure. The gopuram was added in 1936. Inside are some spectacular paintings that have been recently restored by Tamil craftsmen brought over from southern India.

If you take the next right, onto Temple Street, you may be fortunate enough to see one of the few remaining practitioners of a dying profession. Often found sitting on a stool here is a scribe, an old man to whom other elderly Chinese, who have not perfected the art of writing, come to have their letters written. Today all Singaporean children are required to complete years of schooling, so the scribes will soon be out of work.

At the junction of Trengganu Street, notice the old building on **10** the corner. Reliable sources say this was a famous **brothel** in its time. Opium dens and brothels played important roles in the lives of Chinese immigrants, who usually arrived alone, leaving their families behind, and worked long days, with little time for relaxation or pleasure. Many immigrants took to soothing their aching minds and bodies at opium dens; since only 12% of the Chinese émigré community were women, men often sought female comfort from professionals.

Gambling was another popular pastime. Except for the state lottery and the official horse-race betting system, gambling is now outlawed by the government. But you can be sure that when you hear the slap of mah-jongg in a coffee house, a wager or two has been made. Raffles tried to ban gambling, but to no avail—the habit was too firmly entrenched. One legendary figure, Tan Che Seng, who had amassed a fortune by subsidizing junks bringing immigrants to work in his warehouses, resolved to give up gambling and, as a reminder, amputated the first joint of his little finger. Still, he gambled!

You are now in the core of Chinatown, an area known as **Kreta Ayer,** named after the bullock carts that carried water for **11** cleaning the streets. Trengganu Street leads to the new **China-town Centre,** mobbed inside and out with jostling shoppers. At the open-air vegetable and fruit stands, women—toothless and wrinkled with age—sell their wares. Inside, on the first floor, hawker stalls sell a variety of cooked foods, but it is the basement floor that fascinates: Here you'll find a wet market (so called because water is continually sloshed over the floors), where an amazing array of meats, fowl, and fish are bought and sold. Some of the sights are enough to quiet any appetite you may have had. At the far left corner, for example, live pigeons, furry white rabbits, and sleepy turtles are crammed into cages, awaiting hungry buyers.

Leaving the market, walk up **Sago Street** to see more family factories that make paper houses and cars to be burned for good fortune at funerals. A cake shop at No. 36 is extremely popular for fresh baked goods, especially during the Mooncake Festival. Two doors up, at No. 32, is a store selling dry snakes and lizards, for increasing fertility, and powdered antelope horn, for curing headaches and cooling the body.

Parallel to Sago Street is **Sago Lane.** There's nothing to see here now, but the street was once known for its death houses, where Chinese would go to die. It was not regarded as callous to have one's relative moved to a death house. Usually, the family home was noisy and overcrowded, so the death house supplied a peaceful place where the dying could wait out their last days.

If you turn right onto South Bridge Road, you'll come to the intersection of Tanjong Pagar and Neil roads. The old **Jinriksha Station** here was once the bustling central depot for Singapore's rickshaws, which numbered more than 9,000 in 1919. Now there is nary a one. The station has been converted into a food market on one side and an office block on the other.

Tanjong Pagar Road is the center of an area of redevelopment in Chinatown. Thirty-two shophouses have already been restored to their 19th-century appearance and now house teahouses, calligraphers, mah-jongg makers, and other shops. More than 100 shophouses are currently being restored, but public opinion of the high rents and modern substitutes, which give an air of inauthenticity, suggests that only very up-market boutiques and restaurants can afford to set up business if the area is to succeed. One particularly good restaurant serving Italian fare is **Da Paolo's,** 66 Tanjong Pagar Road (*see* Chapter 5). For more casual refreshments, a collection of small restaurants and a food court of fancy hawker stands are at 51 Neil Road. If not for a meal, you may want to drop in for tea and snacks at the **Delicious Kitchen** (24-38 Tanjong Pagar, tel. 226–0607) or browse the wares at **Hua Tuo Herbal Products** (tel. 221–2432) next door.

Also worth visiting are the renovated shophouses on Duxton Road off Tanjong Pagar and the **Pewter Museum** at No. 49A, which houses a private collection of 75 antique pewter items and the tools that were used to make them. You can also watch a demonstration of traditional and modern methods of making pewter (open 9–5:30; admission free). Also on Duxton Road is the **Duxton Inn,** a new boutique hotel with a refined French restaurant, **L'Aigle d'Or.** Duxton Hill, a short street off Duxton Road, has several lively bars and eating establishments: the **Pig and Whistle** at No. 10, **Barnacle Bill's** at No. 10A, and, for blues and jazz, the **Chicago Bar & Grill** at No. 8.

Retrace your steps to South Bridge Road. **Smith Street,** on the left, has stores selling chilis, teas, and soybeans, and a medicine hall that offers ground rhinoceros horn to help overcome impotency and pearl dust to help ladies' complexions.

Recross South Bridge Road and walk down Ann Siang Road. On the left, at No. 3, is a shop selling superb lion-head costumes and other masks. A left up Club Street takes you past old buildings that continue to house many clan associations. Here, too, you'll see the professional **guild for amahs.** Though their numbers are few today, these female servants were once an integral part of European households in Singapore.

Like the *samsui* women—a few of whom can still be observed in their traditional red headdresses passing bricks or carrying buckets at construction sites—the amahs choose to earn an independent living, however hard the work, rather than submit to the servitude of marriage. (In traditional Chinese society, a daughter-in-law is considered the lowest-ranking member of the family.) In the past, when a woman decided to become an amah or samsui, she would go through a ritual that was a sort of substitute marriage. Family and friends would gather—even bring her gifts—and she would tie up her hair to indicate that she was not available for marriage. She would then move to a *gongxi*, or communal house, where she would share expenses and household duties and care for her sisters.

A right off Club Street takes you to Gemmill Lane and several small shops where sculptures of deities are carved from sandalwood. Clients from all over Southeast Asia place orders for (13) statues and temple panels at the **Say Tian Hong Buddha Shop,** at No. 6. Continue along Club Street and turn left onto Ramah Street, where, at No. 12, paper-thin pancakes are cooked on a griddle and sent to restaurants to be turned into spring rolls.

On the other side of Cross Street, Club Street becomes China Street. Here, at another pancake shop, **Chop Chuan An,** you can watch spring rolls being made—and sample the finished products. To the left off China Street are Chin Chew, Nankin, and Hokkien streets; all have a number of well-preserved shophouses selling coffees, Chinese wines, birds' nests, herbal medicines, candy, and funeral paper.

To the right off China Street is Pekin Street, with its share of shophouses. At No. 8 you can buy superb enameled tea boxes, ideal gifts to take home. Back on China Street, opposite (14) Nankin Street, is the **Jen Foh Medical Hall,** where salespeople are very helpful in suggesting cures for diseases or inadequacies you never knew you had. A few yards farther on is the bakery **Gim Tim,** known for its special cakes said to bring the eater prosperity and a long life.

Where China Street ends, turn right onto Church Street, then (15) take the first left onto Phillip Street. Here you'll find the **Wak Hai Cheng Bio Temple,** built between 1852 and 1855 by Teochew Chinese from Guangdong Province and dedicated to the goddess of the sea. The wonderfully ornate roof is covered with decorations—including miniature pagodas and human figures—depicting ancient Chinese villages and scenes from opera.

Chinese temples, incidentally, are invariably dusty, thick with incense, and packed with offerings and statuary—evidence of devotees asking for favors and offering thanks for favors granted. To a Chinese, a sparkling clean, Spartan temple would suggest unsympathetic deities with few followers. Where burning joss sticks have left a layer of dust and continue to fill the air with smoky scent, the gods are willing to hear requests and grant wishes. If word spreads that many wishes have been realized by people visiting a particular temple, it can, virtually overnight, become the most popular temple in town.

From Wak Hai Cheng Bio, retrace your steps to Telok Ayer Street. On the next block is the Taoist **Fuk Tak Chi Temple,** built by Hakka and Cantonese immigrants. Show deference to the two sinister gods on the left as you enter or risk losing your spirit to them. In front of you are small statues representing some of the many Chinese deities. In the far right corner is one of Tua Pek Kong, to whom this temple is dedicated. Represented as a bearded sailor dressed in mourner's sackcloth, this deity is appealed to by those hoping for a prosperous and safe voyage. Here, the deities are sympathetic—dust and the heavy fumes from burning incense weigh heavily in the air. Buying joss sticks to place before the various deities has a good chance of paying off.

Continue south on Telok Ayer; at Cross Street, notice the **Hakka Clan Hall** (Ying He Hui Guan), on the right-hand corner. It is set in a courtyard and features intricate wood carvings on its gables. At No. 134 is **Meow Choon Foh Yit Ken,** a store well known for traditional medicines.

Past the **Nagore Durghe Shrine,** an odd mix of minarets and Greek columns built by southern Indian Muslims between 1828 and 1830, is the **Thian Hock Keng Temple** (Temple of Heavenly Happiness), completed in 1841 to replace a simple shrine built 20 years earlier. This Chinese temple is one of Singapore's oldest and largest, built on the spot where, prior to land reclamation, immigrants stepped ashore from their hazardous journey across the China Sea. In gratitude for their safe passage, the Hokkien people dedicated the temple to Ma Chu P'oh, the goddess of the sea.

Thian Hock Keng is richly decorated with gilded carvings, sculptures, tiled roofs topped with dragons, and fine carved-stone pillars. The pillars and sculptures were brought over from China, the cast-iron railings outside were made in Glasgow, and the blue porcelain tiles on an outer building came from Holland.

Outside, on either side of the entrance, are two stone lions. The one on the left is female and holds a cup, symbolizing fertility; the other, a male, holds a ball, a symbol of wealth. As you enter the temple you must step over a high threshold board. This serves a dual function. First, it forces devotees to look downward, as they should, when entering the temple. Second, it keeps wandering ghosts out of the temple—ghosts tend to shuffle their feet, so if they try to enter, the threshold board will trip them.

Inside, a statue of a maternal Ma Chu P'oh, surrounded by masses of burning incense and candles, dominates the room. On either side of her are the deities of health (on the left if your back is to the entrance) and of wealth. The two tall figures you'll notice are her sentinels: One can see for 1,000 miles, the other can hear for 1,000 miles. The gluey black substance on their lips—placed there by devotees in days past—is opium, to heighten their senses.

While the main temple is Taoist, the temple at the back is Buddhist and dedicated to Kuan Yin, the goddess of mercy. Her many arms represent how she reaches out to all those who suffer on earth. This is a good place to learn your fortune. Choose a number out of the box, then pick up two small, stenciled pieces of wood at the back of the altar and let them fall to the ground. If they land showing opposite faces, then the number you have picked is valid. If they land same-side up, try again. From a valid number, the person in the nearby booth will tell you your fate, and whether you like it or not, you pay for the information. Leave the grounds by the alley that runs alongside the main temple. The two statues to the left are the gambling brothers. They will help you choose a lucky number for your next betting session; if you win, you must return and place lighted cigarettes in their hands.

⓴ Again going south on Telok Ayer Street, you'll come to the **Al Abrar Mosque,** also known as Kuchu Palli (Tamil for "small mosque"). The original atap mosque, built in 1827, was one of the first for Singapore's Indian Muslims. The present structure dates from 1850. Walk east along McCallum Street toward the bay and take a right up Shenton Way. At Boon Tat Street you'll ㉑ see the **Telok Ayer Market,** the largest Victorian cast-iron structure left in Southeast Asia. Already a thriving fishmarket in 1822, it was redesigned as an octagonal structure by George Coleman in 1894. Now it has reopened as a planned food court, with hawker stalls offering the gamut of Asian fare. By day it's busy with office workers. After 7 PM Boon Tat Street closes to traffic and the mood turns festive: The hawkers wheel out their carts, and musicians give street performances until midnight. Because it just opened in 1992, backed by an investment of S$8.3 million for marketing and development, Singaporeans are coming to satisfy their curiosity; only time will tell whether the high prices will drive away the locals.

From Telok Ayer, S$.60 will take you on the MRT subway one stop north to Raffles Place on Collyer Quay, another S$.10 on up to Orchard Road.

Tour 3: Little India

Indians have been part of Singapore's development from the beginning. While Singapore was administered by the East India Company, headquartered in Calcutta, Indian convicts were sent there to serve their time. These convicts left an indelible mark on Singapore, reclaiming land from swampy marshes and constructing a great deal of the city's infrastructure, including public buildings, St. Andrew's Cathedral, and many Hindu temples. The enlightened penal program permitted convicts to study a trade of their choice in the evenings. Many, on gaining their freedom, chose to stay in Singapore.

Other Indians came freely to seek their fortunes as clerks, traders, teachers, and moneylenders. The vast majority came from the south of India—both Hindu Tamils and Muslims from the Coromandel and Malabar coasts—but there were also Gujeratis, Sindhis, Sikhs, Parsis, and Bengalis. Each group brought its own language, cuisine, religion, and social customs, and these divisions remain evident today. The Indians also brought their love of colorful festivals, which they now celebrate more frequently and more spectacularly than is done in India itself. The gory Thaipusam and the festival of lights, Deepavali, are among the most fascinating (*see* Festivals and Seasonal Events in Chapter 1).

The area Raffles allotted to the Indian immigrants was north of the British colonial district. The heart of this area—known today as Little India—is Serangoon Road and the streets east and west of it between Bukit Timah and Sungei roads to the south, and Perumal Road to the north. Although new buildings have replaced many of the old, the sights, sounds, and smells will make you believe you are in an Indian town.

Numbers in the margin correspond to points of interest on the Tour 3: Little India map.

A good starting point for a tour of Little India is the junction of Serangoon and Sungei roads. As you walk along Serangoon, your senses will be sharpened by the fragrances of curry powders and perfumes, by tapes of high-pitched Indian music, by jewelry shops selling gold, and stands selling garlands of flowers. (Indian women delight in wearing flowers and glittering arm bangles, but once their husbands die, they never do so again.) Other shops supply the colorful dyes used to mark the *tilak*—the dot seen on the forehead of Indian women. Traditionally, a Tamil woman wears a red dot to signify that she is married; a northern Indian woman conveys the same message with a red streak down the part of her hair. However, the modern trend is for an Indian girl or woman to choose a dye color to match her sari or Western dress. Occasionally you will see an unmarried woman with a black dot on her forehead: This is intended to counter the effects of the evil eye.

❶ In the first block on the left is **Zhu Jiao Centre,** one of the largest wet markets in the city. The array of fruits, vegetables, fish, herbs, and spices is staggering. On the Sungei Road side of the ground floor are food stalls that offer Chinese, Indian, Malay, and Western foods. Upstairs are shops selling brass goods, "antiques," porcelains, and textiles. On the right, just past Hastings Street, is **P. Govindasamy Pillai,** at No. 48/50, famous for Indian textiles, especially saris. Farther along, after Dunlop Street, at No. 82, is **Gourdatty Pillai,** with baskets filled with spices of every kind.

The streets to the right off Serangoon Road—Hastings Road, Campbell Lane, and Dunlop Street—are also filled with shops, many of them open-fronted, selling such utilitarian items as pots and pans, plus rice, spices, brown cakes of palm sugar, and every other type of Indian grocery item imaginable. You'll see open-air barbershops and tailors working old-fashioned treadle sewing machines, and everywhere you go you'll hear sugar-sweet love songs from Indian movies.

Along Buffalo Road, to the left off Serangoon, are shops specializing in saris, flower garlands, and electronic equipment. Above the doorways are strings of dried mango leaves, a customary Indian sign of blessing and good fortune. Also along this short street are a number of moneylenders from the Chettiar caste—the only caste that continues to pursue in Singapore the role prescribed to them in India. You'll find them seated on the floor before decrepit desks, but don't let the simplicity of their style fool you: Some of them are very, very rich. Next to the **Sri Ganapathy** flower shop at No. 16 is the shop of **Mr. Saminathan,** one of the last practitioners of fine handwork in gold.

Continuing down Serangoon Road, you'll pass poster shops; the **Mi Ramassy Flour Mill** (at No. 92), where customers come for

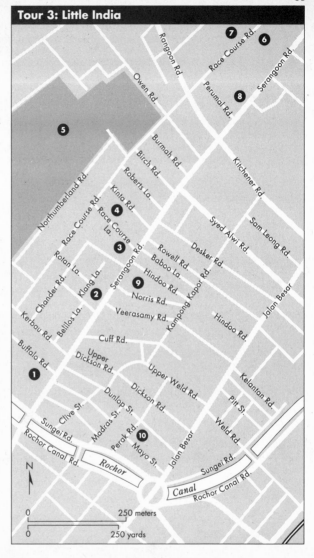

Tour 3: Little India

freshly ground flour; and shops selling silver charms and flower garlands. Down Cuff Road on the right, simple restaurants serve superb chicken, mutton, or fish curries, often on banana leaves with great mounds of boiled rice and an assortment of condiments.

A little farther down Serangoon Road on the left (opposite Veerasamy Road) you'll notice the elaborate gopuram— adorned with newly repainted sculptures—of the **Sri Veeramakaliamman Temple,** built in 1881 by indentured Bengali laborers working the lime pits nearby. It is dedicated to Kali the Courageous, a ferocious incarnation of Shiva's wife, Parvati the Beautiful. Inside is a jet-black statue of Kali, the fiercest of the Hindu deities, who demands sacrifices and is often depicted with a garland of skulls. More cheerful is the shrine to Ganesh, the elephant-headed god of wisdom and prosperity. Perhaps the most popular Hindu deity, Ganesh is the child of Shiva and Parvati. (He was not born with an elephant head but received it in the following way: Shiva came back from a long absence to find his wife in a room with a young man. In a blind rage, he lopped off the man's head, not realizing that it was his now-grown-up son. The only way to bring Ganesh back to life was with the head of the first living thing Shiva saw; he saw an elephant.) Unlike Singapore's other temples, which are open all day, this one is open 8 AM–noon and 5:30–8:30 PM. At these times, you will see Hindus going in to receive blessings: The priest streaks devotees' foreheads with *vibhuti*, the white ash from burned cow dung.

❸ At the corner of Race Course Lane you'll find the **Mahatma Gandhi Memorial Hall,** whose foundation stone was laid by Prime Minister Nehru in 1950. Kinta Road follows Race Course Lane, and here you'll discover a small **Burmese Buddhist Temple,** built in 1878. The temple houses a 3.3-meter (11-foot) Buddha carved from a 10-ton block of white marble from Mandalay (in Burma). The other, smaller Buddhas were placed here by Rama V, the king of Siam, and high priests from Rangoon.

❺ Kinta Road continues down to Race Course Road. **Farrer Park** here is the site of Singapore's original racetrack and where the first aircraft to land in Singapore came to rest en route from England to Australia in 1919. A right at Race Course Road will bring you to the Sakya Muni Buddha Gaya Temple. It is popularly known as the **Temple of 1,000 Lights** because, for a small donation, you can pull the switch that lights countless bulbs around a 15-meter (50-foot) Buddha. The entire temple, as well as the Buddha statue, was built by the Thai monk Vutthisasala, who, until he died at the age of 94, was always in the temple, ready to explain Buddhist philosophy to anyone who wanted to listen. The monk also managed to procure relics for the temple: a mother-of-pearl-inlaid cast of the Buddha's footstep, and a piece of bark from the bodhi tree under which he received Enlightenment. Around the pedestal supporting the great Buddha statue is a series of scenes depicting the story of his search for Enlightenment; inside a hollow chamber at the back is a re-creation of the scene of the Buddha's last sermon.

❼ Across the road is the charming **Leong San See Temple.** Its main altar is dedicated to Kuan Yin—also known as Bodhisattva Avalokitesvara—and framed by beautiful ornate carvings of flowers, a phoenix, and other birds.

Backtrack on Race Course Road to Perumal Road; to the left is the **Sri Srinivasa Perumal Temple.** Dedicated to Vishnu the Preserver, the temple is easy to recognize by the 18-meter-high (60-foot-high) monumental gopuram, with tiers of intricate sculptures depicting Vishnu in the nine forms in which he has appeared on earth. Especially vivid are the depictions of Vishnu's manifestations as Rama, on his seventh visit, and as Krishna, on his eighth. Rama is thought to be the personification of the ideal man; Krishna was brought up with peasants and, therefore, was a manifestation popular with laborers in the early days of Singapore.

Sri Perumal is very much a people's temple. Inside you will likely find devotees making offerings of fruit to one of the manifestations of Vishnu. This is done either by handing the coconuts or bananas, along with a slip of paper with one's name on it, to a temple official, who will chant the appropriate prayers to the deity and place holy ash on your head; or by walking and praying, coconut in hand, around one of the shrines a certain number of times, then breaking the coconut (a successful break symbolizes that Vishnu has been receptive to the incantation).

Time Out If you continue on Race Course Road to No. 56, you can find excellent South Indian curries at **Banana Leaf Apollo,** tel. 298–5054. Be sure to try their specialty of rice with vegetables and spiced sauces served on a banana leaf. The food is extremely cheap—lunch for two is under S$10, and the atmosphere is strictly casual. (*See* Chapter 5.)

From Sri Perumal head back down Serangoon Road and make a left turn onto Norris Road. Here you'll find many open-air cafés specializing in *chapati,* flat Indian bread. At No. 39 is one of
9 Singapore's last remaining *dhobi-wallahs,* traditional Indian laundries where clothes are boiled in a cauldron and beaten on stone slabs. Farther down Serangoon Road, turn left onto Campbell Lane to pass shops selling spices, nuts, flower garlands, plastic flowers, and plastic statues. At Clive Street take another left to see shops selling sugar, prawn crackers, rice, and dried beans. The older Indian women you'll notice with red lips and stained teeth are betel-nut chewers. If you want to try the stuff, you can buy a mouthful from street vendors.

If you turn right at Dunlop Street, you can finish this walking
10 tour of Little India at the small and personable **Abdul Gaffoor Mosque,** which has none of the exotic, multicolor statuary of the Hindu temples but woos you with an intricately detailed facade in the Muslim colors of green and gold.

Tour 4: The Arab District

Long before the Europeans arrived, Arab traders plied the coastlines of the Malay Peninsula and Indonesia, bringing with them the teachings of Islam. By the time Raffles came to Singapore in 1819, to be a Malay was also to be a Muslim. Traditionally, Malays' lives have centered on their religion and their villages, known as *kampongs.* These consisted of a number of wood houses, with steep roofs of corrugated iron or thatch, gathered around a communal center, where chickens and children would feed and play under the watchful eye of mothers and the village elders while the younger men tended the fields or took to the sea in fishing boats. The houses were usually built on stilts above marshes and reached by narrow planks serving as bridges. If the kampong was on dry land, flowers and fruit trees would surround the houses.

Except for the Malay community on Pulau Sakeng (*see* Tour 9), all traditional kampongs have fallen to the might of the bulldozer in the name of urban renewal. Though all ethnic groups have had their social fabrics undermined by the demolition of their old communities, the Malays have suffered the most since social life centered around the kampong.

The area known as the Arab District, or Little Araby, while not a true kampong, remains a Malay enclave, held firmly together by strict observance of the tenets of Islam. At the heart of the community is the Sultan Mosque, or Masjid Sultan, originally built with a grant from the East India Company to the Sultan of Jahore. Around it are streets whose very names—Bussorah, Baghdad, Kandahar—evoke the fragrances of the Muslim world. The pace of life is slower here: There are few cars; people gossip in doorways; and closet-size shops are crammed with such wares as Javanese batiks, leather bags from Yogyakarta, *songkok* hats (the white skullcaps presented to those who have made the pilgrimage to Mecca), and Indonesian herbs whose packages promise youth and beauty or lots of children.

The Arab District is a small area, bounded by Beach and North Bridge roads to the south and north, and spreading a couple of blocks to either side of Arab Street. It is a place to meander, taking time to browse through shops or enjoy Muslim food at a simple café. This tour begins at the foot of Arab Street, just across Beach Road from the Plaza Hotel. (From Collyer Quay, take bus No. 20 or No. 50; from Raffles Boulevard or the Stamford and Orchard roads intersection, take No. 107.)

Numbers in the margin correspond to points of interest on the Tour 4: The Arab District map.

The first shops on Arab Street are bursting with baskets of every description, either stacked on the floor or suspended from the ceiling. Look for **Habib Handicrafts** at 18 Arab Street for leather goods, especially those made from camel hides. Farther along, shops selling fabrics—batiks, embroidered table linens, rich silks and velvets—dominate. However, don't go all the way up Arab Street yet. First turn right onto Baghdad Street (with more shops) and watch for the dramatic view of the Sultan Mosque when Bussorah Street opens up to your left. On Bussorah Street itself, on the right-hand side, are some interesting shops, including a Malay bridal shop and purveyors of batiks and Arab-designed cushion covers; on the left is an importer of leather goods from Yogyakarta (Indonesia). Closer to the mosque, at No. 45, is the Malay-crafts store of **Haija Asfiah,** who will gladly explain in detail the origin and traditional uses of his goods.

● The first mosque on the site of the **Sultan Mosque** was built early in the 1820s with a S$3,000 grant from the East India Company. The current structure, built in 1928 by the same architects who designed the Victoria Memorial Hall, is a dramatic building with golden domes and minarets that glisten in the sunlight. The walls of the vast prayer hall are adorned with green and gold mosaic tiles on which passages from the Qur'an are written in decorative Arab script. The main dome boasts an odd architectural feature: Hundreds of brown bottles, stacked five or more rows deep, are seemingly jammed in neck first between the dome and base. No one seems to understand the point.

Five times a day—at dawn, 12:30 PM, 4 PM, sunset, and 8:15 PM—the sound of the muezzin, or crier, calls the faithful to prayer. At midday on Friday, the Islamic sabbath, seemingly every Malay in Singapore enters through one of the Sultan Mosque's 14 portals to recite the Qur'an. During Ramadan, the month of fasting, the nearby streets, especially Bussorah, and the square before the mosque are lined with hundreds of stalls selling curries, cakes, and candy; at dusk, Muslims break their day's fast

62

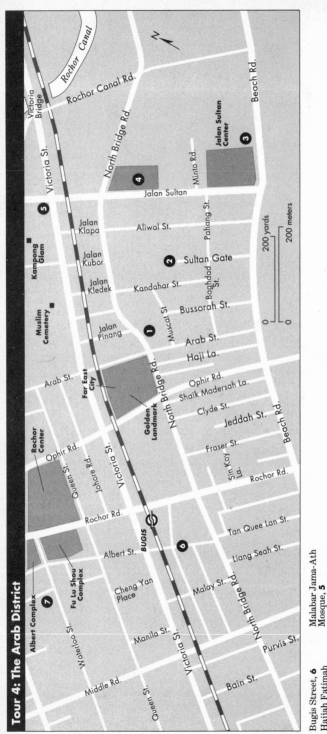

Tour 4: The Arab District

Bugis Street, **6**
Haijah Fatimah Mosque, **3**
Istana Kampong Glam, **2**
Kuan Yin Temple, **7**

Malabar Jama-Ath Mosque, **5**
Sultan Mosque, **1**
Sultan Plaza, **4**

in this square. Non-Muslims, too, come to enjoy the rich array of Muslim foods and the party atmosphere.

② Two blocks east of the mosque, on Sultan Gate, is **Istana Kampong Glam,** the sultan's Malay-style palace. Rebuilt in the 1840s on a design by George Coleman, it is in a sad state of repair today. Next door, faring only slightly better, is another grand royal bungalow: the home of the sultan's first minister. Notice its gateposts surmounted by green eagles. Neither building is open to the public, but through the gates you can get a glimpse of the past. There is talk of this complex being restored, but for now there is little to see.

Baghdad Street becomes Pahang Street at Sultan Gate, where traditional Chinese stonemasons create statues curbside. At the junction with Jalan Sultan, turn right and, at Beach **③** Road, left, to visit the endearing **Hajjah Fatimah Mosque.** In 1845 a wealthy Muslim woman, wife of a Bugis trader, commissioned a British architect to build this mosque. The minaret is reputedly modeled on the spire of the original St. Andrew's Church in colonial Singapore, but it leans at a 6-degree angle. No one knows whether this was intentional or accidental, and engineers brought in to see if the minaret could be straightened walked away shaking their heads.

To non-Muslims, mosques tend to have less personality than other houses of worship, in part because Islam forbids carved images of Allah. The only decorative element usually employed is the beautiful flowing Arabic script in which quotations from the Qur'an are written across the walls. The same may be said of the Hajjah Fatimah Mosque, but because it is relatively small, it is very intimate and an oasis of quiet in bustling Singapore. It is extremely relaxing to enter the prayer hall (remember to take your shoes off!) and sit in the shade of its dome. For some unaccountable reason, the mosque seems to reflect a woman's touch, and not just because it was built by a woman: the Malaccan Hajjah Fatimah. (*Haj* is the honorific title given a man who makes the pilgrimage to Mecca; *hajjah* is the title given to a woman.) French contractors and Malay artisans rebuilt the mosque in the 1930s. Hajjah Fatimah, her daughter, and her son-in-law lie buried in an enclosure behind the mosque.

Return to Jalan Sultan and take a right. Past Minto Road is the **④** **Sultan Plaza.** Inside, dozens of traders offer batiks and other fabrics in traditional Indonesian and Malay designs, and one store on the third floor (No. 26) sells handicrafts from the Philippines.

Continue along Jalan Sultan to the junction of Victoria Street **⑤** for the **Malabar Jama-Ath Mosque.** The land on which it is built was originally granted to the Muslim Kling community in 1848 by Sultan Ally Iskander Shah as a burial ground. The mosque they erected here was abandoned and later taken over by the Malabar Muslims, who rebuilt it in 1963.

Return to North Bridge Road and take a right back to Arab Street. North Bridge Road is full of fascinating stores selling costumes and headdresses for Muslim weddings, clothes for traditional Malay dances, prayer beads, scarfs, perfumes, and much more. Interspersed among the shops are small, simple restaurants serving Muslim food. Toward the Sultan Mosque, the shops tend to concentrate on Muslim religious items, including *bareng haji*, the clothing and other requisites for a pilgrimage to Mecca.

Across Arab Street, Haji Lane, Shaik Madereah Lane, and Clyde Street offer a maze of small shops to explore. The shop at 626 North Bridge Road, **Lean Hen,** cluttered with antique silver, is a delightful place to browse. As you walk southeast along North Bridge Road you'll start seeing fewer signs in Arabic and fewer Malay names. Rochor Road is an unofficial boundary of the Arab District. The next right will bring you to **Bugis Street**—until recently, the epitome of Singapore's seedy but colorful nightlife.

Tourists (and Singaporeans, too, for that matter) used to delight in Bugis Street's red lights and bars, where transvestites would compete with the most attractive women for attention and favors. The government was *not* delighted, though, and so the area was razed to make way for a new MRT station. So strong was the outcry that Bugis Street has been re-created, approximately 137 meters (150 yards) from its original site, between Victoria and Queen streets, Rochor Road, and Cheng Yan Place. The shophouses have been resurrected; hawker food stands compete with open-fronted restaurants (Kentucky Fried Chicken has a dominant corner). The streets in the center of the block are closed to traffic. But pedestrians look in vain for the old Bugis: Plain-clothes security staff make sure that the drunken brawls and general sleaziness remain things of the past. The area has failed to attract the night revelers and performers, and trade hasn't boomed as anticipated. Still, it's convenient for lunch or an early evening meal.

Three blocks beyond where Bugis Street becomes Albert Street—past the **Fu Lu Shou** shopping complex (mostly for clothes) and the food-oriented **Albert Complex**—is Waterloo Street. Near the corner is the **Kuan Yin Temple,** one of the most popular Chinese temples in Singapore. The dusty, incense-filled interior, its altars heaped with hundreds of small statues of gods from the Chinese pantheon, transports the visitor into the world of Chinese mythology.

Of the hundreds of Chinese deities, Kuan Yin is perhaps most dear to the hearts of Singaporeans. According to legend, she was about to enter Nirvana when she heard a plaintive cry from Earth. Touched with compassion, she gave up her place in Paradise to devote herself to alleviating the pain of those on earth; thereupon, she took the name Kuan Yin, meaning "to see and hear all." People in search of help and advice about anything from an auspicious date for a marriage to possible solutions for domestic or work crises come to her temple, shake *cham si* (bamboo fortune sticks), and wait for an answer. The gods are most receptive on days of a new or full moon.

For more immediate advice, you can speak to any of the fortune tellers who sit under umbrellas outside the temple. They will pore over ancient scrolls of the Chinese almanac and, for a few dollars, tell you your future. If the news is not good, you may want to buy some of the flowers sold nearby and add them to your bathwater. They are said to help wash away bad luck.

Time Out A small vegetarian restaurant next to the temple serves Chinese pastries, including mooncakes out of season.

Tour 5: Orchard Road

If "downtown" is defined as where the action is, then Singapore's downtown is Orchard Road. Here are some of the city's most fashionable shops, hotels, restaurants, and nightclubs. The street has been dubbed the Fifth Avenue or Bond Street of Singapore, but in fact, it has little in common with either of those older, relatively understated marketplaces for the wealthy besides the air of luxury. A much more apt comparison would be the Ginza, for, like its Tokyo counterpart, Orchard Road is an ultra-high-rent district that is very modern and very, very flashy, especially at night, when millions of lightbulbs, flashing from seemingly every building, assault the senses.

In addition to all those glittering lights and windows, Orchard Road offers a number of sights with which to break up a shopping trip. We'll start at the bottom of Orchard Street (nearest subway stop: Dhoby Ghaut) and head toward the junction with Scotts Road, the hub of downtown. (Shops and complexes mentioned in this tour are discussed in detail in Chapter 3.)

Numbers in the margin correspond to points of interest on the Tour 5: Orchard Road map.

❶ Leaving the MRT station, with the **Plaza Singapura** shopping complex on your right, you'll see the enormous **Istana**, once the official residence of the colonial governor and now that of the president of the republic. It is open to the public only on National Day. On the first Sunday of each month, there's a changing-of-the-guard ceremony: The new guards leave Bideford Road at 5:30 PM and march along Orchard Road to the Istana, reaching the entrance gate punctually at 6.

❷ On the other side of Orchard Road and a few steps on Clemenceau Avenue is the lovely old **Tan Yeok Nee House.** It was built around 1885 for Tan Yeok Nee (1827–1902), a wealthy merchant from China who started out here as a cloth peddler and became a very wealthy man through trading in opium, gambier, and pepper. Whereas most homes built in Singapore at that time followed European styles, this town house was designed in a style popular in South China—notice the keyhole gables, terra-cotta tiles, and massive granite pillars. After the railway was laid along Tank Road in 1901, the house became the station master's. In 1912, St. Mary's Home and School for Girls took it over. Since 1940 the Salvation Army has made the place its local headquarters. *207 Clemenceau Ave., tel. 734–3358. Admission free. Open weekdays 8:30–4:30, Sat. 9–noon, Sun. 8:30–6.*

❸ Turn onto Tank Road and continue to the **Chettiar Temple,** which houses the image of Lord Subramaniam. The temple is a recent (1984) replacement of the original, built in the 19th century. The 21-meter-high (70-foot-high) gopuram, with its many colorful sculptures of godly manifestations, is astounding. The chandelier-lit interior is lavishly decorated; 48 painted-glass panels are inset in the ceiling and angled to reflect the sunrise and sunset. *Open daily 8 AM–noon and 5:30–8:30.*

Return to Orchard Road and turn left. On the right you'll pass the **Meridien Hotel,** above the **Printemps** department store. If you're an art lover, you might want to take the store's elevator to the Meridien lobby on the fourth floor to see whether one of

Tour 5: Orchard Road

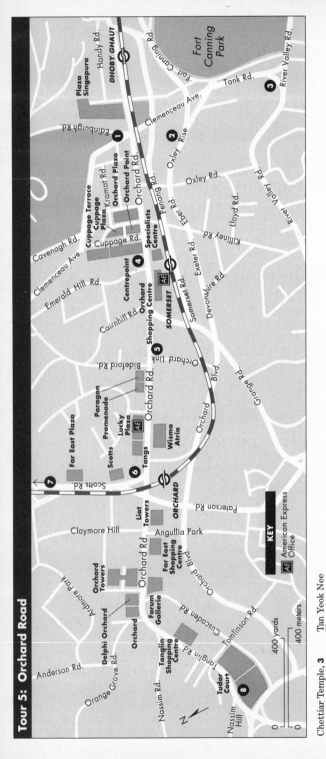

Chettiar Temple, **3**
Dynasty Hotel, **6**
Istana, **1**
Mandarin Hotel, **5**
Newton Circus, **7**
Peranakan Place, **4**
Singapore Handicraft
Centre, **8**

Tan Yeok Nee
House, **2**

KEY

A E American Express
Office

the hotel's frequent exhibitions of local and international artists is under way. A bit farther along is Cuppage Road, with a **market** (open every morning) known for imported and unusual fruit, a row of shops with a good selection of antiques, and the **Saxophone** jazz club.

Time Out For a quick break, try the **Cuppage Food Centre,** next to the Centrepoint shopping complex. Many of the stalls open out onto an attractive tree-lined walkway. The **Selera Restaurant** (No. 01-16) is famous for its Hainanese curry puffs.

Returning once more to Orchard Road, you'll pass the block-long **Centrepoint;** immediately after it is **Peranakan Place,** a celebration of Peranakan (also called Straits-born Chinese, or Baba) culture. This innovative blending of Chinese and Malay cultures emerged in the 19th century as Chinese born in the Straits Settlements adopted Malay fashions, cuisine, and architectural style, adapting them to their own satisfaction. At Peranakan Place, six old wooden shophouses, with fretted woodwork and painted in pastel colors, have been beautifully restored. Notice the typical Peranakan touches, like the distinctive use of decorative tiles and unusual fence doors.

Inside the buildings, ranged around a cobblestone forecourt, are shops selling Baba crafts; **Ba Chik's Foto Saloon,** where you can have a sepia-toned print of yourself, dressed in Peranakan clothing, taken; and restaurants serving Nonya food, the distinctive cuisine of the Straits-born Chinese: Keday Kopi (*see* Chapter 5) and Bibi's (*see below*), both with outdoor tables. Costumed guides conduct tours through the **Show House Museum,** a re-creation of a turn-of-the-century Peranakan home. The unique mixture of Malay, Chinese, and European styles that characterizes Peranakan decor is represented by such furnishings as a Malay bed, a large Chinese altar, and an English sporting print. *180 Orchard Rd., tel. 732–6966. Admission free. Show House Museum tour: S$4 adults, S$2 children under 12. Open daily 11–6:30.*

Time Out In **Bibi's** charming colonial-style dining room one floor up, overlooking Peranakan Place, meals are served on porcelain dishes in the Nonya style. The bar is good for light snacks anytime, and the antiques decorating the walls supply an Old World atmosphere. At midday, the buffet luncheon is a good way to experience the marriage between Chinese (in this case Hokkien) and Malay cuisines. *Tel. 732–6966. Open daily noon–3 PM and 6:45–11 PM. AE, DC, V.*

A bit farther on, across the street, is the **Mandarin Hotel.** In the main lobby is an exquisite mural delineated by real gold etched into white marble. The 21-meter-long (70-foot-long) mural, by Yuy Tang, is called the *87 Taoist Immortals* and is based on an 8th-century Tang scroll. It depicts 87 mythical figures paying homage to Xi Wangmu, Mother of God, on her birthday.

While in the Mandarin, you may want to wander around to see the other works of art displayed. In the Mezzanine Lounge is Gerard Henderson's floor-to-ceiling mural *Gift to Singapore.* Henderson, half Chinese and half Irish, also created a powerful series of eight canvases titled *Riders of the World.* Five of these dominate the wall adjoining the lobby. These vibrant paintings depict the untamed and unconquered, including a 13th-century

Japanese samurai, a Mandarin of the Ming Dynasty, a 9th-century Moor, and a 20th-century cossack. Don't miss the huge abstract batik mural by Seah Kim Joo, one of Singapore's best-known contemporary artists, that adorns three walls of the Mandarin's upstairs gallery.

Recrossing Orchard Road, walk past the **Lucky Plaza** shopping center, packed with camera, electronic, and watch shops, to the corner of Orchard and Scotts roads. You are now at the heartbeat of downtown Singapore. Here, in the lobby of the ❻ **Dynasty Hotel,** you'll find a very special attraction: two facing walls of magnificently executed murals.

These murals are, in fact, 24 gigantic panels of intricately carved teakwood, each 1.2 meters (4 feet) wide and three stories high. Viewed as a whole, they present a vast panorama of 4,000 years of Chinese history and legend. The carving was done in China by 120 master carvers, mostly between 60 and 75 years old, on teak imported from the Burma-Thai border. The vertical panels are unified by the organization of each into horizontal bands. The top band of each panel is devoted to sky and clouds, the central band portrays a hero in a scene, and the lowest band shows the same hero in a different scene. At the base of each panel is the title of the story the panel illustrates. (A book called *Tales of the Carved Panels* is available at the hotel desk.)

Time Out   A detour up Scotts Road past the Hyatt and the Far East Plaza leads to the **Goodwood Park Hotel** (tel. 737–7411). Not as well-known as the Raffles and 30 years younger, this landmark hotel offers the most civilized afternoon tea in town, accompanied by a string quartet. Tea is served from 3:30 to 6 and costs about S$18.

Beyond the Goodwood Park is the Sheraton Towers' **Terrazza** lounge, another fine place for high tea. At the bottom of Scotts ❼ Road is **Newton Circus,** one of the best-known hawker centers in town. (The "circus" refers to the rotary, as in Piccadilly Circus.) Some of the stalls are open all day, but the best times to go are either around 9 AM, when a few stalls serve Chinese breakfasts, or after 7 PM, when all the stores are open and the Circus is humming with the hungry. (*Also see* the introduction to Chapter 5.)

Retrace your steps to the intersection of Scotts and Orchard roads and continue up Orchard Road. Things quiet down a bit now. Walk on the left-hand side of the street past the **Liat Towers** complex (Hermès and Chanel are here), the **Far East Shopping Center,** the **Hilton** and its gallery of boutiques, and the **Orchard Parade Hotel** (the former Ming Court Hotel). On the right-hand side of the street opposite the Hilton is the newest shopping center, the **Palais Renaissance** (390 Orchard Road). The Palais Renaissance is chic, opulent, and overpriced but a delight to wander through. Boutiques such as Ralph Lauren, Dunhill, Christian Lacroix, Chanel, Gucci, and Karl Lagerfeld are for the Japanese shopper seeking status labels at high prices.

Time Out   Turn right at the Orchard Hotel, and take a 10-minute walk up Orange Grove Road to the **Shangri-La** (tel. 737–3644), one of the top three luxury hotels in Singapore. If it's lunchtime, try the excellent dim sum lunch at the hotel's **Shang Palace** restaurant.

At the Orchard Hotel, veer left onto Tanglin Road, another main thoroughfare. Past the **Tudor Court Shopping Gallery,** featuring a number of high-fashion boutiques, is the **Singapore Handicraft Centre,** with more than 40 shops showcasing the crafts of Asia, both contemporary and traditional. On Wednesday, Saturday, and Sunday nights (6–10 PM), a *pasar malam* (Malay for "night bazaar") is held here. The mall and courtyard outside are jammed with stalls selling souvenirs and various and sundry wares. The event is designed for tourists, and to encourage them to buy there are demonstrations of brush painting, Chinese embroidery, and other crafts. On Saturdays there is usually a live show as well—perhaps a lion dance or a performance of a scene from a Chinese opera. One story up from the Handicraft Centre toward the Regent Hotel is a small hawker center, good for light Chinese fare but rather overpriced.

Time Out If you have not yet had tea, you might pay a visit to **Upstairs,** between the Handicraft Centre and the Tudor Court. It is a wonderful ye-olde-style tearoom, a nice contrast to the modernity of Singapore and a pleasant respite from the glitter of Orchard Road.

Tour 6: The East Coast

Two decades ago, Singapore's eastern coastal area contained only coconut plantations, rural Malay villages, and a few undeveloped beaches. Now it has been totally transformed by the dramatic changes that have altered every aspect of Singapore. At the extreme northeastern tip of the island is Changi International Airport, one of the finest in the world. Between the airport and the city, numerous satellite residential developments have sprung up, and vast land-reclamation projects along the seashore have created a park 8 kilometers (5 miles) long, with abundant recreational facilities.

An excursion along the east coast can make for a relaxing and enjoyable morning or afternoon out of the bustling metropolis. A number of sightseeing tours are available through the tour-booking desk of any hotel (*see* Guided Tours in Chapter 1). Alternatively, you can travel by taxi, which can get expensive (a cab to the farthest point, Changi Prison, takes about 40 minutes and costs S$16), or by public bus, an easy and inexpensive way to get around.

Numbers in the margin correspond to points of interest on the Tours 6–8: The East and West Coasts and the Green Interior map.

Our tour starts at the junction of Nicoll Highway and Bras Basah Road, near the Raffles Hotel and Marina Square. Nicoll Highway leads onto East Coast Road, and heading east along it, you come to the Kallang area. Cross the Rochar and Kallang rivers by the Merdeka (Independent) Bridge and you'll see, to the left and right, an estuary that was once the haunt of pirates and smugglers. A few shipyards can be seen to the left where the old Bugis trading schooners used to anchor. (The Bugis, a seafaring people from Celebes, Indonesia, have a long history as great sea traders; their schooners, called *prahus*, still ply the Indonesian waters.) To the right is the huge **National Stadium,** where major international sporting events are held. Just past the stadium, Mountbatten Road crosses Old Airport Road, once the runway of Singapore's first airfield. One of the old British colonial residential districts, this area is still home to the wealthy, as attested by the splendid houses in both traditional and modern architectural styles. Out of Katong, along the East Coast Road, there are still a couple of old-style seafood restaurants, worth visiting for a dinner of chili crab. This area was once close to the seashore, and the restaurants and older bungalows were seaside-vacation destinations.

As you near Bedok you will start to move into more-rural areas and see some of the newer and larger high-rise residential developments. Some of these are mammoth minicities—complete with shopping, recreational, and community services—providing homes for thousands of families. In this part of the island, there were once many traditional Malay kampongs, but virtually all of them have been demolished. Some tour guides will point out the remains of one or two, but shut your eyes—these do not give a true picture of a kampong. Left untended, and probably themselves awaiting the bulldozer, the houses have been vandalized and the community spirit broken.

❶ Changi Prison is well worth a visit. This sprawling, squat, and sinister-looking place, built in 1927 by the British, was used by the Japanese in World War II to intern some 70,000 prisoners of war, who endured terrible hardships here. Today it is still a prison, housing some 2,000 convicts, many of whom are here under Singapore's strict drug laws. This is where serious offenders are executed. A few organized tours can take you into a part of the prison (but not on Saturdays, Sundays, or public holidays)—if you're interested, check itineraries before choosing a tour.

On organized tours you may also pass through the old British barracks areas to the former RAF camp at Changi. Here, in Block 151—a prisoners' hospital during the war—you can see the simple but striking murals painted by a British POW, bombardier Stanley Warren. In going through this area, one marvels at the huge scale of military spending in the 1930s by the British, who put up these well-designed barracks to accommodate tens of thousands of men. It is hardly surprising that the British believed Singapore to be impregnable! This is still a military area; most of the barracks are used by Singapore's servicemen during their 2½-year compulsory military duty.

Most tour groups and all visitors not part of a tour are allowed to see only the **Changi Prison Chapel,** whose walls hold poignant memorial plaques to the regiments and individuals interned here during the war. It is a replica of one of 14 chapels where 85,000 Allied prisoners of war and civilians gained faith and courage to overcome the degradation and deprivation inflicted upon them by the Japanese. Next door is the **Chapel Prison Museum,** with drawings, sketches, and photographs by the POWs depicting their wartime experiences. *Tel. 545–1441. Donations accepted. Chapel and museum open weekdays 8:30 AM–12:30 PM and 2–4:45 PM, Sat. 8:30 AM–12:30 PM. Visitors are welcome at the Sunday service at 5:30 PM. Bus No. 13 from Orchard Rd., with a transfer to bus No. 1 or No. 2 at Victoria St. or Bus No. 1 or No. 2 from Raffles City, will get you here.*

Return to the city via the East Coast Parkway, which is bordered on both sides by landscaped gardens. Between the highway and the sea is **East Coast Park,** with a wide variety of recreational facilities (for more information, *see* Chapter 4; for locations, *see* East Coast Parkway map). Also along here are the **Food Centre,** with alfresco dining from many stalls, and the **UDMC Seafood Centre,** a gathering of eight outdoor restaurants that is a popular evening destination (*see* Chapter 5).

The attraction nearest the city is the **Crocodilarium,** where more than 1,000 of the jaw-snapping creatures are bred to be skinned. Feeding time is 11 AM every Tuesday, Thursday, and Saturday. Watch crocodile wrestling Tuesday through Sunday at 1:15 and 4:15 PM. Naturally, there is a place to buy crocodile-skin bags and belts—at inflated prices. *Tel. 447-3722. Admission: S$2 adults, S$1 children. Open daily 9–5:30.*

Tour 7: The West Coast

The satellite city of **Jurong** is Singapore's main industrial area. It is estimated that more than 70% of the nation's manufacturing work force is employed here by more than 3,000 companies on some 20 industrial estates. One would think this an unlikely tourist area, except perhaps for visitors specializing in industrial design or city planning. However, a number of attractions have been created in or around Jurong as part of the overall planning of the island, and the concept of the garden environment has been continued here to demonstrate that an industrial area does not have to be ugly.

Some of the main tourist attractions in and around Jurong are covered in tours that may be booked at the travel desk of any major hotel. Or you can easily use the new MRT subway or public buses to reach whichever attractions interest you.

Haw Par Villa (Tiger Balm Gardens), near the West Coast Highway, is a modern rendition of Chinese folklore presented in a Disney-type fashion. The half dozen attractions take three to four hours to see, so you may want to make Haw Par Villa a separate excursion. The original Haw Par Villa was an estate owned by two eccentric brothers in the 1930s. After World War II, the gardens were open to the public. The gardens fell into disarray and were sold to a soft-drink bottling company to create a theme park. After S$85 million, the Haw Par Villa reopened in late 1990 as a cross between an amusement park and a multimedia presentation of Chinese mythology. The most popular attractions are a boat ride ("Tales of China") through the inside of a dragon whose entrails have scenes from the 10 courts of hell; slide presentation ("Legends and Heroes") of Chinese mythology that explains why we have only one sun; the tragedy of the Lady White Snake; the heroic Nezha, a 3-dimensional movie ("Creation of the World") of how Pan Gu created the world and Nu Wa created human beings; and a ride on the water roller coaster ("Wrath of the Water Gods Flume Ride"). These and six other attractions to wander through are excellent for keeping your child's interest, though you will be either bored or amused by the corniness of the sanitized production sets. The best time to start your visit is at 9:30 AM, before the crowds and long lines. *262 Pasir Panjang Rd., tel. 774-0300. Open daily 9–6. Admission (which covers entrance to all attractions): S$16 adults, S$10 children under 16. A taxi from Orchard Rd.*

Tours 6-8: The East and West Coasts and the Green Interior

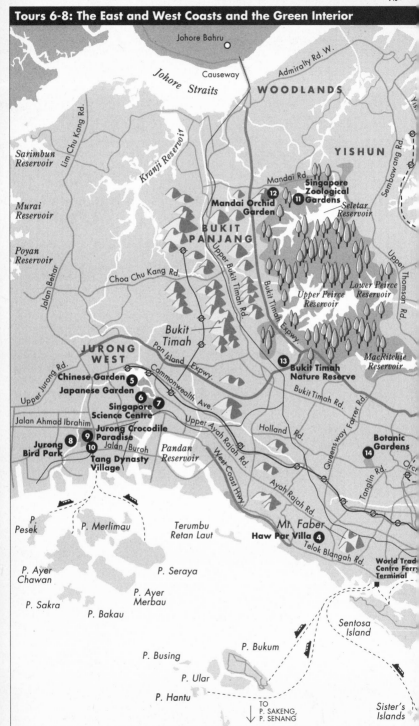

Johore Bahru

Causeway

Johore Straits

Admiralty Rd. W.

WOODLANDS

Sarimbun Reservoir

Lim Chu Kang Rd.

Kranji Reservoir

YISHUN

Yis...

Sembawang Rd.

Murai Reservoir

Mandai Rd.

Singapore Zoological Gardens

⑫ ⑪

Mandai Orchid Garden

Seletar Reservoir

Poyan Reservoir

Jalan Behar

BUKIT PANJANG

Upper Bukit Timah Rd.

Choa Chu Kang Rd.

Upper Peirce Reservoir

Lower Peirce Reservoir

Upper Thomson Rd.

JURONG WEST

Bukit Timah

Pan Island Expwy.

Bukit Timah Expwy.

MacRitchie Reservoir

Upper Jurong Rd.

Chinese Garden ⑤

Japanese Garden ⑥ ⑦

Commonwealth Ave.

⑬ **Bukit Timah Nature Reserve**

Bukit Timah Rd.

Singapore Science Centre

Jalan Ahmad Ibrahim

Upper Ayah Rajah Rd.

Holland Rd.

Queensway Farrer Rd.

Botanic Gardens

Jurong Crocodile Paradise

⑧ ⑨

Jurong Bird Park

⑩

Jalan Buroh

Pandan Reservoir

West Coast Hwy.

Ayah Rajah Rd.

Tanglin Rd.

⑭

Orch...

Tang Dynasty Village

P. Pesek

P. Merlimau

Terumbu Retan Laut

Haw Par Villa ④

Telok Blangah Rd.

Mt. Faber

World Trade Centre Ferry Terminal

P. Ayer Chawan

P. Seraya

P. Sakra

P. Ayer Merbau

P. Bakau

Sentosa Island

P. Busing

P. Bukum

P. Ular

P. Hantu

TO
↓ P. SAKENG,
P. SENANG

Sister's Islands

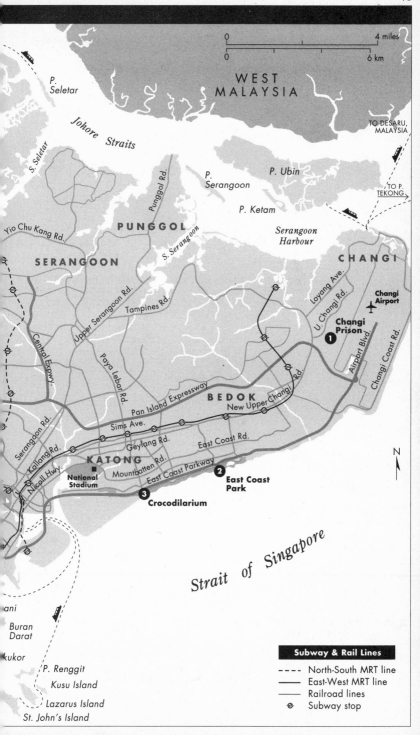

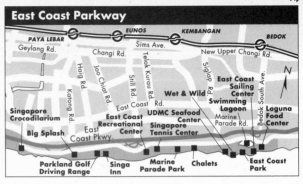

East Coast Parkway

will run S$10, or you can take Bus No. 10 or No. 30 from the Padang for S$.80.

Three popular west-coast attractions, relatively close to one another, are the Chinese Garden, the Japanese Garden, and the Jurong Bird Park. The easiest way to get to them is by air-conditioned express bus. The **Bird Park/Road Runner Service,** operated by Journey Express (tel. 339-7738), departs twice daily, in the morning and afternoon, from hotels along Orchard and Havelock roads. The round-trip fare is S$10 for adults, S$6 for children; there is also a shuttle service three times daily between the Bird Park and the Chinese Garden. Alternatively, you can take either the MRT (get off at Clementi Station) or the public bus (take the No. 10 or No. 30 from Clifford Pier or the No. 7 from Orchard Road to the Jurong Interchange; from the Interchange, you can walk to the gardens or take the No. 240, 242, or 406 bus). A taxi costs about S$12 to the Bird Park or the gardens from Orchard Road.

⑤ The 34.6-acre **Chinese Garden** (Yu Hwa Yuan) reconstructs an ornate Chinese Imperial garden, complete with temples, courtyards, bridges, and pagodas. (One inspiration was the garden of the Beijing Summer Palace.) Within the main garden are theme areas, such as the Ixora Garden, with several varieties of the showy flowering ixora shrub; the Herb Garden, showcasing plants used in herbal medicines; and the Garden of Fragrance, where many newlyweds have their photographs taken against stone plaques with auspicious Chinese engravings. The Chinese Garden is beautifully landscaped, with lotus-filled lakes, placid streams overhung by groves of willows, and twin pagodas. Rental rowboats allow a swan's-eye view of the gardens, and refreshment facilities are available. The garden is especially popular during such festive occasions as Chinese New Year and the Lantern Festival. *Off Yuan Ching Rd., Jurong, tel. 265–5889. Admission: S$2 adults, S$1 children. (Combined ticket with Japanese Garden: S$2.50 adults, S$1.20 children.) Open Mon.–Sat. 9–7, Sun. 8:30–7.*

⑥ Adjacent to the Chinese Garden and connected with it by a walkway is the **Japanese Garden.** This delightful formal garden is one of the largest Japanese-style gardens outside Japan. Its classic simplicity, serenity, and harmonious arrangement of plants, stones, bridges, and trees induce tranquillity. (Indeed, the garden's Japanese name, Seiwaen, means "Garden of Tranquillity.") A miniature waterfall spills into a pond full of water lilies and lotus. *Off Yuan Ching Rd., Jurong, tel. 265–5889. Admission: S$1 adults, S$.50 children. (Combined ticket with Chinese Garden: S$2.50 adults, S$1.20 children.) Camera charge: S$.50. Open Mon.–Sat. 9–7, Sun. 8:30–7.*

⑦ Across the water from the gardens is the **Singapore Science Centre,** dedicated to the space age and its technology. Subjects such as aviation, nuclear sciences, robotics, astronomy, and space technology are entertainingly explored through audiovisual aids and computers that you operate. Visitors can walk into a "human body" for a closer look at the vital organs; there is also a flight simulator of a Boeing 747, plus computer quiz games and other computer/laser displays. The Omni-Theatre presents two programs: "Oasis in Space," which travels to the beginning of the universe, and "To Fly," which simulates the feel of travel in space. The center is designed as a learning experience for schoolchildren, but children of any age are sure to get a thrill from the brave new world of science presented here. *Science Centre Rd., off Jurong Town Hall Rd., tel. 560–3316. Admission: S$2 adults, S$.50 children. Open Tues.–Sun. 10–6. From Orchard Blvd., take bus No. 174 to Coronation Shopping Plaza, then change to the No. 157. From the bird park or the gardens, take bus No. 157 or 178 from the Jurong Interchange.*

⑧ The **Jurong Bird Park,** on 50 landscaped acres, boasts the world's largest walk-in aviary, complete with a 30-meter (100-foot) man-made waterfall that cascades into a meandering stream. More than 3,600 birds from 365 species are here, including the colorful, the rare, and the noisy. It is quite a shock to stand atop Jurong Hill, amid the park's twittering birds and lush green vegetation, and look down on the factories cranking out Singapore's economic success.

If you get to the bird park early, try the breakfast buffet from 9 to 11 at the Song Bird Terrace, where birds in bamboo cages tunefully trill as you help yourself to sausages, eggs, and toast. From there you can walk over to the Free Flight Show (held at 10:30), featuring eagles and hawks. In the afternoon, at 3:30, you might catch the Parrot Circus, complete with bike-riding bird-gymnasts—if you can stand the jabbering. The nocturnal-bird house allows a glimpse of owls, night herons, frogsmouth, kiwi, and other birds usually cloaked in darkness. Pelicans get fed at 10:15 AM and 2:15 PM; visitors can do so throughout the day at the Waterfront Cafe or the Burger King. *Jurong Hill, Jalan Ahmad Ibrahim, tel. 265–0022. Admission: S$6 adults, S$2.50 children. Open daily 9–6. Take the westbound MRT to Boon Lay Station and transfer to SBS bus No. 251, 253, or 255 from the interchange, or use the Road Runner Coach Service (S$10) by booking through Journey Express (tel. 339–7738) or the concierge at your hotel.*

⑨ Next to the bird park is the **Jurong Crocodile Paradise.** Singaporeans seem to be fascinated with crocs, for at this five-acre park you'll find 2,500 of them in various environments—in landscaped streams, at a feeding platform, in a breeding lake. You can feed the crocodiles, watch muscle-bound showmen (and a show*lady*) wrestle crocodiles, or buy crocodile-skin products at the shop. You can also watch the beasts through glass, in an underwater viewing gallery. A seafood restaurant and fast-food outlets provide refreshments, and there is an amusement center with rides for children. *241 Jalan Ahmad Ibrahim, tel.*

261–8866. Admission: S$4.50 adults, S$2.50 children under 12. Crocodile-wrestling shows are at 11:30 AM and 3 PM. Open daily 9–6.

⑩ Yet another theme park, the **Tang Dynasty Village**, re-creates the 7th-century Chinese village of Chang 'An (present-day Xian) with pagodas, gilded imperial courts, and an underground palace of the royal dead guarded by 1,000 terra-cotta warriors. The Imperial Palace includes a cluster of six palaces built to original scale. Restaurants and entertainment facilities are modern intrusions, but artisans make and sell traditional wares, and acrobats, rickshaws, and oxcarts all add to the authenticity. The easiest way out on public transport is the MRT to Boon Lay Station. *Admission: S$15 (S$40 with tour). Open daily 9 AM–10 PM.*

Tour 8:
Into the Garden Isle

Singapore is called the Garden Isle, and with good reason. Obsessed as it is with ferroconcrete, the government has also established nature reserves, gardens, and a zoo. This excursion from downtown Singapore takes you into the center of the island to enjoy some of its greenery. If you have only a little time to spare, do try to fit in the zoo, at least—it is exceptional.

The quickest way to reach the zoo is a 20-minute taxi ride (the fare is about S$11). Bus No. 171 (*Singapore Explorer*) from Orchard Boulevard and Raffles City or No. 137 from Upper Thomson Road will take you to the zoo in under 40 minutes for S$.80 any time of the day; other buses (*see below*) connect the nearby tourist sites.

Alternatively, the air-conditioned **Zoo Express** bus (tel. 235–3111 or 777–3897) takes about 30 minutes, depending on which hotel you're collected from, and includes a short stopover at the Mandai Orchid Garden (*see below*). The bus makes two runs a day, starting at 8:30 AM and at 1 PM. Cost (including round-trip and admission to the zoo and the Mandai gardens) is S$20 adults, S$14 children under 12. The **Zoo Road Runner Service** (tel. 339–7738) makes three runs a day, picking up at seven hotels. It also takes about 30 minutes and includes a stop at Mandai Orchid Garden. Cost (bus fare only): S$10 adults, S$6 children under 12.

⑪ Cliché though it may be, at the **Singapore Zoological Gardens,** humans visit animals as guests in their habitat. One gets the impression that animals come here for a vacation and not, as is often the case elsewhere, to serve a prison sentence. What makes the Singapore zoo different is that it is designed according to the open-moated concept, wherein a wet or dry moat separates the animals from the people. (Interestingly, a mere 1-meter-deep [3-foot-deep] moat will keep humans and giraffes apart, for a giraffe's gait makes even a shallow trench impossible to negotiate. A narrow water-filled moat prevents spider monkeys from leaving their home turf for a closer inspection of visitors.)

Few zoos have found it possible to afford the huge cost of employing this system, developed by Carl Hagenbeck, who created the Hamburg (Germany) zoo at the turn of the century: Moated exhibits take up much more space per animal than cages do. The Singapore zoo has managed by starting small and expanding as more funds became available. It now sprawls over 69 acres of a 220-acre forested area, and the visitor has the pleasurable feeling that the animals are in their natural environments and having a good life.

Try to arrive at the zoo in time for the buffet breakfast. The food itself is not special, but the company is. At 9:30 AM, Ah Meng, a 24-year-old orangutan, comes by for her repast. She weighs about 250 pounds, so she starts by taking a table by herself, but you are welcome to join her for a snack. Afterward, from glass windows beneath their watery grotto, you can watch the polar bears dive for their own fishy breakfast. At the reptile house, be sure to see the Komodo dragon lizards, which can grow to 3 meters (10 feet) in length. Then it will be time for the primate-and-reptile show, in which monkeys, gibbons, and chimpanzees have humans perform tricks, and snakes embrace volunteers from the audience.

There are performances by fur seals, elephants, free-flying storks, and other zoo inhabitants at various times throughout the day. In numerous miniparks reproducing different environments, giraffes, Celebese apes, bearded pigs, tigers, lions, and other of the zoo's 1,700 animals from among 160 species take life easily. Elephant rides are available for S$2 adults, S$1 children. For S$1.50, visitors can travel from one section of the zoo to another by tram. *80 Mandai Lake Rd., tel. 269–3411. Admission: S$5 adults, S$2.50 children under 16. Extra charge of S$2 adults, S$1 children, for the animal shows. Open daily 8:30–6. Breakfast with an orangutan Tues.–Sat. 9–10 AM; high tea at 3.*

⑫ The **Mandai Orchid Garden,** a half-mile down the road from the zoo (bus No. 171 links the two), is a commercial orchid farm. The hillside is covered with the exotic blooms, cultivated for domestic sale and export. There are many varieties to admire, some quite spectacular. However, unless you are an orchid enthusiast, and since it is a good 30-minute taxi ride from downtown, a visit here is worth it only when combined with a visit to the zoo. The Botanic Gardens (*see below*) are closer to downtown and also have orchids. *Mandai Lake Rd., tel. 269–1036. Admission: S$1 adults, S$.50 children (refunded if you make a purchase). Open weekdays 9–5:30.*

For those who prefer their nature a little wilder than what the
⑬ carefully manicured parks around the city can offer, the **Bukit Timah Nature Reserve** is the place. In these 148 acres around Singapore's highest hill (175 meters, or 574 feet), the tropical forest runs riot, giving a feel for how things were before anyone besides tigers roamed the island. Wandering along structured, well-marked paths, you may be startled by flying lemurs, civet cats, or—if you're *really* lucky—a troupe of long-tailed macaques. The view from the hilltop is superb. Wear good walking shoes—the trails are not smooth gravel but rocky, sometimes muddy, paths. *Km 12, Upper Bukit Timah Rd., no tel. Admission free. Open dawn to dusk. From the zoo or the Mandai Orchid Garden, take bus No. 171. The same bus departs from the Orchard and Scotts Rds. intersection.*

⑭ Back toward the city center are the **Botanic Gardens,** an ideal place to escape the bustle of downtown Singapore (and only a short bus ride away). The gardens were begun in Victorian times as a collection of tropical trees and plants. (Today a 19th-century bandstand perpetuates the image of carefully conceived British gardens.) Later, botanist Henry Ridley came here to experiment with rubber-tree seeds from South America; his experiments led to the development of the region's huge rubber industry and the decline of the Amazon basin's importance as a source of the commodity.

The beautifully maintained gardens are spread over some 74 acres, with a large lake, masses of shrubs and flowers, and magnificent examples of many tree species, including 30-meter-high (98-foot-high) fan palms. Locals come here to stroll along nature walks, jog, practice *tai chi* (the Chinese shadow-boxing exercise), feed the geese that inhabit the small pond, or just enjoy the serenity. An extensive orchid bed boasts specimens representing 250 varieties, some of them very rare. The combined fragrances of frangipani, hibiscus, and aromatic herbs that pervade the gardens are a delight. *Corner of Napier and Cluny Rds., tel. 474–1163. Admission free. Open weekdays 5 AM–11 PM, weekends 5 AM–midnight. Via bus No. 7 it's a 10-min ride to the Botanic Gardens from the top of Orchard Rd.*

Tour 9: The Islands

Singapore consists of one large island and 57 smaller ones. Though the STPB, ever striving to make Singapore more attractive to tourists, has begun targeting the islands for development as beach destinations, most of them are still off the beaten track, with few facilities for visitors. Exceptions are Sentosa (the largest and most highly developed), Kusu, and St. John's.

Sentosa

In 1968, the government decided that Sentosa, the Isle of Tranquillity, would be transformed from the military area it was into the Disney-type resort playground it is, with museums, parks, golf courses, restaurants, and hotels. A tremendous amount of money has been poured into the island's development, and some Singaporeans find Sentosa an enjoyable place to spend some of their free time. More attractions are planned, and a causeway linking Sentosa to the main island will facilitate travel to and from the island. However, this "pleasure park" is likely to hold little interest for travelers who have come 10,000 miles to visit Asia. Though Sentosa is certainly not a must-see in Singapore, there are two good reasons to go: the visual drama of getting there and the fascinating wax museum.

Getting There To reach Sentosa from Singapore, you can take either the 1.8-kilometer (1.1-mile) cable car (with small gondolas holding four passengers each) or the ferry. Traveling out by cable car, the more dramatic method, heightens the anticipation; for variety, return by ferry. The new causeway, which will open a rail-and-pedestrian (and probably taxi-) crossing to the island from the World Trade Centre, should be completed in 1993.

The **cable car** picks up passengers from two terminals: the Cable Car Towers, next to the World Trade Centre, and the Mt. Faber Cable Car Station. Since the trip from Cable Car Towers starts at the edge of the sea and is a bit shorter, it does not afford the spectacular, panoramic views you get swinging down from Mt. Faber. At 113 meters (377 feet), **Mt. Faber** is not particularly high, but it offers splendid views of Singapore city to the east and of industrial Jurong to the west. At sunset it is a very romantic spot. A small café offers simple fare.

There is no bus to the Mt. Faber Cable Car Station, and it's a long walk up the hill, so a taxi is the best way to get there. The Cable Car Towers station *is* accessible by bus: from Orchard Road, take No. 10 or 143; from Collyer Quay, No. 10, 20, 30, 97, 125, or 146. *Off Kampong Bahru Rd., tel. 270–8855. Cost: S$6.50 round-trip, S$4.50 one way. Open Mon.–Sat. 10–7, Sun. and public holidays 9–9.*

Ferries ply between Jardine Steps at the World Trade Centre and Sentosa every 15 minutes from 7:30 AM, seven days a week; the crossing takes four minutes. The last ferry back from Sentosa departs at 11 PM Monday through Thursday. From Friday through Sunday and on public holidays, there are two extra return ferries, one at 11:15 PM, the other at midnight. Cost: S$2 one way.

While at the World Trade Centre you may want to visit the **Guinness World of Records Exhibition,** where recordbreaking feats that have made the famed book are the subject of hundreds of displays. *02–70 World Trade Centre, tel. 271–8344. Admission: S$4 adults, S$3 children. Open daily 9–5:50.*

The World Trade Centre is also opening the **Singapore Maritime Showcase,** with high-tech interactive exhibits and displays designed to enlighten visitors about the past, present, and future of Singapore's shipping industry. The Shipbridge Simulator lets visitors operate sophisticated navigational controls to guide megaton ships through computerized versions of famous waterways. Another exhibit shows how Singapore could become a space port. At the TechnoPort, visitors play simulated games working dockside equipment in a detailed model of Singapore's Tajong Pagar and Brani terminals. *Admission free. Open daily 9–5.*

Getting Around Once on Sentosa, there is a **monorail** system—the first of its kind in Southeast Asia—whose six stations cover most of the major attractions (operates daily 9AM–10 PM). Unlimited rides are included in the price of the admission ticket—you may get on and off at any of the stations at will. A free bus (daily 9–7) also provides transportation to most of the attractions. Bicycles are available for rent at kiosks throughout the island. And of course you can walk.

Admission There are two main types of all-day (8:30 AM–10 PM) admission passes to the island, plus cheaper evening-only (5–10 PM) versions of the same. The **Day Charges Ticket** covers round-trip ferry, unlimited monorail and bus rides, swimming in the lagoon, and admission to the fountain shows and the Maritime Museum. Cost: day, S$3.50 adults, S$2 children under 12; night, S$3, S$2. The **Day Package Ticket** includes the above, plus admission to the Pioneers of Singapore/Surrender Chambers, the Coralarium, and Fort Siloso. Cost: day, S$7 adults, S$3.50 children under 12; night, S$5, S$3. Call if you need further information about Sentosa and its facilities (tel. 270–7888). You may also choose the **Sentosa Discovery Package,** which includes transfer to and from the city's major hotels and admission to major attractions. Reservations may be made through your hotel desk or by telephoning 235–3111.

Guided Tour A three-hour guided tour of Sentosa covers the major attractions, including the wax museum, the Maritime Museum, Fort Siloso, and the Coralarium. Cost: S$15 adults, S$11.50 children under 12. These tours depart daily at 10:30 AM. Tickets may be purchased at the Sentosa Cable Car Station ticket booth. You can certainly do as well on your own, however: A recording on the monorail points out sights as you pass, and audiovisual displays accompany many exhibits in the museums.

Exploring Sentosa *Numbers in the margin correspond to points of interest on the Sentosa Island map.*

❶ In front of the ferry terminal are the **Fountain Gardens;** here, several times each evening, visitors are invited to dance along with the illuminated sprays from the fountains to classical or pop music. Performances by traditional-dance groups are sometimes held during the evening.

❷ The **Butterfly Park and World Insectarium** has a collection of 2,500 live butterflies from 50 species, 4,000 mounted butterflies and insects, plus lots of insects—like tree-horn rhino beetles, scorpions, and tarantulas—that still creep, crawl, or fly. The park is landscaped on an Oriental theme, with moon gate, streams, and bridges. *Admission: S$2.50 adults, S$1.50 children. Open weekdays 9:30–5:30, weekends and holidays 9:30–7.*

❸ **Fort Siloso** covers 10 acres of gun emplacements and tunnels created by the British as a fortress against invasion by the Japanese. Unfortunately, the Japanese arrived by land (through Malaysia) instead of by sea, so the huge guns were pointed in the wrong direction. (In fact, the guns could have been redirected, but they were designed to fire shells that pierced ships' armor, not to deal with land forces.) Gun buffs will enjoy the range of artillery pieces in the fort. Photographs document the history of the war in the Pacific, and dioramas depict the life of POWs during the harsh Japanese occupation. *Admission: S$1 adults, S$.50 children. Open daily 9–7.*

The one Sentosa attraction that stands out from all the rest is
❹ the **Pioneers of Singapore/Surrender Chambers** wax museum. A series of galleries traces the development of Singapore and portrays the characters whose actions profoundly influenced the island's history. Though the wax figures are not the most lifelike you'll ever see, the scenes and audio narrative offer a vivid picture of life in Singapore in the 19th century and a rare opportunity, in the modernized Singapore of today, to ponder the diversity of cultures that were thrust together in the pursuit of trade and fortune. The second part of the museum is the Surrender Chambers, with wax tableaux depicting the surrender of the Allies to the Japanese in 1942 and the surrender of the Japanese in 1945. Photographs, documents, and audiovisuals highlight significant events in the Japanese occupation of Singapore and the various battles that led to the eventual defeat. Originally, there was only the scene representing the Japanese surrender; as Japan became the number-one source of foreign visitors to Singapore, it was wisely decided to show both surrenders. *Admission: S$2 adults, S$1 children. Open daily 9–9.*

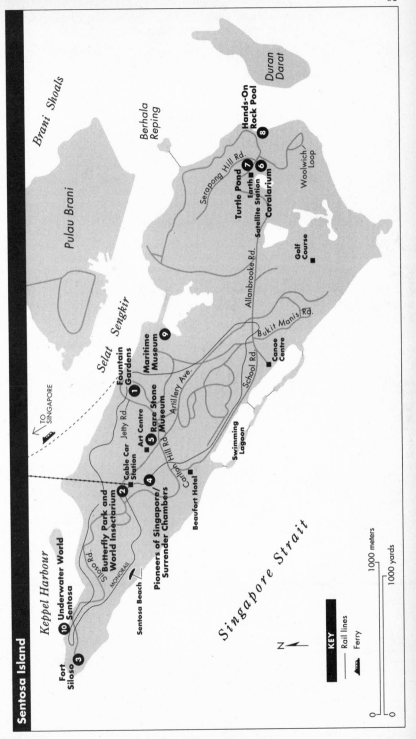

Sentosa Island

Brani Shoals

Pulau Brani

Keppel Harbour

Selat Sengkir

Duran Darat

Berhala Reping

Serapong Hill Rd.

TO SINGAPORE

Fountain Gardens ①

Cable Car Jetty Rd.

Art Centre

Cable Car Station ②

Rare Stone Museum ⑤

Artillery Ave.

Maritime Museum ⑨

Turtle Pond ⑦

Earth ■

Satellite Station

Hands-On Rock Pool ⑧

Coralarium ⑥

Woolwich Loop

Golf Course ■

Allanbrooke Rd.

Bukit Manis Rd.

School Rd.

Canoe Centre ■

④

Pioneers of Singapore/ Surrender Chambers

Caliban Hill Rd.

Beaufort Hotel ■

Swimming Lagoon

Siloso Rd.

MONORAIL

Butterfly Park and World Insectarium

Sentosa Beach

Underwater World Sentosa ⑩

Fort Siloso ③

Singapore Strait

KEY
— Rail lines
— Ferry

N

0 ____ 1000 meters
0 ____ 1000 yards

5 The **Rare Stone Museum** is exactly what its name implies. Here you'll find some 4,000 rare and unique stones and other rocks that have been given interesting designs and shapes by nature. Among these shapes, the imaginative have recognized deities, animals, and historical figures, including Confucius and Winston Churchill. The collection is the work of five generations and includes a display of large rocks, such as 600,000-year-old stalactites and stalagmites, and of fossils and dinosaur bones. *Admission: S$3 adults, S$1 children. Open daily 9–7.*

6 The **Coralarium** has more than 2,500 specimens of seashells and corals on display. In an artificial cave, unusual fish and live fluorescent coral can be viewed. Exhibits demonstrate how coral grows, how shells have evolved, and how typical coral reefs
7 are structured. Admission includes a visit to **Turtle Pond** (open daily 11 AM), where you can feed the turtles with watercress, and
8 to the **Hands-On Rock Pool**, with crabs, corals, and other denizens of the not-so-deep to pick up and have a look at. *Admission: S$1.50 adults, S$.50 children. Open daily 9–7.*

9 The **Maritime Museum** offers a small but interesting collection of ship models, pictures, and other items documenting Singapore's involvement with the sea in business and in war. A fishing gallery displays nets, traps, and spears used in the area throughout the centuries; a collection of full-size native watercraft traces the development of local boatbuilding from dugout canoes to Indonesian *prahus*. *Admission: S$1 adults, S$.50 children. Open daily 10–7.*

10 **Underwater World Sentosa,** completed in 1991, reverses the traditional aquarium experience by placing the visitor right in the water. Two gigantic tanks house thousands of Asian Pacific fish and other marine life; visitors walk through a 91-meter (100-yard) acrylic tunnel that curves along the bottom. *Admission: S$9 adults, S$4 children. Open daily 9–9.*

In addition to historical and scientific exhibitions, Sentosa offers a nature walk through secondary jungle; a *pasar malam* (night market) with 40 stalls (open Fri.–Sun. 6–10 PM); campsites by the lagoon and tent rentals; and a wide range of recreational activities. Canoes, paddleboats, and bicycles are available for hire. There is swimming in the lagoon and at a small ocean beach, though the waters leave a lot to be desired, considering the hundreds of cargo ships at anchor off the coast. Golf is available at the Tanjong Course, and for anyone with balance, there is a roller-skating rink, said to be the largest in Southeast Asia. (For detailed information on Sentosa's recreational offerings, *see* Chapter 4.)

Time Out You may want to enjoy high tea or an early dinner at the **Rasa Sentosa Food Centre** (open 10 AM–10:30 PM), next to the ferry terminal. More than 40 stalls offer a variety of foods for alfresco dining amid groomed tropical surroundings. Two stalls worth noting are **Fatty's from Albert Street,** for Cantonese, and **Charlie's Peranakan,** for authentic Nonya food.

The intent has been to make Sentosa a resort destination, not just an afternoon's outing, and with that in mind, the 175-room **Beaufort Hotel** has opened (*see* Chapter 6). It will be joined in 1993 by the 450-room **Shangri-La International.** Should you wish to visit the Beaufort for lunch by the pool, looking out to the sea, there's a frequent shuttle bus between the hotel and

Sentosa's ferry terminal. (The Shangri-La also promises a shuttle service.)

Kusu Island

Approximately 30 minutes away by ferry from Jardine Steps is the small island of Kusu. There are two ferries, at 10 AM and 1:30 PM, Monday through Saturday. On Sundays and public holidays there are nine, the first departing at 9 AM and the last at 8 PM. Round-trip fare is S$5 adults, S$2.50 children.

Several companies offer day cruises to Kusu and the other islands (*see* Guided Tours in Chapter 1), a convenient and pleasant way to see the islands. Tours are designed to suit a variety of interests and budgets. Most tour boats give sufficient time to visit only the Malay shrine and the Chinese temple. If you want to swim, you'll have to visit the island by ferry.

Kusu, also known as Turtle Island, is an ideal retreat (except on weekends) from the traffic and concrete of Singapore. There is a small coffee shop on the island, but you may want to bring a picnic lunch to enjoy in peace on the beach.

A number of different stories explain the association with turtles, all in some way relating to a turtle that saved two shipwrecked sailors, one Chinese and one Malay, who had washed up on the island. Turtles now are given sanctuary here, and an artificial pond honors them with stone sculptures.

Next to the coffee shop is a small, open-fronted Chinese temple, **Tua Pek Kong,** built by Hoe Beng Watt in gratitude for the birth of his child. The temple is dedicated to Da Bo Gong, the god of prosperity, and the ever-popular Kuan Yin, goddess of mercy. Here she is also known by her Chinese surname, Sung Tzu Niang ("giver of sons"), and is associated with longevity, love of virtue, and fulfillment of destiny. Sung Tzu had a difficult childhood. She was determined to become a nun, but her father forbade it. When she ran away to join an order, he tried to have her killed. In the nick of time she was saved by a tiger and was able to fulfill her destiny. In gratitude, she cut off her arm as a sacrifice. This so impressed the gods that she was then blessed with many arms. Hence, when you see her statue in many of the Chinese temples in Singapore, she is depicted with six or eight arms.

This temple has become the site of an annual pilgrimage. From late October to early November, some 100,000 Taoists bring exotic foods, flowers, joss sticks, and candles, and pray for prosperity and healthy children. The Chinese believe in covering all bases, so while they are here, they will probably also visit the **Malay shrine** on top of the hill.

The shrine (called a *keramat*) is dedicated to a Malay saint, a pious man by the name of Haji Syed Abdul Rahman, who, with his mother and sister, is said to have disappeared supernaturally from the island in the 19th century. To reach the shrine, you must climb the 122 steps that snake their way up the hill through a forest of trees. Plastic bags containing stones have been hung on the trees by devotees who have come to the keramat to pray for forgiveness of sins and the correction of wayward children. If his wishes are granted, the believer must return the following year to remove his bag and give thanks.

St. John's

St. John's is the most easily reached island for beach activities, and the one to which Singaporeans go for weekend picnics. The same ferries that go to Kusu go to St. John's. The trip takes an hour from Jardine Steps.

St. John's was first a leper colony, then a prison camp for convicts. Later it became a place to intern political enemies of the republic, and now it has become an island for picnicking and overnight camping. Without any temples or particular sights, it is quieter than Kusu. There are plans to develop camping facilities, which will surely take away some of the peaceful solitude one can experience here now.

Pulau Sakeng

Pulau Sakeng is off the tourist track. Indeed, no public ferries cross to the island. You'll need to hire a bumboat (at S$30 an hour) from Jardine Steps for the 45-minute passage. The islanders have resisted change; the Malay fishing village on stilts is much as it was a century ago. About 150 families—all Malay, except for the friendly Chinese who own the grocery store—live in the kampong. Residents pay the Singapore government only S$3 a year in property taxes, but they have to bring their own fresh water over from the main island. Aside from a small, simple mosque to visit and local crafts to buy, there is little to do but enjoy the warmth and hospitality of the villagers. The Malay is a natural and giving host.

It is possible to go swimming off the shore, but there are no facilities. If you're changing on the beach, do remember to respect the Malays' sense of propriety.

Other Islands

There are innumerable other islands—uninhabited and very small—to explore. **Pulau Senang,** near the picturesque old Raffles Lighthouse, is fairly large for exploring. Closer to the lighthouse are the smaller **Pulau Jong** and **Pulau Bola. Pulau Hantu** ("Hantu" in Malay means "ghost") is where Malay warriors went to duel to the death. **Sisters' Island** is one of the beautiful southern islands and is also one of the best for snorkeling and diving. **Lazarus Island** is slated for development into a resort area.

Since no regular ferry service goes out to these islands, they require hiring a bumboat *(see* Getting Around Singapore by Bumboat in Chapter 1) or taking an organized day cruise *(see* Guided Tours in Chapter 1). Some of the boatmen know where to find the best coral beds, but the quality of these is not outstanding compared with the quality of those in nearby Malaysia. If you dive off the islands to the south, be careful of the currents—they can be very strong. With a picnic hamper, some champagne, and someone you love, spending the afternoon on a deserted beach could be pure paradise. One word of caution: Make sure you arrange to have the bumboat come back for you!

What to See and Do with Children

Butterfly Park and Insectarium, Sentosa (*see* Tour 9).

Coralarium, Sentosa (*see* Tour 9).

Crocodilarium (*see* Tour 6).

East Coast Park (*see* Chapter 4).

Haw Par Villa (*see* Tour 7).

Jurong Bird Park (*see* Tour 7).

Jurong Crocodile Paradise (*see* Tour 7).

Sentosa Island (*see* Tour 9).

Singapore Crocodile Farm (*see* Birds, Animals, and Reptiles in Sightseeing Checklists, *below*).

Singapore Science Centre (*see* Tour 7).

Singapore Zoological Gardens (*see* Tour 8).

Van Kleef Aquarium (*see* Birds, Animals, and Reptiles in Sightseeing Checklists, *below*).

Off the Beaten Track

A special Sunday-morning treat is to take breakfast with the birds at a **bird-singing café.** Bird fanciers bring their prize specimens, in intricately made bamboo cages, to coffee shops and hang the cages outside for training sessions: By listening to their feathered friends, the birds learn how to warble. Bird-singing enthusiasts take their hobby very seriously and, incidentally, pay handsomely for it. For you, it costs only the price of a coffee to sit at a table and listen to the birds. One place to try is the coffee shop on the corner of Tiong Bahru and Seng Poh roads—get there around 9 AM on Sunday.

With Bugis Street cleaned up, those in search of a risqué evening out might consider taking the causeway into **Johore Bahru, Malaysia.** Start with a Cantonese seafood dinner at **Jaws 5** (Jalan Skudar, Johore Bahru, tel. 07/236062) and take a window table overlooking the Straits of Johore. Then wander up the hill to **Machinta Nightclub** (tel. 07/221400), which offers cabaret acts with transvestites—no doubt those who used to work the nightclubs on Bugis Street.

Near the Mandai Orchid Garden is **The Artists Village,** where Singaporean and expatriate artists work together in a cluster of huts on a working farm. Shows and workshops are held from time to time, but in the artists' desire to involve the viewer in the process of creating art, they welcome visitors anytime. *61-B Lorong Gambas, tel. 257–2503. The nearest MRT stop is Yi Shun; from there, take a taxi.*

Sightseeing Checklists

Amusement and Recreation Parks

CN West Leisure Park (*see* Chapter 4).

East Coast Park (*see* Chapter 4).

Haw Par Villa (Tiger Balm Gardens; *see* Tour 7).

Sentosa Island (*see* Tour 9).

Animals

Butterfly Park and Insectarium, Sentosa (*see* Tour 9).

Crocodilarium (*see* Tour 6).

Jurong Bird Park (*see* Tour 7).

Jurong Crocodile Paradise (*see* Tour 7).

Singapore Crocodile Farm. Yet more of these popular creatures—plus alligators, snakes, and lizards—are on view at this 1-acre breeding farm. Feeding time is 11 AM Tuesday through Sunday. At the factory, observe the process of turning hides into accessories that are sold at the farm shop, along with imported eelskin products. *790 Upper Serangoon Rd., tel. 288–9385. Admission free. Open daily 8:30–5:30.*

Singapore Zoological Gardens (*see* Tour 8).

Underwater World Sentosa (*see* Tour 9).

Van Kleef Aquarium. Some 4,500 specimens of fish, coral, and marine life are exhibited in 71 tanks. *River Valley Rd., tel. 337–6271. Admission: S$.60 adults, S$.40 children. Open daily 9:30–9.*

Buildings

City Hall (*see* Tour 1).

Hakka Clan Hall (*see* Tour 2).

Istana (*see* Tour 5).

Istana Kampong Glam (*see* Tour 4).

Parliament House (*see* Tour 1).

Raffles Hotel (*see* Tour 1).

Supreme Court (*see* Tour 1).

Tanjong Pagar (*see* Tour 2).

Tan Yeok Nee House (*see* Tour 5).

Thong Chai Medical Institute (*see* Tour 2).

Victoria Memorial Hall and Victoria Theatre (*see* Tour 1).

Churches, Mosques, and Temples

Al Abrar Mosque (*see* Tour 2).

Armenian Church (*see* Tour 1).

Burmese Buddhist Temple (*see* Tour 3).

Chettiar Temple (*see* Tour 5).

Convent of the Holy Infant Jesus (*see* Tour 1).

Fuk Tak Chi Temple (*see* Tour 2).

Hajjah Fatimah Mosque (*see* Tour 4).

Jamae Mosque (*see* Tour 2).

Keramat, Kusu (*see* Tour 9).

Kong Meng San Phor Kark See Temple. This relatively modern complex of Buddhist temples on Bright Hill Drive is typical of the ornate Chinese style, with much gilded carving.

Kuan Yin Temple (*see* Tour 4).

Leong San See Temple (*see* Tour 3).

Malabar Jama-Ath Mosque (*see* Tour 4).

Nagore Durghe Shrine (*see* Tour 2).

St. Andrew's Cathedral (*see* Tour 1).

Siong Lim Temple. This is the largest Buddhist temple complex in Singapore, built by two wealthy Hokkien merchants between 1868 and 1908. Set among groves of bamboo, the temple (184 E. Jalan Toa Payoh) is guarded by the giant Four Kings of Heaven, in full armor. There are a number of shrines and halls, with many ornate features and statues of the Lord Buddha. The goddess of mercy, Kuan Yin, has her shrine behind the main hall; another hall houses a number of fine Thai Buddha images. The oldest building in the complex is a small wood shrine containing antique murals of the favorite Chinese legend "Pilgrimage to the West."

Sri Mariamman Temple (*see* Tour 2).

Sri Srinivasa Perumal Temple (*see* Tour 3).

Sri Veeramakaliamman Temple (*see* Tour 3).

Sultan Mosque (*see* Tour 4).

Tan Si Chong Su Temple. Built for the Tan family in 1876, this small, very personable Chinese temple on Magazine Road was designed in the style of a Chinese palace. It is elaborately decorated with rows of inscribed tablets to honor deceased clansmen.

Temple of 1,000 Lights (*see* Tour 3).

Thian Hock Keng Temple (*see* Tour 2).

Tua Pek Kong, Kusu (*see* Tour 9).

Wak Hai Cheng Bio Temple (*see* Tour 2).

Parks and Gardens

Botanic Gardens (*see* Tour 8).

Bukit Timah Nature Reserve (*see* Tour 8).

Chinese Garden (*see* Tour 7).

Farrer Park (*see* Tour 3).

Fort Canning Park (*see* Tour 1).

Haw Par Villa (Tiger Balm Gardens; *see* Tour 7).

Japanese Garden (*see* Tour 7).

MacRitchie Reservoir. This park surrounding a reservoir in the center of the island (Lornie Rd., near Thomson Rd.) is popular with joggers and those seeking greenery in the rough.

Mandai Orchid Garden (*see* Tour 8).

Merlion Park (*see* Tour 1).

Mt. Faber (*see* Tour 9).

Seletar Reservoir. Larger and wilder than the MacRitchie Reservoir, the Seletar (on Mandai Rd., near the zoo) is the largest and least developed natural area on the island.

Tang Dynasty Village (*see* Tour 7).

Museums, Monuments, and Memorials

Cenotaph War Memorial (*see* Tour 1).

Changi Prison (*see* Tour 6).

Coralarium, Sentosa (*see* Tour 9).

Empress Place (*see* Tour 1).

Fort Siloso, Sentosa (*see* Tour 9).

Kranji War Memorial. This cemetery, a tribute to the forces who fought to defend Singapore in World War II, is in the north of the island, off Woodlands Road. Rows of Allied dead are grouped with their countrymen in plots on a peaceful, well-manicured hill. This is a touching experience, a reminder of the greatness of the loss in this and all wars.

Lim Bo Seng Memorial (*see* Tour 1).

Mahatma Gandhi Memorial (*see* Tour 3).

Maritime Museum, Sentosa (*see* Tour 9).

National Museum and Art Gallery (*see* Tour 1).

New Ming Village. At this small complex of buildings not far from the Jurong Bird Park, demonstrations of the art of Chinese pottery making are given, and copies of Ming Dynasty blue and white porcelain are produced and sold. *32 Pandam Rd., tel. 265–7711. Admission free. Open daily 9–5:30.*

Peranakan Place (*see* Tour 5).

Pioneers of Singapore/Surrender Chambers, Sentosa (*see* Tour 9).

Rare Stone Museum, Sentosa (*see* Tour 9).

Singapore Mint Coin Gallery. Minting operations can be viewed here, along with coins, medals, and medallions from Singapore and around the world. *249 Jalan Boon Lay, Jurong, tel. 265–3907. Admission free. Open weekdays 9:30–4:30.*

Singapore Science Centre (*see* Tour 7).

Statue of Sir Thomas Stamford Raffles (*see* Tour 1).

Tomb of Iskandar Shah (*see* Tour 1).

Victorian Fountain (*see* Tour 1).

War Memorial (*see* Tour 1).

3 Shopping

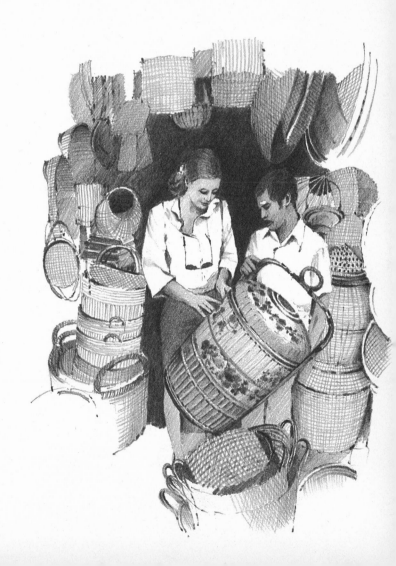

Singapore is truly a shopping wonderland. What makes it so is the incredible range of goods brought in from all over the world to be sold in an equally incredible number of shops. Unfortunately, though, the bargain prices for which Singapore was once famous no longer exist. The intense competition among shops prevents them from buying and selling in volume. Also, with a growing economy and a standard of living second in Asia only to Japan's, Singapore has a strong dollar and high overheads for importing agents and retail outlets.

There are still bargains, but the savings may not be great. You should know the prices of goods you intend to buy before you leave home. This is especially true of photographic and electronic equipment. Prices do not vary a great deal from shop to shop. Compare a few shops to feel secure about your price. Good values are found in fashion goods (Singapore has become a fashion contracting center, since it does not have the quota restrictions Hong Kong and other Asian cities do), handcrafted rosewood furniture, Chinese objets d'art, and carpets.

When shopping, look for the Singapore Tourist Promotion Board logo—a gold Merlion (a lion's head with a fish tail) on a red background. This signifies that the retailer is recommended by the STPB and the Singapore Retail Merchants Association. Members are required to sell at "reasonable prices," give receipts, and display price tags indicating the discount as well as what is included in the price. If the object is a camera, for example, the price tag must say whether the camera bag, lenses, etc., are included in the displayed price.

Electrical Goods Singapore's current is 220–240 volts at 50 cycles, similar to Australia's, Great Britain's, and Hong Kong's. Canada, Japan, and the United States use 110–120 volts at 60 cycles. When buying electrical equipment, verify that you can acquire special adapters, if required, and that these will not affect the equipment's performance.

Imitations Copyright laws passed in early 1987 impose stern penalties on the selling of pirated music tapes and computer software. However, Singapore still has a reputation for pirated goods. If you are buying a computer, for example, stores are quite amenable to loading it with all the software you want.

Street stalls or bargain shops have designer-label merchandise for ridiculously low prices; they are all fakes. Sport shirts with famous-name labels and logos—Lacoste, Pierre Cardin, Giordano—filter in from Thailand and Hong Kong. Deeply discounted leather goods with such labels as Cartier, Etienne Aigner, and Gucci at these shops are most certainly frauds.

Street peddlers sell quartz watches, mainly from Taiwan, bearing the names of great Swiss or French watchmakers or European design houses for about S$30; they are fakes. The greatest of the fakes is the "solid gold Rolex," which comes complete with serial number for S$100. It looks so good you could have a problem at Customs—though you're more likely to have a Customs problem (either in Singapore or at home) if you're discovered to have purchased a counterfeit item.

Touts Touting—soliciting business by approaching people on the street with offers of free shopping tours and special discounts—is illegal (maximum fines were raised from S$200 to S$5,000 in 1989, and prison sentences of up to six months are possible). Nevertheless, it continues outside one or two shopping centers, especially the Far East Shopping Centre and Lucky Plaza. Some taxi drivers tout as well. Avoid all touts and the shops they recommend. The prices will end up being higher—reflecting the tout's commission—and the quality of the goods possibly inferior. Any reputable shop does not need touts.

Bargaining Bargaining is widely practiced in Singapore; the type of store determines the potential "discount." Only the department stores do not offer discounts—their items are tagged with fixed prices. It's a good idea to visit a department store first to establish the base price of an item, then shop around. If you do not like to bargain, stick to the department stores, which usually have the lowest initial ("first") price.

Shops in upscale shopping complexes or malls tend to give a 10% discount, sometimes 15%, on clothes. However, at a jewelry store, the discount can be as high as 50%. At less-upscale complexes, the discounts tend to be greater, especially if they view you as a tourist—that will boost their initial asking price. Stalls and shops around tourist attractions have the highest initial prices and, consequently, can be bargained down to give the greatest discounts.

Everyone has his or her own method of bargaining, but in general, when a vendor tells you a price, ask for the discounted price, then offer even less. The person will probably reject your offer but come down a few dollars. With patience, this can continue and earn you a few more dollars off the price. If you don't like haggling, walk away after hearing the discounted price. If the vendor hasn't hit bottom price, you'll be called back.

How to Pay All department stores and most shops accept credit cards— American Express, Diners Club, MasterCard, and Visa—and many tourist shops also accept Carte Blanche. Traveler's checks are readily accepted, and many tourist shops will also accept foreign currency, but it is better to change traveler's checks and foreign currency at a bank before shopping. Retailers work at a low profit margin and depend on high turnover; they assume you will pay in cash. Except at the department stores, paying with a credit card will mean that your "discounted price" will reflect the commission the retailer will have to pay the credit card company.

Receipts Be sure to ask for receipts, both for your own protection and for Customs. Though shopkeepers are amenable to stating false values on receipts, Customs officials are wary and knowledgeable.

Guarantees Make sure you get international guarantees and warranty cards with your purchases. Check the serial number of each item against its card, and don't forget to mail the card in. Sometimes guarantees are limited to the country of purchase. If the dealer cannot give you a guarantee, he is probably selling an item intended for the domestic market in its country of manufacture; if so, he has bypassed the authorized agent and should be able to give you a lower price, but that is not always the case. Though your purchase of the item is not illegal, you have no guarantee. If you decide to buy it anyway, be sure to check that the item is in working order before you leave the shop.

Complaints Complaints about either a serious disagreement with a shop-keeper or the purchase of a defective product should be lodged with the STPB (#01-19 Raffles City Tower, Singapore 0617, tel. 339–6622). Give full details of the complaint, and the STPB's Tourism Services Division will pursue it. The Consumers Association of Singapore (Trade Union House Annex, Shenton Way, Singapore 0106, tel. 221–6238) can also advise you regarding a vendor-related complaint.

Shipping All stores that deal with valuable, fragile, or bulky merchandise know how to pack well. Ask for a quote on shipping charges, which you can then double-check with a local forwarder. Check whether the shop has insurance covering both loss and damage in transit. You might find you need additional coverage.

Shopping Districts

Throughout the city are complexes full of shopping areas and centers. Many stores will have branches carrying much the same merchandise in several of these areas.

Orchard Road The heart of Singapore's preeminent shopping district, Orchard Road is bordered on both sides with tree-shaded tiled sidewalks lined with modern shopping complexes and deluxe hotels that house exclusive boutiques. Also considered part of this area are the shops on Scotts Road, which crosses Orchard, and two shopping centers—Supreme House on Penang Road and Singapore Shopping Centre on Clemenceau Avenue—at the end of Orchard Road, where it detours at Plaza Singapura, next to the Istana.

Orchard Road is known for fashion and interior design shops, but you can find anything from Mickey Mouse watches to Chinese paper kites and antique Korean chests. The interior design shops have unusual Asian bric-a-brac and such original items as a lamp stand made from an old Chinese tea canister or a pair of bookends in the shape of Balinese frogs. Virtually every Orchard Road complex, with the exception of the Promenade, has a clutch of department stores selling electronic goods, cigarette lighters, pens, jewelry, cameras, and so on. Most also have money changers, a few inexpensive cafés, and snack bars.

Though there is reference to an "Orchard Road price," which takes into account the astronomical rents some shop tenants have to pay, the department stores have the same fixed prices here as at all their branches. Small shops away from the center may have slightly cheaper prices.

Chinatown Once Singapore's liveliest and most colorful shopping area, Chinatown lost a great deal of its vitality when the street stalls were moved indoors, but it is still fun to explore. The focus is on the Smith, Temple, and Pagoda street blocks, but nearby streets—Eu Tong Sen Street, Wayang Street, and Merchant Road on one side, and Ann Siang Hill and Club Street on another—can yield some interesting finds.

The old street vendors have moved into the **Kreta Ayer Complex,** off Neil Road; the **Chinatown Complex,** off Trengganu Street; and the **People's Park Centre,** on Eu Tong Sen Street. Most sell market goods, but here and there you'll find a booth with odds and ends of jade or porcelain.

Chinese kitchenware can be fascinating. On Temple Street in particular you can find a wealth of unusual plates, plant pots, teapots, lacquered chopsticks, and so on.

All the paraphernalia for Chinese funerals is sold in a number of shops in Chinatown, especially around Sago Street. (Nearby Sago Lane was lined, not so long ago, with "death houses," where elderly people went to await death.) This may sound gruesome, but these funerary items are among the most creative examples of folk art in the world. They include paper replicas of life's necessities, to serve the dead in their afterlife. You can even buy paper servants, a paper Mercedes, or—the height of this artwork—a paper Boeing 747. There are some famous funeral-paper craftsmen on Ann Siang Hill, where there is also a shop that can sell you a lion's head (made of fabric over a wire frame) like those used in the Chinese lion dance.

Just around the corner, on Club Street, are several woodcarvers who specialize in creating idols of Chinese gods. On Merchant Road, a vendor of costumes for Chinese operas welcomes customers. And on Chin Hin Street, you can buy a package of fragrant Chinese tea direct from the merchant.

South Bridge Road in Chinatown is the street of goldsmiths. There are dozens of jewelers here, specializing in 22K and even 24K gold ornaments in the characteristic orange color of Chinese gold. Each assistant, often shielded by a metal grill, uses an abacus and a balance to calculate the value of the piece you wish to buy. You *must* bargain here.

At **Fook On** (83-85 South Bridge Rd., tel. 532–3239) you can buy all your winter clothes, whether you prefer Chinese or Western styles. On the same street, there are many art galleries, such as the **Seagull Gallery** (#62B, tel. 532–3491) and the **Wenian Art Gallery** (#95, tel. 538–3750); and seal carvers in the **Hong Lim Shopping Centre** will carve your name into your own personal "chop."

Of the shopping areas along Eu Tong Sen Street, the most famous is the **People's Park Complex,** where every shop promises a bargain. There are lots of watch and camera shops here, and the **Overseas Emporium** (tel. 535–0555) is a wonderful place to explore. In the next block is **People's Park Centre,** which is not as lively but has an emporium, too, as well as shopkeepers who are easier to deal with. Neither complex opens before noon.

Little India   Serangoon Road is affectionately known as Little India. For shopping purposes, it begins at the **Zhu Jiao Centre,** on the corner of Serangoon and Buffalo roads. Some of the junk dealers and inexpensive-clothing stalls from a bazaar known as Thieves Market were relocated here when the market was cleared out. It's a fun place to poke about.

All the handicrafts of India can be found here: intricately carved wood tables, shining brass trays and water ewers, hand-loomed table linens, fabric inlaid with tiny mirrors, brightly colored pictures of Hindu deities, and even garlands of jasmine for the gods.

And the sari shops! At dozens of shops here you can get the 6 meters (6.5 yards) of voile, cotton, Kashmiri silk, or richly embroidered Benares silk required to make a sari. For the variety, quality, and beauty of the silk, the prices are very low. Other Indian costumes, such as long or short *kurtas* (men's

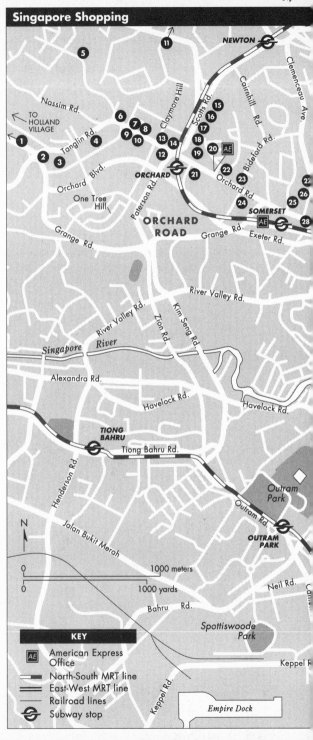

Singapore Shopping

KEY

AE American Express Office

North-South MRT line

East-West MRT line

Railroad lines

Subway stop

95

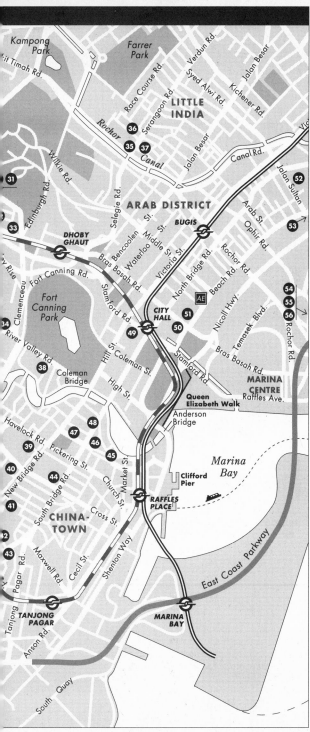

collarless shirts) and Punjabi trouser sets, are unusual and attractive buys.

Just off Serangoon Road is a Chinese business that can provide you with some good souvenirs. At 18 Birch Road is a shop where figures of pressed sawdust, painted to look as if they're wearing makeup and Chinese costumes, are made to ornament giant Chinese joss (incense) sticks.

Should you overspend and find yourself with excess baggage, there are several luggage shops on Serangoon Road where you can buy an old-fashioned tin trunk big enough to hide a body in.

Arab Street   The Arab Street shopping area really begins at Beach Road, opposite the Plaza Hotel. This old-fashioned street is full of noteworthy buys. A group of basket and rattan shops first catches your eye. There are quite a few jewelers here, and even more shops selling loose gems and necklaces of garnet and amethyst beads. The main business is batiks (textiles bearing hand-printed designs) and lace.

Brassware, prayer rugs, carpets, and leather slippers are sold in abundance on Arab Street and its side streets, which have appealing names like Muscat Street and Baghdad Street. Two noteworthy complexes in the vicinity are the **Golden Mile Food Centre,** on Beach Road, devoted to good food on the lower floors and junk and antiques on the top floors; and the **Textile Centre,** on Jalan Sultan, offering a wide variety of batiks.

Katong   The quiet east-coast suburb of Katong, just 15 minutes from town via the expressway, has old-fashioned shophouses along its main street, some selling inexpensive children's clothes and one dealing in antiques. Off the main road is an even more old-fashioned street called Joo Chiat Road, which gets more and more interesting as it approaches Gelang Road. Its shops sell Chinese kitchenware, antiques, and baby clothes, and lots of offbeat items.

Holland Village   Holland Village, 10 minutes from town by taxi, is a bit of a Yuppie haunt, but it is the most rewarding place to browse for unusual and inexpensive Asian items, large and small. Many shops here specialize in Korean chests. Behind the main street is Lorong Mambong, a street of shophouses jammed with baskets, earthenware, porcelain, and all sorts of things from China and Thailand. The **Holland Village Shopping Centre** on Holland Avenue has quite a few shops, including **Lim's Arts and Crafts** (tel. 467–1300), selling inexpensive gifts and souvenirs; there always seems to be something out of the ordinary to pick up here. A 10-minute walk away is **Cold Storage Jelita** (293 Holland Rd.), with several stores, including **Jessica Art 'N Craft** (tel. 469–0689).

Shopping Centers

Note: Shops in multilevel buildings and shopping complexes are often listed with a numerical designation such as #00-00. The first part of this number indicates what floor the shop is on. The second part indicates its location on the floor. When the phone number of an individual shop is not given, you'll find it listed with the shop under a specific merchandise category, below.

Centrepoint   This spacious and impressive center (176 Orchard Rd.) has the **Robinsons** department store as its anchor tenant. One of the

SOME OF THE BEST KNOWN SIGHTS IN ASIA.

Forty-five years of flying to Asia has made Northwest a familiar face. Especially when you consider we've been flying there longer than any other airline.

And now the leading airline to Asia can get you there faster. With new schedules that reduce travel time by as much as three hours.

We've even enhanced our fleet of 747s. So you'll find spacious surroundings, elegant meals and state-of-the-art audio and video programming.

Northwest flies to more cities in Asia from the U.S. than any other airline. And when you fly to Asia on Northwest, you'll be able to earn free travel with Northwest WorldPerks® after only 20,000 miles.

Be sure to ask your travel agent about the great savings on our Northwest WorldVacations℠ customized vacation packages to Asia, too.

To put yourself in the picture, call your travel agent or Northwest at 1-800-447-4747.

NORTHWEST AIRLINES
Some People Just Know How To Fly.

CALL YOUR TRAVEL AGENT OR NORTHWEST
1-800-447-4747

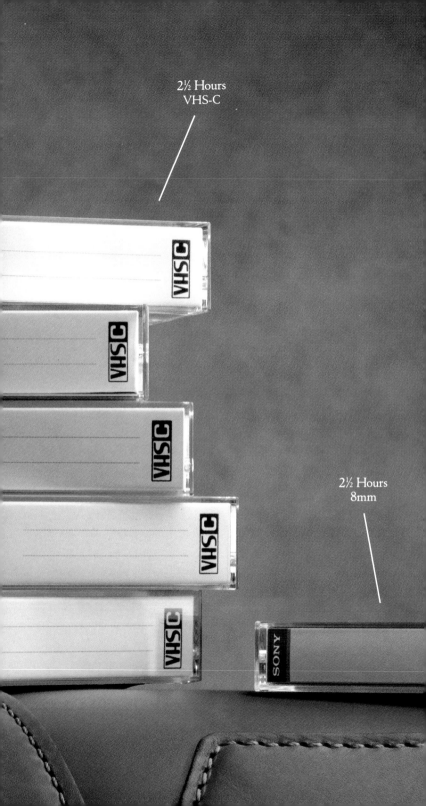

2½ Hours
VHS-C

2½ Hours
8mm

PACK WISELY.

Given a choice, the seasoned traveler always carries less.
Case in point: Sony Handycam® camcorders, America's most
popular. They record up to 2½ hours on a single tape.
VHS-C tapes record only 30 minutes.* And why carry five tapes
when you can record everything on one? Which brings us
to the first rule of traveling: pack a Sony Handycam camcorder.

American Express offers Travelers Cheques built for two.

American Express® Travelers Cheques *for Two*. The first Travelers Cheques that allow either of you to use them because both of you have signed them. And only one of you needs to be present to purchase them.

Cheques *for Two* are accepted anywhere regular American Express Travelers Cheques are, which is just about everywhere. So stop by before your next trip and ask for Cheques *for Two*.

Travelers Cheques

liveliest complexes, Centrepoint also has jewelry, silverware, and fashion shops; furniture stores selling Philippine bamboo and Korean chests; and a large basement supermarket.

Delfi Orchard Also on Orchard Road (at #402), Delfi has a very Japanese bias influenced by the recent opening of the **Meitetsu** department store, but **Waterford Wedgwood** is also here, along with a well-stocked golf shop.

Far East Plaza This center (at 14 Scotts Rd.) is where the young and trendy gather to see and be seen. The shops are geared to them, and there's a bargain-basement atmosphere about the place. A forecourt offers fast-food restaurants (including a McDonald's), outdoor tables, and entertaining people-watching.

Forum Galleria This center (at 583 Orchard Rd.) boasts a huge **Toys 'R' Us** (tel. 235–4322), as well as an assortment of boutiques.

Liang Court Complex Liang Court (177 River Valley Rd.) is off the beaten track but only five minutes by cab from Orchard Road and worth the drive. The department store **Daimaru** is here, with half of its floor transformed into selected designer boutiques, a pearl specialist, a bookstore, and a silk store.

Lucky Plaza At this center (304 Orchard Rd.), which includes two department stores, the tenant mix is aimed specifically at the tourist market. This is a place to bargain furiously. The many jewelers here are involved in a perpetual price-cutting war, to the delight of shoppers.

Marina Square Part of an elegant complex, this shopping center includes two department stores, **Metro** (tel. 337–2868) and **Tokyu** (tel. 337–0077), and 200 smaller shops, including the English stores **Habitat** (tel. 337–0688) and **Mothercare** (tel. 337–0388).

Orchard Point and Orchard Plaza Side by side on Orchard Road (#220 and #150), these centers don't have the popular appeal of some other complexes but will reward dedicated shoppers with good finds. **Euvon** (tel. 235–1375), a reptile-skin shop on the second floor of Orchard Plaza, can whip up a snakeskin bag to your specifications for S$100. More reptile bags can be found in the basement shops of Orchard Point, next to the art-supply shop **Grafitti** (tel. 732–5984).

Palais Renaissance Across the road from the Hilton Hotel (390 Orchard Rd.) is Singapore's newest haute-fashion center. Targeted at the Japanese shopper seeking status labels at high prices, the Palais Renaissance is chic, opulent, and overpriced but a delight to wander through. Boutiques for Ralph Lauren, Dunhill, Christian Lacroix, Chanel, Gucci, and Karl Lagerfeld compete as much in the design of their store as in the design of their merchandise. Perfumes, jewelry, and travel accessories are also expensively represented in this extravagant marbled emporium to make it a one-stop shopping spree for the well-heeled.

The Paragon As one of the glossiest of the shopping centers, the Paragon (290 Orchard Rd.) has more than 15 men's fashion boutiques and numbers among its more popular tenants **Gucci** (tel. 734–2528) and the **Metro** department store (tel. 235–2811).

Parkway Parade This excellent and very attractive center is on Marine Parade Road, 15 to 20 minutes east of town by expressway. On weekdays you can shop here in peace and quiet; on weekends, it is uncomfortably crowded. The focus is on up-to-date and affordable fashions. Things get started around noon.

People's Park Complex This Chinatown center (Eu Tong Sen St.) has an international reputation. It's not new and glossy like most of the other complexes, but it's always entertaining. Everything is sold here: herbs, Chinese medicines, cameras, stereo equipment, clothes, luggage. Shopkeepers are much more aggressive here than in town, and if you haven't done your homework, you can get taken.

The Promenade The Promenade (300 Orchard Rd.) is Singapore's most elegant shopping center, in both design (a spiral walkway with a gentle slope instead of escalators) and tenants. Its fashion stores carry some of the hottest names; **Issey Miyake** (tel. 732–0364) chose it for his first boutique outside Japan. Home-decor shops sell a superb collection of Asian odds and ends.

Raffles City Bordered by Stamford, North Bridge, and Bras Basah roads, this complex has a confusing interior. If you get lost, you're sure to come across many shopping finds, many of them in the Japanese department store **Sogo.** Also here are a **Times** bookshop, fashion boutiques, a post office, and the STPB on the ground floor next to Singapore Airlines. Across the road is the **Raffles Hotel Shopping Complex,** with 60 boutiques selling high fashion and art.

Scotts Shopping Centre One of the best places in Singapore for affordable fashion that stops just short of haute couture, Scotts (6–8 Scotts Rd.) also has a basement food court with local and delicatessen food, plus activities and demonstrations to keep shoppers entertained.

Shaw Centre This center (at 1 Scotts Rd.) has been around since the tourist boom of the early 1970s. Among its offerings are a rosewood showroom, a quaint antiques shop, and **Ming Blue** (tel. 734–6541), a super place for knickknacks from all over the Orient.

Singapore Handicraft Centre This center at the junction of Grange and Tanglin roads showcases the handicrafts of Malaysia, Indonesia, Sri Lanka, the Philippines, and India. The batik shops are especially good. In some units you can see craftsmen demonstrating their skills. Good buys can be found here in Oriental carpets, rosewood, ivory, and Chinese porcelain. You'll also find a fun souvenir shop— **Waldon's** (tel. 253–5283)—the gallery of Chinese artist Chen Wen Hsi.

On Wednesday and from Friday through Sunday, the Handicraft Centre is the site of a *pasar malam* (a Malay night market) that is touristy but fun. The mall outside and the courtyard inside are jammed with stalls selling ballpoint pens with Merlion emblems, key rings, Chinese fans, batik dresses, and other souvenirs. There is music in the mall from 5:30 PM on, and entertainment—perhaps a Malay pop band, an excerpt from a Chinese opera, a lion dance, or a martial-arts demonstration—in the courtyard from around 7 PM.

Specialists Centre This center (277 Orchard Rd.) is the home of the **John Little** department store (tel. 727–2222), better known as JL, and assorted boutiques. There is also a **Times** bookshop, where you can pick up something to read over tea and scones at nearby **Fosters** (tel. 737–8939).

Tanglin Shopping Centre This center, where Orchard Road meets Tanglin Road, is too big to generalize about, but it does have a good selection of antiques shops, especially in a small, self-contained section at ground level. **Moongate,** one of the oldest dealers in fine antique porcelain in Singapore, is here, as is **Antiques of the Ori-**

ent, the city's only shop specializing in antique maps. The contemporary interior-design shops are excellent, too.

Wisma Atria Also on Orchard Road (#435), this center has several fashion names, such as **Dior** (tel. 734–0374), and the **Isetan** department store. An added attraction of the complex is an aquarium that wraps around the elevator.

Department Stores

Singapore has two homegrown chains, quite different in character. **Metro** stores are of two types: Regular Metros offer a wide range of affordable fashions and household products; Metro Grands focus on upmarket fashion. When shopping for locally designed and manufactured fashion as well as brands such as Esprit, Metro is the best bet. The designs are up-to-the-minute, and the prices are good by local standards and unbelievably good by international standards. Look for Metros in Supreme House, Far East Plaza, Marina Square, the Paragon, and the Holiday Inn Building (25 Scotts Rd.). There is a Metro Grand in the Scotts Shopping Centre and another in Lucky Plaza. **Klasse** department stores put the accent on budget buys but are best for Chinese imports. The most interesting Klasse store for tourists is at Lucky Plaza (tel. 235–0261).

Tang's (tel. 737–5500), also known as Tang's Superstore or C.K. Tang's, is also locally owned, with just one branch, next to The Dynasty hotel on Orchard Road (#320). It looks upmarket, but some of the best buys in town are found here. Its fashions are, at best, improving, but its accessories are excellent—especially the costume jewelry—and its household products are unsurpassed.

Other stores that are good for Chinese products are the emporiums. One in the International Building (360 Orchard Rd.), simply called the **Chinese Emporium** (tel. 737–1411), is under the same ownership as Klasse. Two others, under different ownership, are the **Overseas Emporiums** in the People's Park Complex (tel. 535–0555) and the People's Park Centre (tel. 535–0967). These stores all offer basically the same goods: Chinese silk fabric, silk blouses, brocade jackets, crafts, children's clothes, and china. Every department holds its own fascination because the Chinese products, even the humdrum sheets and towels, seem so different to Western eyes.

Singaporeans enjoy Japanese department stores. **Isetan**—in Wisma Atria (435 Orchard Rd., tel. 733–7777), the Apollo Hotel (Havelock Rd., tel. 733–1111), and Parkway Parade (Marine Parade Rd., tel. 345–5555)—always has good specials, and the fashion departments for men and women are well stocked. **Daimaru** (tel. 339–1111), in Liang Court, has some very unusual goods. **Yaohan,** whose biggest store is in Plaza Singapura (tel. 337–4061; others are at Parkway Parade and at Thomson Plaza on Thomson Rd.), is by far the most popular chain; its appliances and audio equipment are very competitive in price. **Sogo** (tel. 339–1100) has opened in Raffles City, and the giant **Tokyu** (tel. 337–0077) has opened at Marina Square. **Meitetsu** (tel. 732–0222) has a store at the Delfi Orchard complex.

The French have not ignored Singapore. **Printemps** (tel. 733–9722), in the Hotel Meridien on Orchard Road, is good for lingerie and other women's fashions. **Galeries Lafayette** (tel. 732–9177) is at Liat Towers (541 Orchard Rd.).

The English **Robinsons** (tel. 733–0888), in Centrepoint, is Singapore's oldest department store. It recently shed its fuddy-duddy image and rethought its pricing and is once again one of the best. **John Little** (tel. 727–2222), at the Specialists Centre, has a full range of offerings but is now targeting the young and trendy.

Hotel Shopping Arcades

Most of Singapore's hotels have one or two boutiques in their lobbies, but the Hilton and the Mandarin have extensive shopping arcades with designer boutiques.

The **Hilton Shopping Gallery** (581 Orchard Rd.), is home to a number of top designer names—Giorgio Armani, Matsuda, Valentino—and, through a boutique called Singora, many other Italian and French fashion houses. Among its other top-flight tenants are Gucci, Davidoff, Louis Vuitton, L'Ultimo, Daks of London, and Dunhill.

The **Mandarin Shopping Arcade,** in the Mandarin Singapore (333 Orchard Rd.), has Courrèges, Givenchy, Ungaro, Versace, and Ferraud, plus two shops, **Link** and **Club 21,** that offer a selection of haute couture names. Also here are Hermès, A. Testoni, and Bally, along with several other shops selling a variety of quality leather goods, and a Georg Jensen for silver.

Other hotels with shopping arcades include **The Dynasty** (320 Orchard Rd.), with a boutique for Porsche luggage and accessories, and the **Hyatt Regency** (10-12 Scotts Rd.), with a large shop for Lanvin.

Markets

Food Markets Stalls crowd upon stalls in a covered, open space to make a hectic, colorful scene where everything edible is sold. The range of foodstuffs is staggering and some of the items may turn your stomach. The live animals eyed by shoppers will tug at your heartstrings. Usually a food market is divided into two sections: the dry market and the wet market. It is in the latter that squirming fish, crawling turtles, strutting chickens, and cute rabbits are sold for the pot, and the floors are continually being sluiced to maintain hygiene. The wet market at the **Chinatown Centre** is the most fascinating, while **Cuppage Centre** (on Cuppage Rd., off Orchard Rd.), where the flower stalls are particularly appealing, is best for the squeamish.

Street Markets Old-style street bazaars have gone now, but in the **Sungei Road area,** site of the once-notorious Thieves Market, a few street vendors creep back each weekend. The stalls sell mainly inexpensive shirts, T-shirts, children's clothes, and underwear, as well as odds and ends such as inexpensive watches, costume jewelry, and sunglasses. A few sell plastic household items.

The **Kreta Ayer** complex in Chinatown may be modern, but it has all the atmosphere of a bazaar. All the street vendors from Chinatown were relocated here. The shops sell cassette tapes, clothing from China, toys, and a lot of gaudy merchandise.

Some of Chinatown's elderly junk peddlers refuse to leave the streets. In the afternoon, they line up along **Temple Street** and lay out a strange variety of goods—old bottles, stamps, bits of porcelain or brass, old postcards, etc.—on cloths.

The bazaar at the **Singapore Handicraft Centre,** held from 6:30 to 10 PM on Wednesdays and from Friday through Sunday, is meant for tourists but attracts a fair number of Singaporeans as well. It is a good place to buy souvenirs. Shops and stalls also cluster at the new **Bugis Street** and at **Telok Ayer,** but the merchandise tends to be overpriced.

There is a small market of souvenir stalls near the food center on **Sentosa Island** on Friday and Saturday nights.

Specialty Shops

Antiques
Some curio dealers style themselves as antiques shops, as do some vendors selling rosewood items or reproduction furniture. Good places to see the genuine articles, if you have no time to explore outside Orchard Road, are the Tanglin Shopping Centre's **Antiques of the Orient** (tel. 734–9351), specializing in maps; **Funan Selected Works of Art** (tel. 737–3442), with Buddhas and other religious items; and **Moongate** (tel. 737–6771), for porcelain. For museum-quality Asian antiques, visit the **Paul Art Gallery** in Holland Park (62–72 Greenleaf Rd., tel. 468–4697). Off Orchard Road on Cuppage Road is a row of restored shophouses. Here, **Babazar** (31A–35A Cuppage Terr., tel. 235–7866) is full of wonderful finds in jewelry, furniture, clothes, art, knickknacks, and antiques; and **Aizia Discoveries** (29B Cuppage Rd., tel. 734–8665) has yet more antiques. **Keng of Tong Mern Sern** (226 River Valley Rd., tel. 734–0761), near the Chettiar Temple, has a rabbit warren full of antiques. The store's sign says, "We buy junk, we sell antiques." Strictly speaking, antiques in Singapore are defined as being more than 80 years old.

Most antiques stores have a variety of small items—porcelain, brassware, idols, and so on—as well as Chinese furniture, which may be of blackwood inlaid with mother of pearl, or namwood stained red with elaborate carvings picked out in gold. There is a fashion now for Chinese "country furniture," which is carried by **Aizia.** For primitive art and antique Indonesian batik and ikat (a woven fabric of tie-dyed yarns), there is **Tatiana** (tel. 235–3560) in the Tanglin Shopping Centre.

Art
Singapore has more than its share of fine artists. Established names, such as Chen Wen Hsi (who has a gallery at the Singapore Handicraft Centre) for Chinese brush painting, Thomas Yeo for abstract landscapes, and Anthony Poon for contemporary graphics, fetch high prices. Among the artists who are gaining recognition are Wan Soon Kam, Ng Eng Teng (a sculptor who re-creates the human figure in cement, stoneware, and bronze), James Tan (known for his traditional and abstract Chinese brush paintings), and Teng Juay Lee (who specializes in orchids). Nostalgic scenes of the Singapore of yesteryear are captured in watercolors and oils by artists such as Gog Sing Hoi, Ang Ah Tee, and Ong Kim Seng, known for his scenes of the Singapore River and Chinatown. Some delightful paintings can be had for as little as S$300.

For a range of art, try **Art Forum** (tel. 737–3448) and **Raya Gallery** (tel. 732–0298), both in the Promenade; for local Singapore artists, **Sun Craft** (tel. 737–1308), in the Tanglin Shopping Centre, and **Collectors Gallery** (tel. 339–8007), in Raffles City. There are also many galleries on South Bridge Road in Chinatown (*see* Chinatown, *above*). **Della Butcher** is the grande dame of the Singapore art scene and maintains a gallery at 39A Cuppage Terrace (tel. 235–7107) on the second floor. If you wish to see Chinese calligraphy in action, Yong Cheong Thye works his art at the **Yong Gallery** (#02-149A Raffles Blvd., tel. 339–2648) in Marina Square.

Batik   A traditional craft item of Singapore, Malaysia, and Indonesia, batik is now also important in contemporary fashion and interior design. **Blue Ginger** (tel. 235–6295) and **Design Batik** (tel. 235–5468), both in the Handicraft Centre, sell clothes and fabrics in modern designs. Blue Ginger is especially innovative. Traditional batik sarong lengths can be bought in the shops on **Arab Street** and in the **Textile Centre** on Jalan Sultan—try **Eng Leong Seng** (#01-37, tel. 294–4945). **Tang's** stores sell inexpensive batik products, including a good range of men's shirts.

Perhaps the most fun designs and products are to be found at **CGB Creations** (12 Ewe Boon Rd., tel. 732–2929). Owned by American Carolyn Batey, the store commissions local artists to let their imaginations rip. You must call for an appointment, since there is not always somebody minding the store.

Cameras   Photographic equipment may not be the bargain it once was, but the range of cameras and accessories available can be matched only in Hong Kong. It is especially important that you establish the price at home before buying here. Film and film processing remain excellent buys. All department stores carry cameras, and there are so many in Lucky Plaza that you can do all your comparison-shopping in one spot. **A&P Photo** in Lucky Plaza (#B1-87, tel. 737–9933) is one of the few tourist-oriented stores that carry only photographic equipment.

If you do not care for negotiating prices, **Cost Plus Electronics** (#B1–21 Scotts Shopping Centre, tel. 235–1557), something of a supermarket of cameras and electronics, is a good place to shop. The prices are just about as low as you'll find listed in Singapore; no further discounts are given. For more-personalized service try **Cathay Photo** (tel. 339–6188) in Marina Square or **Bobby O Store** (Guan Hua Bldg., 133 Middle Rd., tel. 337–2191) between Raffles City and the Allson Hotel for attentive (albeit pressured) service and discounts. For camera repairs, **Goh Gin Camera Service Center** (160 Orchard Rd., tel. 732–6155) may be able to help you.

Carpets   Carpets are very attractively priced in Singapore. Afghan, Pakistani, Persian, Turkish, and Chinese carpets—both antique and new—are carried by reputable dealers. Carpet auctions, announced in the newspapers, are good places to buy if you know your stuff.

Carpets from Tientsin are superb. At **Chinese Carpets** (tel. 235–6548), in the Handicraft Centre, goods range from wool rugs for a few hundred dollars to large carpets in silk for thousands. Also in the center is the **Oriental Carpet Palace** (tel. 235–8259), selling everything from new Pakistani rugs to antique Persians. The kilim collection here is worth a look.

Other good shops include **Qureshi's** (#05-12, tel. 235–1523) in Centrepoint, **Hassan's** (#01-15, tel. 737–5626) in the Tanglin Shopping Centre, and **Amir & Sons** (#03-01, tel. 734–9112) in Lucky Plaza. It is quite acceptable to bargain in these shops—in fact, it's integral to the rather lengthy proceedings.

Curios Falling halfway between souvenir shops and antiques stores, curio shops sell a fascinating variety of goods, mainly from China. Reverse-glass paintings, porcelain vases, cloisonné, wood carvings, jewelry (agate, jade, lapis lazuli, malachite), ivory carvings, embroidery, and idols represent just a fraction of the treasure trove. These shops, such as the International Building's **Asia Arts** (#01-02, tel. 737–3631) and Orchard Towers' **Chen Yee Shen** (#01-12, tel. 737–1174) and **Ivory Palace** (tel. 737–1169), are great places for those who seek the unusual.

Fun Fashion In department stores and small boutiques all over the island—but especially on Orchard Road—locally made ladies' fashions and Japanese imports sell for a song. Brands like Chocolate and Ananas, as well as Hong Kong's Esprit, offer colorful, reasonably made, very fashionable garments. Three of the better-known boutiques are **Mondi** (#02-13 Scotts, tel. 235–1812; #03-36 Centrepoint, tel. 734–9672), **Man and His Woman** (#02-07 The Promenade, tel. 737–9492), and **Trend** (Centrepoint, tel. 235–9446; Plaza Singapura, tel. 337–1038). **Options** (#03-23 Scotts Shopping Centre, tel. 732–3335) is also excellent.

Shoes are good buys, too, especially in the **Metro** and **Tang's** department stores, but sizes here are smaller than in the West, and some women have a problem getting the right fit.

High Fashion Singapore has its own designers: **Tan Yoong** has his shop in Lucky Plaza (tel. 734–3783), **Lam** has his in Liang Court (tel. 336–5974), and **Benny Ong** (who is based in London) sells through Tang's and China Silk House (*see* Silk, *below*).

For European couture, check the arcades of the **Hilton International** and the **Mandarin,** as well as the more fashionable shopping centers. **Kenzo** (tel. 734–4738) is at Galeries Lafayette in Liat Towers; **Lanvin** (tel. 235–4039) is at the Hyatt Regency; **Gucci** is in the Hilton (tel. 732–3298) and the Paragon (tel. 734–2528); **Loewe's** (tel. 737–0058), **L'Ultimo** (tel. 734–0456), and **Karl Lagerfeld** (tel. 734–5858) are in the Hilton; **Sonia Rykiel** (tel. 737–9747) is in the Mandarin; **Dior** (tel. 734–0374) is in Wisma Atria; **Nina Ricci** (tel. 734–2792) is in Galeries Lafayette; and **Emanuel Ungaro** (tel. 734–2259) is in the Paragon. Boutiques carrying a number of designers include **Singora** (tel. 737–0768) in the Hilton; **Link** (tel. 235–4648) and **Club 21** (tel. 235–0753) in the Mandarin; and **Glamourette** (tel. 734–3137) in the Promenade. For resort clothing and swimwear, stop in at the **Lingerie Shop** (tel. 732–5437) in the Promenade.

The boutiques of the **Tudor Court Shopping Gallery** on Tanglin Road carry most of the top European designers. Check out the **Krizia Boutique** (tel. 732–2141), **Maxims de Paris** (tel. 732–5109), and **Luciano Soprani** (tel. 733–9959).

Men's fashions are represented by **Dunhill** (tel. 737–8174) in the Hilton; **Mario Valentino** in the Scotts Shopping Centre (tel. 235–0876) and Marina Square (tel. 338–4457); **Hermès** (tel. 734–1353) in Liat Towers; **Ralph Lauren** (tel. 732–0608) in the Promenade; and **Melwani** (tel. 339–6075) in the Metro department store at Marina Square. The Wisma Atria department store also carries Ralph Lauren, Givenchy, and Valentino.

Don't forget the high-price but extremely fashionable collection of designer-name boutiques for both men and women in the new Palais Renaissance shopping center on Orchard Road across from the Hilton.

Ivory Singapore has accepted the international ban on ivory imports, so demand for antique ivory may increase. Be aware that ivory can be smoked to make it appear old, so it is prudent to buy from an established dealer such as **Bin Gei** (tel. 733–8915) at the Specialists Shopping Centre. A lot of curio shops carry ivory, too: Souvenir shops have ivory jewelry; high-class curio shops have carved tusks and figurines. Japanese *netsuke* (small carved figures) in ivory are found in the better curio shops.

Jewelry Singapore is a reliable place to buy jewelry, and there are so many jewelers that prices are competitive. Never accept the first price offered, no matter how posh the store. All jewelers give enormous discounts, usually 40% or more, but some, especially in hotels, don't mention this until pressed.

The Singapore Assay Office hallmarks jewelry, though the procedure is time-consuming and not many jewelers submit to it unless required for export. There are a number of gem-testing laboratories as well.

In Chinatown, particularly along South Bridge Road and in People's Park, there are dozens of Chinese jewelers selling 22K gold. Many of these, such as **Poh Heng** (27/28 N. Canal Rd., tel. 535–4933), are old family firms. Chinese jewelers of this kind can be found in all the suburbs and are patronized by all ethnic groups. Prices are calculated by abacus based on the weight of the ornament and the prevailing price of gold. The bargaining procedure can take quite some time.

On Orchard Road, the jewelry shops are often branches of Hong Kong firms or are local firms modeled along the same lines. They sell 18K set jewelry, often in Italian designs, as well as loose investment stones. **Larry's** (tel. 734–8763), with branches in Orchard Towers and Lucky Plaza, is one popular store. One of the many other small jewelers in Lucky Plaza is **The Hour Glass** (tel. 734–2420), which carries a large selection of designer watches. **Je T'Aime** (tel. 734–2275) in Wisma Atria is also a reputable firm. **Cartier** has shops in Lucky Plaza (tel. 734–2427) and in the Hilton (tel. 235–0295).

Antique European jewelry is not often seen in Singapore, but the antique silver jewelry of the Straits Chinese can be seen in **Petnic's** (41A Cuppage Rd., tel. 235–6564).

Like other forms of jewelry, pearls are a good buy in Singapore. **Miyako,** with a store in the Regent hotel (tel. 732–7266), is just one of a number of brands of simulated Japanese pearls on the local market. Small jewelers in Lucky Plaza and other complexes use freshwater pearls as "loss leaders," selling a strand for just a few dollars. Mikimoto pearls are available at **Kampooli Jewelers** (tel. 336–1381) in the Singapura Plaza.

Luggage and Accessories It is not well known that luggage is a bargain in Singapore. Every complex boasts several stores carrying all the designer names in luggage and leather accessories. Department stores carry such brands as Samsonite and Delsey.

Dunhill (tel. 737–8174) is in the Hilton; **Etienne Aigner** is in Shaw Centre (tel. 737–6141), Scotts Shopping Centre (tel. 235–2742), and Delfi Orchard (tel. 732–9700); **Louis Vuitton** (tel. 737–5820) is in the Hilton; **Hermès** is at Liat Towers (541 Orchard Rd., tel. 734–1353) and at Daimaru in Liang Court, tel. 339–1111); and **Charles Jourdan** (tel. 737–4988) is in the Promenade. The **Escada** boutique (tel. 734–7624) at Delfi Orchard has a range of accessories and custom-made luggage.

Pewter and Dinnerware Malaysia is the world's largest tin producer, and pewter is an important craft item in the region. **Selangor Pewter,** the largest pewter concern in Singapore, has a great product range displayed at the main showrooms in the Singapore Handicraft Centre (tel. 235–6634), and Raffles City (tel. 339–3958). The main office is at 7500A Beach Road (tel. 293–3880).

Modern pewter items are heavily influenced by Scandinavian design. Items range from jewelry and tiny figurines to coffee and tea sets. Sake sets, bowls, vases, ornamental plates, clocks, and traditional beer tankards are also available. Some items are specifically aimed at the tourist trade, such as Raffles plates and Chinese zodiac plaques.

For dinnerware, **Christofle** (tel. 733–7257) has a boutique in the Hilton. Also try the **Waterford Wedgwood Shop** (#01-01 Delfi Orchard, tel. 734–8375).

Reptile-Skin Products Check the import restrictions on these goods. Singapore issues no export certificate for these or for ivory. The price of alligator, crocodile, and snake skins is lower here than anywhere else except Hong Kong.

In the old shops around the Stamford Road–Armenian Street area, hard bargaining will yield dividends. The range is widest at big stores such as the showroom at the **Crocodilarium** (730 East Coast Pkwy., tel. 447–3722). You can have bags and belts made to your specifications. The existing designs, especially for shoes, are often old-fashioned. For smarter styles, try the **Leather Hut** (tel. 733–1445) in the Shangri-La hotel. In Marina Square, visit the **Shanghai Fushang House of Reptile and Leather Goods** (tel. 339–8268).

Silk Indian silk, in sari lengths, is found in the dozens of sari shops in the Serangoon Road area. For 6 meters (6.5 yards) of silk, which could be the thin Kashmiri silk or the heavier, embroidered Benares silk, you pay only a fraction of what you would pay elsewhere. Especially for saris, you may want to try **Maharanee's** (Blk. 664, #01-05 Buffalo Rd., tel. 294–9868). The major store for Indian textiles is **P. Govindasamy Pillai** (48/50 Serangoon Rd., tel. 337–2050), opposite the Zhu Jiao Centre.

Chinese silk is easy to find in Singapore. All the emporiums have special departments for fabrics and tailored clothes. **China Silk House** (Tanglin Shopping Centre, tel. 235–5020, and Centrepoint, tel. 733–0555) has a wide range of fabrics in different weights and types, plus silk clothing, including a line designed for the shop by Benny Ong.

Thai silk, in different weights for different purposes, comes in stunning colors. Specialty shops sell it by the meter or made up into gowns, blouses, and dresses. **Design Thai** (tel. 235–5439) in the Tanglin Shopping Centre is one of the largest such shops. There are **Miss Ming** shops in the Mandarin Hotel Shopping Arcade (tel. 737–1342) and in Orchard Towers (tel. 235–2865).

Tailoring There are tailors and tailors—what you end up with depends on how well you choose. Tailors who offer 24-hour service rarely deliver, and their quality is pretty suspect. Another indication of danger is not seeing a tailor on the premises. Anyone can set up shop as a tailor by filling a store with fabrics and then subcontracting the work; the results from such places are seldom felicitous. Allow four to five days for a good job. **Justmen** (tel. 737–4800) in the Tanglin Shopping Centre is one of a number of excellent men's tailors. For ladies, shops such as the Tanglin branch of **China Silk House** (tel. 235–5020) and the Specialists Centre's **M.B. Melwani** (tel. 737–5342) and **Bagatelle Shoppe** (tel. 737–7090) offer good tailoring.

4 Sports, Fitness, Beaches

Participant Sports and Fitness

Archery The **Archery Club of Singapore** (5 Binchang Walk, tel. 258–1140) welcomes enthusiasts.

Bicycling You can rent a bike from the **Bicycle Hire Centre** (tel. 443–2325), next door to the Food Centre on the East Coast Parkway. Rates are about S$1 an hour, and special bike paths run the length of East Coast Park. Cycling along the beaches and parks along the highway to the airport is a very pleasant way to see this part of the island. There are also bicycles for rent on Sentosa Island.

Bowling There are a number of bowling centers in Singapore. **Kallang Bowl** (Leisure-Dome, 5 Stadium Walk, Kallang Park, tel. 345–0545), with 62 lanes, claims to be the largest in Southeast Asia. Under the same ownership and in the same building is the **Kallang Bowlers Dome,** with 30 computerized lanes. Other alleys: **Jackie's Bowl** (452B East Coast Rd., tel. 241–6519; 8 Grange Rd., tel. 737–4744), **Pasir Panjang Bowl** (269 Pasir Panjang Rd., tel. 775–5555), and **Plaza Bowl** (8th floor, Textile Centre, Jalan Sultan, tel. 292–4821). The cost per string is about S$2.20 on weekdays before 6 PM, S$3 on weekends and after 6 PM weekdays.

Canoeing At the **East Coast Sailing Centre** (1210 East Coast Pkwy., tel. 449–5118), canoes may be rented for S$3 an hour. Open daily 9:30–6:30. Canoes and rowboats may be rented on Sentosa Island (*see* Beaches and Water Parks, *below*).

Flying The **Republic of Singapore Flying Club** (East Camp Bldg., 140B Seletar Airbase, tel. 481–0502 or 481–0200) offers visiting membership to qualified pilots and has aircraft available for hire (cost: approximately S$200 per hour). A piloted ride for up to three people can be arranged for about S$250 an hour and is a superb way to see the island.

Golf Some of the top Singapore hotels, including the Oriental, have special arrangements for guests at local golf clubs. For example, they may make all the necessary bookings, including equipment reservations, at the club of your choice and arrange for a limousine to take you there (cost: about S$175 for a round). You might check before leaving home to see whether your club has any reciprocal arrangements with a Singapore club. Several excellent Singapore golf clubs accept nonmembers, though some limit this practice to weekdays.

Changi Golf Club is a hilly nine-hole course on 50 acres. *345 Netheravon Rd., tel. 545–1298. Greens fee: S$30 weekdays, S$150 weekends and public holidays. Caddy fee: S$13.*

Jurong Country Club has an 18-hole, par 71 course on 120 acres. Half the holes are on flat terrain and the other nine over small hills. *9 Science Centre Rd., tel. 560–5655. Greens fee: S$80 weekdays, S$120 weekends and public holidays. Caddy fee: S$22.*

Keppel Club is the nearest 18-hole course to the city. *Bukit Chermin, tel. 273–5522. Greens fee: S$90 Tues.–Fri., S$150 weekends and public holidays. Closed Mon. Caddy fee: S$25.*

Seletar Country Club is considered the best nine-hole course on the island. The course was laid out in 1932 by the Royal Air Force. *Seletar Airbase, tel. 481–4746. Greens fee: S$80 (for 18 holes) Tues.–Fri. only. Caddy fee: S$20.*

Sembawang Country Club is an 18-hole, par 70 course. It is known as the commando course for its hilly terrain. There are also squash courts available. *17km Sembawang Rd., tel. 257–0642. Greens fee: S$60 weekdays, S$100 weekends and public holidays. Caddy fee: S$24.*

Sentosa Golf Club permits visitors to play on the 18-hole, par 71 Tanjong course on the southeastern tip of the island. The Serapong Course is restricted to members. *Sentosa Island, tel. 275–0022. Greens fee: S$60 weekdays, S$120 weekends and public holidays. Caddy fee: S$24. Golf clubs: S$15.*

Singapore Island Country Club has four 18-hole, par 71 courses: two at Upper Thomson Road and two (including the world-class Bukit course) on Sime Road. There are clubhouse facilities at both locations. *180 Island Rd., tel. 459–2222; the Bukit clubhouse is at 240 Sime Rd., tel. 466–2244. Greens fee: S$130 weekdays only. Caddy fee: S$25.*

Horseback Riding There is no organized riding stable for visitors. However, arrangements may be made through the **Singapore Polo Club** (Thomson Rd., tel. 256–4530) or the **Saddle Club,** which is associated with the Singapore Turf Club (Bukit Timah Rd., tel. 469–3611, ext. 295). Cost: around S$30 for 45 minutes.

Hotel Health Facilities The **Shangri-La** has a good-size outdoor pool and a smaller one indoors; a modern health club with a universal gym, stationary bikes, running treadmills, and other equipment; tennis and squash courts; and a three-hole golf course, where you can jog in the early morning. The **Oriental** has a jogging track; tennis and squash courts; and a splendid outdoor pool with an underwater sound system and a view of the harbor. The fifth-floor health club includes a Jacuzzi, massage, steam and sauna rooms for men and for women, free weights, a universal gym, stationary bikes, running treadmills, and individual trainers. The **Mandarin** has squash and tennis courts, an outdoor pool, a gym with Nautilus-type equipment, a universal gym, a running treadmill, free weights, individual trainers, steam room, sauna, massage, and a minigolf course suitable for a quick jog. The **Pan Pacific** has a modern fitness center with computer-monitored equipment, free weights, Nautilus, and trainers on duty, plus an outdoor pool and tennis courts; it is on the bay, a good place for an invigorating jog. The **Hyatt Regency** has a kidney-shaped pool, tennis courts, and an ultramodern fitness center with Nautilus equipment, free weights, universal gym, sauna, massage, and trainers on duty. For all addresses and telephones, *see* Chapter 6, Lodging.

Jogging Singapore is a great place for joggers. There are numerous parks, and a number of leading hotels offer jogging maps. Serious joggers can tackle the 10-kilometer (6.2-mile) **East Coast Parkway track,** then cool off with a swim at the park's sandy beach. One of the most delightful places to run is the **Botanic Gardens** (off Holland Road and not far from Orchard Road), where you can jog on the paths or on the grass until 11 at night. The best time to run in Singapore is in the morning or evening; avoid the midday sun. It is safe for a woman to run alone. Remember to look right when crossing the road—in the British manner, driving is on the left. Several full or half marathons are organized in Singapore during the year.

Roller-skating **Sentosa Island** has a rink that is said to be the largest in Southeast Asia. *Admission free. Roller skate rentals: $2 per hr. Open weekdays 9–6, weekends 9–8.*

Sailing If you introduce yourself at the **Changi Sailing Club** (Netheravon Rd., tel. 545–2876), you should be able to find a berth crewing on one of the weekend races. Sunfish and sailboards may be rented at the **East Coast Sailing Centre** (1210 East Coast Pkwy., tel. 449–5118) and on **Sentosa Island** (*see* Beaches and Water Parks, *below*).

Scuba Diving The waters around Singapore are polluted, thanks to the thousands of ships that anchor offshore and to the oil refineries. Better diving is found off the nearby islands, though the currents are treacherous. Contact the **Singapore Club Aquanaut** (c/o 20 Bideford Rd., #11-05 Wellington Bldg., tel. 737–0673) for information on local opportunities.

Squash and Several hotels have their own squash courts (*see* Hotel Health
Racquetball Facilities, *above*), and there are numerous public squash and racquetball courts available, some of which are listed here: **Alexandra Park** (Royal Rd. off York Rd., tel. 473–7236), **Changi Courts** (Gosport Rd., tel. 545–2941), **East Coast Recreation Centre** (East Coast Pkwy., tel. 449–0541), **Farrer Park** (Rutland Rd., tel. 251–4166), **Kallang Squash and Tennis Centre** (National Stadium, Kallang, tel. 348–1258), and **Singapore Squash Centre** (Fort Canning Rise, tel. 336–0155). Court costs range from S$3 to S$6 an hour, depending on the time of day.

Swimming Virtually all Singapore hotels have swimming pools. There are also 19 public swimming complexes, the best of which are superb (*see* Beaches and Water Parks, *below*). The Singapore Swimming Club is at Tanjong Rhu Road (tel. 345–2122).

Tennis The top hotels have their own tennis courts, and several public clubs welcome visitors: **Alexandra Park, Changi Courts, Farrer Park,** and **Kallang Squash and Tennis Centre** (*see* Squash and Racquetball, *above*) all have courts. Also try the **Singapore Tennis Centre** (1020 East Coast Pkwy., tel. 442–5966) and **Tanglin Tennis Courts** (Minden Rd., tel. 473–7236). Court costs range from S$3 to S$5 an hour, depending on the time of day.

Waterskiing The center of activity for waterskiing is Ponggol, a village in northeastern Singapore. **Ponggol Boatel** (17th Ave., Ponggol, tel. 481–0031) charges S$60 an hour for a boat with ski equipment. Some of the local boats are for hire at considerably lower rates—about S$40 an hour. Negotiate directly, and make sure the proper safety equipment is available.

Windsurfing At the **East Coast Sailing Centre** (1210 East Coast Pkwy., tel. 449–5118), sailboards rent for S$20 for two hours, S$10 per hour thereafter. Half-day lessons are available weekdays 2–6 PM for S$50. Windsurfing is available on **Sentosa Island** (*see* Beaches and Water Parks, *below*) from 9:30 to 6:30.

Spectator Sports

In addition to the sports listed below, international matches of golf, tennis, cycling, formula motor racing, swimming, badminton, and squash are held on and off. Some of these attract top professionals from abroad, and it may be easier to see them here than in countries where competitions are more heavily attended. Most events are detailed in the newspapers; information is also available from the **National Sports Council** (tel. 345–7111). A number of tourist-oriented events—such as the International Dragon Boat Races, an international kite-flying festival, and powerboat races—are organized on an annual basis.

Cricket From March through September, games take place on the Padang grounds in front of the old **Cricket Club** (tel. 338–9271) every Saturday at 1:30 PM and every Sunday at 11 AM. Entrance to the club during matches is restricted to members, but you can watch from the sides of the playing field. Refreshments are available in the park on the seaward side of the main road.

Horse Racing The **Singapore Turf Club** (Bukit Timah Rd., tel. 469–3611) was founded in 1842 and in 1933 moved to its present location, about 10 kilometers (6 miles) from the city center. The race course is set in lush parkland, and its facilities are superb. Traffic heading for the track is dense on race days (usually Saturdays), when around eight races are run for fields of up to 14 horses. The first race is usually at 1:30 PM. Horses are often from abroad; local and Australian jockeys compete for some very large prizes, such as the annual Singapore Gold Cup, worth S$250,000. Gambling on the tote system (automatic gambling organized by track operators) is intense. For the S$5 admission price, you can watch the action either live or on a huge video screen opposite the grandstand.

You can get to the races easily by way of an organized tour. An air-conditioned coach picks you up from selected hotels at about 11 AM and takes you to the club for a buffet lunch, followed by an afternoon of races (watched from the members' section) and a guided tour of the paddock. The club maintains a dress code: collared shirt with tie for men, dress or skirt (or slacks) and blouse for women. International passports are required for the tour, for security reasons. *RMG Tours, tel. 337–3377; Singapore Sightseeing, tel. 737–8778. Cost (both): S$68.*

Polo The **Singapore Polo Club** (Thomson Rd., tel. 256–4530) is quite active, with both local and international matches. Spectators are welcome to watch Tuesday, Thursday, Saturday, and Sunday matches, played in the late afternoon.

Rugby Rugby is played on the Padang grounds in front of the Singapore **Cricket Club.** Kickoff is usually at 5:30 PM on Saturdays from September through March.

Soccer Soccer is the major sport of Singapore; important matches take place in the **National Stadium** at Kallang. Details are published in the daily papers, and ticket reservations can be made through the National Sports Council. The main season is September through March.

Track and Field In recent years, most Asian countries have become keen on track-and-field events. Singapore has the **National Stadium** at Kallang for major events, plus nine athletic centers with tracks. International meets are usually detailed in the daily press and arouse considerable nationalistic feeling. For information and details on how to book seats for major meets, call the National Sports Council.

Beaches and Water Parks

CN West Leisure Park. This huge water-sports complex boasts a flow pool, a baby pool with slide, a wave pool, and a 50-meter (164-foot) water slide. Also here are amusement rides, such as minicars and a minijet merry-go-round. *9 Japanese Garden Rd., Jurong, tel. 261–4771. Admission: S$4 adults, S$1 children. Open Tues.–Fri. noon–6, weekends and holidays 9:30–6. Closed Mon.*

East Coast Park. This park stretches for 8 kilometers (5 miles) between the new airport road and the seashore on recently reclaimed land. Here you'll find well-planned recreational facilities, including an excellent beach and a water-sports lagoon where you can rent sailboards, canoes, and sailboats. If you prefer swimming in a pool, the Aquatic Centre has four pools—including a wave pool—and a giant water slide called The Big Splash. "Holiday chalets" set among the palm trees beside the beach can be rented by the day. Restaurants and changing facilities are available. *East Coast Pkwy., tel. 449–5118. Admission to swimming lagoon: S$3 adults, S$2 children. Open Mon., Tues., Thurs., Fri. noon–6; weekends 9–6. Closed Wed.*

Sentosa Island. Billed as Singapore's leisure resort, Sentosa offers a range of recreational facilities in addition to its museums, waxworks, musical fountains, etc. There is a reasonable beach and a swimming lagoon, with changing and refreshment facilities, as well as rowboats, sailboards, and canoes for rent. You can camp here, play golf or tennis, or roller-skate. Do not expect seclusion on the weekend—the island gets very crowded. Midweek is much better. *See* Tour 9 in Chapter 2.

Nearby Islands. The islands of Kusu and St. John's have reasonable small beaches and swimming facilities. On weekends, they are crowded with locals. *See* Tour 9 in Chapter 2.

Desaru, Malaysia. The best beach area near Singapore is on peninsular Malaysia, 100 kilometers (60 miles) east of Johore Bahru. It takes a little over two hours to drive there (slightly longer by bus) but makes a great retreat, especially if you've got a weekend to spare. There are excellent beaches and lots of resort-type activities on the water, as well as an 18-hole golf course. Development is planned that will include three more golf courses, four new beach hotels and a theme recreation park that, surprisingly, will create a winter wonderland of fun and amusement. You can charter a taxi from Johore Bahru for about M$50 (US$20). By 1993, there should be a 200-passenger catamaran service taking 47 minutes to speed over the water between the Marine Terminal at Changi and Desaru. For overnight accommodations, Desaru has two hotels and several chalets (the Desaru View Hotel will collect you from Singapore). For more information, *see* Chapter 8.

5 Dining

Introduction by Violet Oon and Tan Lee Leng

Singapore offers the greatest feast in the East, if not in the world. Here you'll find excellent restaurants specializing in home-grown fare (known as Nonya, or Peranakan cuisine) and in foods from Malaysia, Indonesia, Thailand, Vietnam, Korea, Japan, all parts of China, and north and south India, as well as from France, Germany, Italy, Britain, and the United States. At the hawker centers—semioutdoor markets with as many as 200 vendors selling wonderfully cooked, authentic foods—you can sample all these cuisines in the same meal!

It's not a joke that in Singapore, eating is a national pastime. We eat joyously, taking great pleasure in sharing with friends and family. We also eat around the clock. If we have a yen for breakfast at 5 AM, we head for Chinatown and an old-fashioned Cantonese teahouse like the **New Nam Thong** for tea and *dim sum*—little steamed buns, dumplings, and other finger foods.

So it goes throughout the day, with a mid-morning snack running into lunch and high tea at any of several hotels bridging the gap until dinner. At around 10:30 PM, we may pop out of the house for a quick visit to a hawker center. After the late show on television or the last screening at the cinemas, we may feel the need for a snack before bed and join the crowd that streams out of the nightclubs and bar lounges between 1 and 2 AM to sup leisurely till around 4 at one of the Chinese restaurants that cater to a later crowd. By then it's time for an early breakfast. With the infinite variety of cuisines we have to choose from, is it any wonder we are so moved to sample them all continuously?

The Cuisines of Singapore

Singapore's dining scene reflects the three main cultures that have settled here—Chinese, Indian, and Malay—as well as the many other influences that contribute to the island's diverse cultural mix.

Chinese

Chinese make up about 76% of Singapore's population, and this predominance is reflected in the wide assortment of restaurants representing its ethnic groups. The following is a sampling of the many Chinese cuisines represented in Singapore.

The best-known regional Chinese cuisine is **Cantonese,** with its fresh, delicate flavors. Vegetable oil, instead of lard, is used in the cooking, and crisp vegetables are preferred. Characteristic dishes are stir-fried beef in oyster sauce; steamed fish with slivers of ginger; and deep-fried duckling with mashed taro.

If you walk around Ellenborough Market, you'll notice the importance of dried ingredients in Chinese cooking. The people here are **Teochew** (or Chao Zhou), mainly fisherfolk from Swatow in the eastern part of Guangdong Province. Though their cooking has been greatly influenced by the Cantonese, it is

---

Violet Oon, Singapore's leading culinary authority, is the publisher and editor of a monthly newspaper, The Food Paper, *and author of a cookbook on Nonya (Straits-born Chinese) foods. She is especially interested in chronicling and preserving the diverse food cultures of Singapore. Tan Lee Leng is a Singaporean chef expert in several different styles of cuisine, including regional Chinese and Nonya. She also teaches cooking, writes on food for local publications, and is the author of* A Compendium of Asian Cooking.

quite distinctive. Teochew chefs cook with clarity and freshness, often steaming or braising, with an emphasis on fish and vegetables. Oyster sauce and sesame oil—staples of Cantonese cooking—do not feature much in Teochew cooking; Teochew chefs pride themselves on enhancing the natural flavors of the foods.

Characteristic Teochew dishes are *lo arp* and *lo goh* (braised duck and goose), served with a vinegary chili-and-garlic sauce; crispy liver or prawn rolls; stewed, preserved vegetables; black mushrooms with fish roe; and a unique porridge called *congee*, which is eaten with small dishes of salted vegetables, fried whitebait, black olives, and preserved-carrot omelets.

Szechuan food is very popular in Singapore, as the spicy-hot taste suits the Asian palate. This style of cooking is distinguished by the use of bean paste, chilies, and garlic, as well as a wide, complex use of nuts and poultry. The result is dishes with pungent flavors of all sorts, harmoniously blended. Simmering and smoking are common forms of preparation, and noodles and steamed bread are preferred accompaniments. Characteristic dishes to order are hot-and-sour soup, sautéed chicken or prawns with dried chilies, camphor- and tea-smoked duck, and spicy fried string beans.

Pekingese cooking originated in the Imperial courts. It makes liberal use of strong-flavored roots and vegetables, such as peppers, garlic, ginger, leeks, and coriander. Dishes are usually served with noodles or dumplings and baked, steamed, or fried bread. The most famous dish is Peking duck: The skin is lacquered with aromatic honey and baked until it looks like dark mahogany and is crackly crisp. Other choices are clear wintermelon soup, emperor's purses (stir-fried shredded beef with shredded red chili, served with crispy sesame bread), deep-fried minced shrimp on toast, and baked fish on a hot plate.

The greatest contribution to Singaporean cuisine made by the many arrivals from China's **Hainan** island, off the north coast of North Vietnam, is "chicken rice": Whole chickens are lightly poached with ginger and spring onions; then rice is boiled in the liquid to fluffy perfection and eaten with chopped-up pieces of chicken, which are dipped into a sour and hot chili sauce and dark soy sauce.

Also popular here are **Fukienese** and **Hunanese** restaurants. Fukien cuisine emphasizes soups and stews with rich, meaty stocks. Wine-sediment paste and dark soy sauce are often used, and seafood is prominently featured. Dishes to order are braised pork belly served with buns, fried oyster, and turtle soup. Hunanese cooking is dominated by sugar and spices and tends to be more rustic. One of the most famous dishes is beggar's chicken: A whole bird is wrapped in lotus leaves and baked in a sealed covering of clay; when it's done, a mallet is used to break away the hardened clay, revealing a chicken so tender and aromatic that it is more than worthy of an emperor. Other favorites are pigeon soup in bamboo cups, fried layers of bean-curd skin, and honey ham served with bread.

Hakka food is very provincial in character and uses ingredients not normally found in other Chinese cuisines. Red-wine lees are used to great effect in dishes of fried prawns or steamed chicken, producing gravies that are delicious eaten with rice. Stuffed bean curds and beef balls are other Hakka delicacies.

Indian   Most Indian immigrants to Singapore came from the south, from Madras and Kerala and Tamil Nadu, so the **southern Indian** cultural traditions tend to predominate here. In Little India, many small and humble restaurants can be found. Race Course Road is a street of curries: At least 10 Indian restaurants, most representing this fiery-hot cooking tradition, offer snacks or meals, served on banana leaves. The really adventurous should sample the Singapore Indian specialty fish-head curry. Like all the food served here, this dish, with its hot, rich, sour gravy, is best appreciated when eaten without utensils—somehow, eating with the fingers enhances the flavor!

Southern Indian cuisine is generally more chili-hot, relies on strong spices like mustard seed, and uses coconut milk liberally. Meals are very cheap, and eating is informal: Just survey the cooked food displayed, point to whatever you fancy, then take a seat at a table. A piece of banana leaf will be placed before you, plain rice will be spooned out, and the rest of your food will be arranged around the rice and covered with curry sauce.

Tempting southern Indian dishes include fish *pudichi* (fish in coconut, spices, and yogurt), fried prawns and crabs, mutton or chicken *biryani* (a meat-and-rice dish), *brinjal curry keema* (spicy minced meat), *vindaloo* (hot spiced meat), *dosai* (savory pancakes), *appam* (rice-flour pancakes), sour lime pickle, and *papadam* (flat bread). Try a glass of *rasam* (pepper water) to aid digestion or a glass of beer to cool things down.

More recently, **northern Indian** food has made a mark in Singapore. Generally found in the more posh restaurants, this cuisine blends the aromatic spices of Kashmiri food with a subtle Persian influence. The main differences between northern and southern Indian cuisine are that northern Indian food is less hot and more subtly spiced than southern and that cow's milk is used as a base instead of coconut milk. Northern Indian cuisine also uses yogurt extensively to tame the pungency of the spices and depends more on puréed tomatoes and nuts to thicken gravies.

The signature northern Indian dish is Tandoori chicken (marinated in yogurt and spices and cooked in a clay urn) and fresh mint chutney, eaten with *naan chapati* and *paratha* (Indian breads). Another typical dish is *rogan josh*, lamb braised gently with yogurt until the spices blend into a delicate mix of aromas and flavors. *Ghee*, a nutty clarified butter, is used—often in lavish quantities—to cook and season rice or rice-and-meat dishes (*pulaos* and biryanis).

In general, northern Indian food is served more elegantly than is southern Indian food. The prices are also considerably higher. (Beware of ordering prawns in southern Indian restaurants, though—they often cost as much as S$8 each!)

The **Indian Muslim** tradition is represented in the Arab Street area. Opposite the Sultan Mosque, on North Bridge Road, are small, open-fronted restaurants serving *roti prata* (a sort of crispy, many-layered pancake eaten with curries), *murtabak* (prata filled with a spiced, minced mutton and diced onions), *nasi biryani* (saffron-colored rice with chicken or mutton), and various curries. These places are for the stouthearted only; they are cramped and not really spick-and-span.

Japanese   Over the past few years in Singapore, there has been a sudden interest in all things Japanese, no doubt partly because of the influx of Japanese tourists, but also because of the very large Japanese community here. Japanese restaurants are all over the island, and Singapore can now offer Japanese cuisine equal to the best served in Japan.

The Japanese eat with studied grace, making dining a dramatic event. Dishes look like still-life paintings; flavors and textures both stimulate and soothe. Waitresses quietly appear and then vanish; the cooks welcome and chat with you.

In Singapore you can savor the high art of *kaiseki* (the formal Japanese banquet) in popular family restaurants. It was developed by the Samurai class for tea ceremonies and is influenced by Zen philosophy. The food is served on a multitude of tiny dishes and offered to guests as light refreshments. Regulations govern the types of foods that can be served: The seasoning is light, the color schemes must be harmonious, and the foods, whenever possible, must be in their natural shapes. Everything presented is intended for conscious admiration. This stylistic approach is the perfect way to mark a special occasion.

More fun for some are the forms of Japanese dining in which guests can watch the chef exercise his skills right at the table. At a *sushi* bar, for example, the setting and the performance of the chef as he skillfully wields the knife to create the elegant, colorful pieces of sushi (vinegared rice tinged with *wasabi*, or green horseradish, topped with a slice of raw fish) make the meal special. Savor the rich, incredible flavor and you will be hooked forever. Also watch the chef perform stylistic movements, including knife twirling, at places serving *teppanyaki:* On a large griddle around which diners are seated, fish, meat, vegetables, and rice are lightly seared, flavored with butter and sake. *Sukiyaki* too is grilled at the table, but the meat is strictly beef and the soup is sweeter; noodles and bean curd are served at the end of the meal as fillers.

Yakitori, a Japanese satay, is meat and vegetables grilled to perfection and glazed with a sweet sauce. *Yakiniku* is a grill-it-yourself meal of thin slices of beef, chicken, or Japanese fish. *Shabu-shabu* is a kind of fondue: Seafoods and meats are lightly swished in boiling stock, then dipped in a variety of sauces. *Tempura* is a sort of fritter of remarkable lightness and delicacy; the most popular kinds are made of prawns and vegetables. The dipping sauce is a mix of soy sauce and *mirin* (sweet rice wine), flavored with grated turnip and ginger.

Malay and Indonesian Malay cuisine is hot and rich. Turmeric root, lemon grass, coriander, *blachan* (prawn paste), chilies, and shallots are the ingredients used most often; coconut milk is used to create fragrant, spicy gravies. A basic method of cooking is to gently fry the *rempah* (spices, herbs, roots, chilies, and shallots ground to a paste) in oil and then, when the rempah is fragrant, add meat and either a tamarind liquid, to make a tart spicy-hot sauce, or coconut milk, to make a rich spicy-hot curry sauce. Dishes to look for are *gulai ikan* (a smooth, sweetish fish curry), *telor sambal* (eggs in hot sauce), *empalan* (beef boiled in coconut milk and then deep-fried), *tahu goreng* (fried bean curd in peanut sauce), and *ikan bilis* (fried, crispy anchovies).

Perhaps the best-known Malay dish is *satay*—slivers of marinated beef, chicken, or mutton threaded onto thin coconut sticks, barbecued, and served with a spicy peanut sauce. At one corner of Queen Elizabeth Walk, on the riverbank, you will find the **Satay Club:** row upon row of men hunched over low charcoal fires, fanning the embers to grill sticks of satay. Tell the waiter how many of each type of meat you want, and he'll bring the still-smoking satay to your table.

Unlike the Chinese, who have a great tradition of eating out and a few classical schools of restaurant cooking, most Malay families continue to entertain at home, even when celebrating special events, such as marriages. As a consequence, there are very few stylish Malay restaurants.

Indonesian food is very close to Malay; both are based on rice, and both are Muslim and thus do not use pork. A meal called *nasi padang*—consisting of a number of mostly hot dishes, such as curried meat and vegetables with rice, that offer a range of tastes from sweet to salty to sour to spicy—originally comes from Indonesia. Dishes are usually displayed in glass cases, from which customers make their selections.

Nonya The first Chinese immigrants to this part of the world were the Hokkien. When they settled on the Malay Peninsula, they acquired the taste for Malay spices and soon adapted Malay foods. Nonya food is one manifestation of the marriage of the two cultures, which is also seen in language, music, literature, and clothing. This blended culture was called Baba, as were the men; the women were called *nonya*, and so was the cuisine, because cooking was considered a feminine art.

Nonya cooking combines the finesse and blandness of Chinese cuisine with the spiciness of Malay cooking. Many Chinese ingredients are used—especially dried ingredients like Chinese mushrooms, fungus, anchovies, lily flowers, soybean sticks, and salted fish—along with the spices and aromatics used in Malay cooking. A favorite Chinese ingredient is pork, and pork satay is made for the Peranakan home (you're unlikely to come across Malay pork satay, since Muslims do not eat pork).

The ingenious Nonya cook uses *taucheo* (preserved soybeans), garlic, and shallots to form the rempah needed to make *chap chay* (a mixed-vegetable stew with soy sauce). Other typical dishes are *husit goreng* (an omelet fried with shark's fin and crabmeat) and *otak otak* (a sort of fish quenelle with fried spices and coconut milk). Nonya cooking also features sourish-hot dishes like *garam assam*, a fish or prawn soup made with pounded turmeric, shallots, *galangal* (a hard ginger), lemon grass, and shrimp paste. The water for the soup is mixed with preserved tamarind, a sour fruit that adds a delicious tartness.

A few years ago, Nonya cuisine appeared to be dying, like Peranakan culture itself, but since the publication of many Nonya cookbooks, there has been a resurgence of interest in it. Peranakan Place, a center celebrating Straits-born Chinese culture (*see* Tour 5 in Chapter 2), has also helped save this unique cuisine from extinction, and many hotels include Nonya dishes on their menus.

Thai Thai cuisine, while linked with Chinese and Malay, is distinctly different in taste. Most Thai dishes are hot and filled with exciting spices and fish aromatics. On first tasting a dish, you may find it stingingly hot (tiny chilies make the cuisine so fiery), but the taste of the fresh herbs will soon surface. Thai food's characteristic flavor comes from fresh mint, basil, coriander, and citrus leaves; extensive use of lemon grass, lime, vinegar, and tamarind keeps the sour-hot taste prevalent.

Thai curries—such as chicken curry with cashews, salted egg, and mango—use coconut milk and are often served with dozens of garnishes and side dishes. Various sauces are used for dipping; *nam pla*, one favorite, is a salty, fragrant amber liquid made from salted and fermented shrimp.

A popular Thai dish is *mee krob*, crispy fried noodles with shrimp. Other outstanding Thai dishes: *tom yam kung*, hot and spicy shrimp soup (few meals start without it); *gai hor bai toey*, fried chicken wrapped in pandanus leaves; *pu cha*, steamed crab with fresh coriander root and a little coconut milk; and *khuo suey*, steamed white rice, which you'll need to soothe any fires that may develop in your mouth.

The larger Thai restaurants are actually seafood markets where you can pick your own swimming creature and tell the waitress how you want it cooked. For drinks, try Singha beer, brewed in Thailand, or *o-liang*, the national drink—very strong black iced coffee sweetened with palm-sugar syrup.

European Singaporeans recognize that through the stomach lies the path to all other satisfactions. Culinary skills have been developed to superlative levels—not only for Chinese or Indian or Asian cooking styles but also for European cuisine. If you long for steak or fish-and-chips or fondue, you'll find it here.

The many Continental restaurants have impeccable service and high-quality food. But of all European food that has come to Singapore, French cuisine has made the greatest impact. During the past few years, Singapore has been a burgeoning market for all French products, from name brands in fashion to wines of every hue and flavor, cheese from obscure provinces, and previously unknown vegetables. But perhaps the most important gastronomic gift from France is its famous visiting chefs, who have raised Singapore's standard of French cooking and skill to great heights. Classic or nouvelle cuisine is yours for the ordering, but all good things have their price, so be prepared to pay for what you enjoy.

Except for **Fosters Restaurant** in the Specialists' Shopping Centre, we do not really have a full-fledged English restaurant, but the Goodwood Park Hotel's **Gordon Grill** serves a fantastic sherry trifle, and their English roast beef is famous. The **Baron's Table** offers traditional German and Austrian dishes.

Seafood Seafood is among Singapore's greatest contributions to the gourmet world, and generally very inexpensive (though elegant and expensive seafood meals featuring delicacies like shark's fin, dried abalone, and lobster are served in some Chinese restaurants). The countryside area of Ponggol is famous for seafood, as is the **Seafood Centre** on the East Coast Parkway, with no less than eight restaurants in terracelike pavilions looking out toward the sea. Dishes marked "market price" on the menu are the premium items. Before ordering, be sure to find out exactly how much each dish will cost.

Other Choices In Singapore, you'll find that you can get pretty much whatever kind of cuisine you're in the mood for. Other Asian restaurants include the **Tae Nung** on East Coast Road, with Korean barbecue, and the Vietnamese restaurants **Paregu** and **Saigon,** both in the Orchard Road area. For Mexican food, try **El Filipe Cantina** in Holland Village.

Dining Out

While some cultures consider atmosphere, decor, and service more important than food, in Singapore, the food's the thing. To us, a good meal means good food cooked with fresh ingredients. Gourmet cooking can be found as easily in small, unpretentious, open-front coffee shops as in the most elegant restaurants in the world, with service that's second to none. Most of these are located in hotels—Singaporeans love to make a grand entrance through a sparkling, deluxe hotel lobby. The Shangri-La's **Latour,** Pan Pacific's **Chateaubriand,** and the Goodwood Park's **Gordon Grill** are excellent examples of fine European-style dining, complete with displays of roses and orchids, polished silver and gleaming crystal, waiters dressed in tuxedos, impeccable service in the best French tradition, and soothing music from a grand piano or a string quartet. The food itself is of the highest standards, with ingredients flown in fresh from France, Scotland, Australia, and elsewhere.

Elegant meals can be eaten with jade chopsticks at the Sheraton Towers' **Li Bai** Cantonese restaurant. And the Hyatt's **Ruyi** is a pleasure for the eyes as well as the tastebuds: Its understated yet richly hued Chinese decor envelops you in luxury.

Hawker Centers and Wok-and-Roll

At the other end of the scale are the hawker centers, agglomerations of individual vendor-chefs selling cooked foods in the open air. These vendors originally traveled from door to door selling their wares from portable stalls. Each hawker would serve only one dish, sometimes made from a secret recipe handed down through generations. The hawker would advertise his or her wares by sounding a horn, knocking two bamboo sticks together, or simply shouting. Hearing the sound, people would dash out of the house to place an order. After everyone had eaten, the hawker would collect and wash the crockery and utensils, then continue up the road. As many as 10 different hawkers might pass one's house in a day.

Some years ago, Singapore decided to gather the hawkers in food centers for reasons of hygiene. (And these new centers *are* all perfectly clean—the health authorities are very strict.) Visitors and locals alike find these centers a culinary adventure. You can check out each stall—see the raw materials and watch the cooking methods—then choose whatever strikes your fancy from as many different stalls as you like. Find a seat at any of the tables (the government owns the centers and the seats; the hawkers rent only their stalls). Note the number of your table so you can tell the hawkers where to deliver your orders, then sit down and wait for food to arrive. Someone will come to your table to take your drink order. You pay at the end of the meal. Most dishes cost S$4 or slightly more; for S$12, you can get a meal that includes a drink and a slice of fresh fruit for dessert.

The most touristy center is **Newton Circus.** Many people find Newton *the* place to see life at night—it's raucous and noisy and festive. Go to Newton if you must for the experience, but avoid the seafood stalls: They are known to fleece tourists. Feast, instead, at stalls offering the traditional one-dish meals, such as fried Hokkien noodles, roast-duck rice, *rojak*, or Malay *satay* (*see* Glossary of Food Terms, *below*). These stalls have prices displayed prominently. When you place your order, specify whether you want a S$2, S$3, or S$4 order. An excellent new hawker center is at **Marina South,** where hundreds of stalls in a covered area offer a vast selection of Chinese and Malay foods. The area is not easy to reach by public transport, but if you'd rather not take an S$8 (from Orchard Road) taxi ride, you could take the evening shuttle bus to Marina Village that collects passengers from most major hotels and then walk 10 minutes along the waterfront to the hawker center.

Other centers include **Cuppage Centre,** on Cuppage Road; **Empress Place,** behind the exhibition hall; **Telok Ayer Transit Food Centre,** on Shenton Way in the financial district; and **Bugis Square,** at Eminent Plaza (this one's open 7 AM–3 AM).

Another experience in Singaporean dining is to visit the **stir-fry stalls,** fondly called "wok-and-roll" by Americans. These stalls, most half-restaurant and half-parking lot, can be found in abundance on East Coast Road. They are characterized by open kitchens and a stream of waiters yelling and running about. As a rule of thumb, always follow the crowd to the busiest place and watch gastronomy in action.

The most popular dish at the stir-fry stalls is chili crab, with crusty bread to dip into a hot, rich, tasty sauce. Who can resist it? Other favorites are deep-fried baby squid and steamed prawns or fish, accompanied by fried noodles. There is certainly no elegance here—just good, fresh food cooked according to tried-and-true recipes. Prices are very reasonable. Stalls open for business at 5 PM.

Dim Sum

Called *dian xin* ("small eats") in Singapore, dim sum is a particularly Cantonese style of eating, featuring a selection of bite-size steamed, baked, or deep-fried dumplings, buns, pastries, and pancakes, with a variety of savory or sweet flavorings. Popular items are the *cha shao bao* (a steamed bread bun filled with diced, sweetened barbecued pork) and *shao mai* (a steamed mixture of minced prawns, pork, and sometimes water chestnuts). The selection, which may comprise as many as 50 separate offerings, may also include such dishes as soups, steamed pork ribs, and stuffed green peppers.

Traditionally, dim sum are served three on a plate in bamboo steamer baskets on trolleys that are pushed around the restaurant. You simply wait for the trolleys to come around, then point to whichever item you would like. The more elegant style now is to order dim sum à la carte so that it will be prepared freshly for you. Dim sum is usually served for lunch from noon to 2:30 PM, though in some teahouses in Chinatown, it is served for breakfast from 5 to 9. Dim sum is usually priced between S$1.80 and S$6 per dish of three pieces, though the fancier restaurants will have a higher range. An excellent place for dim sum in the financial district is the **Mayflower Restaurant** (6 Shenton Way, #04-02 DBS Bldg., tel. 220–3133), a huge room heavy with Chinese decor. Also see recommendations in the reviews that follow.

High Tea

High tea has become very popular in Singapore, especially among women of leisure, who find it a pleasant way to pass the time with friends. In many hotels, such as the **Goodwood Park Hotel** and the **Holiday Inn Park View,** high tea is accompanied by light Viennese-style music. Though British-inspired, the Singapore high tea is usually served buffet style and includes dim sum, fried noodles, and other local favorites in addition to the regulation finger sandwiches, scones, and cakes. For delicious pastries and tea or coffee, try the new Canopy Bar at the **Hyatt Regency** on Scotts Road. Teas are usually served between 3 and 6 PM and cost between S$10 and S$16 per person. The **Oriental** at Marina Square has recently initiated its version of high tea, and, with an array of Chinese, Nonya, Malay, Indian, and Western delicacies, it ranks as one of the best around.

The Flavors of Asia

It will not take you long to discover that Singaporeans love spices. This is not surprising in light of Singapore's history as a port through which the products of the famed Spice Islands were traded. But spicy doesn't necessarily mean hot. The dozens of spices used in the various cuisines can yield tastes mellow, as in thick, rich coconut gravies; pungent, as in Indian curries; tart, as in the sour and hot tamarind-, vinegar-, and lime-based gravies of Thailand, Malaysia, Indonesia, and Singapore; or sweet and fragrant, as in Indian desserts and beverages.

Basically, there are two main schools of spicy cooking, both well represented in Singaporean cuisine. The first is the Indian tradition, emphasizing dried-seed spices: cardamom, cloves, cumin, fennel, fenugreek, white and black pepper, chili peppers, dried turmeric root, and mustard and poppy seeds. These spices are sometimes used whole but are more often ground into a powder (broadly referred to as curry powder) or made into a paste used as a base for gravies.

The second tradition is Southeast Asian and depends mainly on fresh root spices and aromatic leaves. Typically, lemon grass, turmeric root, galangal, Chinese ginger, garlic, onions, shallots, and other roots are pounded into smooth pastes with candlenuts and shrimp paste to form a base for gravies and soups. (In Asia, gravies are thickened not by flour or cream but usually by these pastes.) The leaves—turmeric, lime, coriander, several varieties of basil, bay—add a distinctive bouquet. How exciting this juxtaposition of flavors and aromas is!

Glossary of Food Terms

The following are dishes and food names you will come across often at the hawker centers. *Also see* The Cuisines of Singapore, *above,* for descriptions of other dishes.

char kway teow—fried flat rice noodles mixed with soy sauce, chili paste, fish cakes, and bean sprouts and fried in lard.
Hokkien prawn mee—fresh wheat noodles in a prawn-and-pork broth served with freshly boiled prawns.
laksa—a one-dish meal of round rice noodles in coconut gravy spiced with lemon grass, chilies, turmeric, galangal, shrimp

paste, and shallots. It is served with a garnish of steamed prawns, rice cakes, and bean sprouts.

mee rebus—a Malay version of Chinese wheat noodles with a spicy gravy. The dish is garnished with sliced eggs, pieces of fried bean curd, and bean sprouts.

rojak—a Malay word for "salad." Chinese rojak consists of cucumber, lettuce, pineapple, *bangkwang* (jicama), and deep-fried bean curd, tossed with a dressing made from salty shrimp paste, ground toasted peanuts, sugar, and rice vinegar. Indian rojak consists of deep-fried lentil and prawn patties, boiled potatoes, and deep-fried bean curd, all served with a spicy dip sweetened with mashed sweet potatoes.

roti prata—an Indian pancake made by tossing a piece of wheat-flour dough into the air until it is paper-thin and then folding it to form many layers. The dough is fried until crisp on a cast-iron griddle, then served with curry powder or sugar. An ideal breakfast dish.

satay—small strips of meat marinated in fresh spices and threaded onto short skewers. A Malay dish, satay is barbecued over charcoal and eaten with a spiced peanut sauce, sliced cucumbers, raw onions, and pressed rice cakes.

thosai—an Indian rice-flour pancake that is a popular breakfast dish, eaten with either curry powder or brown sugar.

The Nitty-Gritty

Dress Except at the fancier hotel dining rooms, Singaporeans do not dress up to eat out. The weather calls for lighter wear than a jacket and tie. (Some restaurants tried to enforce a dress code for men but found that their customers went elsewhere to eat. Now an open-neck shirt and a jacket represent the upper limit of formality.) Generally, though, shorts, thongs, singlets (sleeveless cotton T-shirts), and track suits are not appropriate. Those sensitive to cold might bring a sweater, since many restaurants are air-conditioned to subarctic temperatures.

Hours Most restaurants are open from noon to 2:30 or 3 for lunch and from 7 to 10:30 PM (last order) for dinner. Seafood restaurants are usually open only for dinner and supper, until around midnight or 1 AM. Some hotel coffee shops (and the Indian coffee shops along Changi Road) are open 24 hours a day; others close between 2 and 6 AM. At hawker centers, some stalls are open for breakfast and lunch while others are open for lunch and dinner. Late-night food centers like Eminent Plaza in Jalan Besar are in full swing until 3 AM.

Ordering Asians, particularly Chinese and not including Japanese, order food to be shared. Generally plan on small servings of four to five dishes for four people, or three dishes for two people. Food is either served family-style—placed all at once at the center of the table so everyone can serve himself—or, for more formal meals, served a course at a time, again with diners sharing from a single dish at the center of the table. Each diner is given a plate or bowl of rice.

Taxes and Charges Hawker stalls and small restaurants do not impose a service charge. Most medium-size and larger restaurants, however, add 10% service charge as well as a 4% government tax to the bill. Most Chinese restaurants also automatically add a charge of about S$2 per person for tea, peanuts, pickles, and rice.

Tipping Tipping is actively discouraged in Singapore. Do not tip in restaurants and hawker centers unless you really feel the service deserves an extra bit of recognition. (The 10% service charge is shared by a restaurant's staff.)

Alcohol Liquor is very expensive in Singapore. A bottle of wine in a restaurant costs about S$36; a carafe, S$20–S$25; a cocktail, S$6–S$8. It generally costs more to drink than to eat.

Smoking Smoking is banned in air-conditioned restaurants and banquet/meeting rooms.

Restaurants

By Violet Oon

Updated by Nigel Fisher

Highly recommended restaurants are indicated by a star ★.

Category	Cost*
Very Expensive	over S$50 (US$25)
Expensive	S$25–S$50 (US$13–US$25)
Moderate	S$10–S$25 (US$5–US$13)
Inexpensive	under S$10 (US$5)

*All prices are per person, including first course, main course, and dessert, excluding tax, tip, and drinks. Unless otherwise stated, restaurants are open daily for lunch and dinner.

American

Moderate **Steeples Deli.** Steeples is much loved by American expatriates and by Singaporean Yuppies who come for the yogurt (with its various toppings), muesli, and corned beef on rye and other sandwiches, which are accompanied by lots of vegetables. The homemade soups, cookies, and cakes are wholesome and good. The atmosphere is casual, with counter service and light pine furniture. *Tanglin Shopping Centre (#02-25), 19 Tanglin Rd., tel. 737–0701. No reservations. Dress: casual. No credit cards. Open Mon.–Sat. 8 AM–9:30 PM, holidays 9–4.*

Chinese: Cantonese

Very Expensive **Hai Tien Lo.** Sit in the right place at this 37th-floor restaurant in the round and you'll get a view of the sea, the Padang, and City Hall. The cuisine, decor, and service are all super-elegant: Plates are changed with every course; waitresses wear *cheong-sams* (traditional Chinese sheath dresses with high collars and side slits) of celadon green, to match the decor; and the delicate white china is hand-painted with cherry blossoms. For lunch, opt for the dim sum, priced at a premium because top-quality ingredients are used. The specialties are Cantonese roast chicken with crispy golden-brown skin and tender, juicy meat; cubes of beef fillet fried with black pepper and oyster sauce; and deep-fried fresh scallops stuffed with minced prawns and tossed in a salty black-bean sauce. The pièce de résistance is Monk Jumps over the Wall—dried abalone, whole chicken, Chinese ham, fish stomach lining, dried scallops, and shark's fin steamed together for hours until tender. At S$90 per serving (or S$900 for 10 people), it is one of the most expensive dishes in town, but the broth is the best in the world—the really rich simply drink it and leave the rest. *Pan Pacific Singapore (#01-300), 6 Raffles Blvd., Marina Square, tel. 336–8111. Reservations advised. Dress: smart casual. AE, DC, MC, V.*

Expensive– Very Expensive ★ **Li Bai.** Its dining room evokes richness without overindulgence: deep maroon wall panels edged with black and backlighted; elaborate floral displays that change with the seasons; jade table settings; ivory chopsticks. The service is very fine, as is the cooking, which is modern and innovative, yet deeply rooted in the Cantonese tradition. The chef's unusual creations include deep-fried diamonds of egg noodles in a rich stock with crabmeat and mustard greens; fried lobster in black bean paste; and double-boiled shark's fin with Chinese wine and *jinhua* ham. The extensive menu also features barbecued sliced duckling with fresh mango; suckling pig on prawn toast; and Monk Jumps over the Wall with abalone, mushrooms, fish maw, sea cucumber, Chinese herbs, and shark's fin. The restaurant is small, seating fewer than 100 people. *Sheraton Towers Hotel, 39 Scotts Rd., tel. 737–6888. Reservations advised. Dress: smart casual to elegant. AE, DC, MC, V.*

Moderate– Very Expensive **Tung Lok Shark's Fin Restaurant.** On the pale blue walls flecked with silver hangs a priceless collection of Chinese paintings—including landscapes and horse studies—and calligraphy. The owner is an avid collector and counts China's leading artists among his friends. As the restaurant's name suggests, the specialty is shark's fin (served with consommé). Some of the other dishes—even simple ones such as spring rolls or sautéed pea pods—don't quite live up to the restaurant's reputation. For lunch, there's dim sum—the selection is considered one of the best. If you're on a budget, ask for the lunch menu of less-pricey dishes. *Liang Court Complex (#04-07), 177 River Valley Rd., tel. 336–6022. Reservations advised. Dress: smart casual. AE, DC, MC, V.*

Moderate– Expensive **Fook Yuen.** The decor is a trifle chichi, with the pink walls, chairs, and Austrian blinds, but the restaurant is considered very elegant by its Chinese clientele. The new-style Cantonese cooking is characterized by a respect for fresh ingredients, clear tastes, and light textures. Steamed fish fresh from the tank—served in a gravy of light soy sauce, vegetable oil, and julienne of spring onions—is a specialty. Garoupa is very popular. Ordering à la carte can be costly, but the dim sum lunch and the excellent set menus are reasonably priced. *Paragon Shopping Centre (#03-05/06), 290 Orchard Rd., tel. 235–2211. Reservations advised. Dress: smart casual. AE, DC, MC, V.*

Ruyi. This is Singapore's most beautiful Chinese restaurant. Such touches as Chinese screens and paintings, porcelain lamps, subdued lighting, and artistic presentation of food combine to make dining out at the Ruyi a memorable experience. The cooking is purist. Try the minced pigeon on lettuce leaves or the beef-and-carrot rolls fried in delicate black-pepper sauce. Instead of Peking duck, try chicken cooked in a similar way; the skin is sliced and enclosed in paper-thin spinach-flavored pancakes with sweet plum sauce and spring onions. There's dim sum at lunch. *Hyatt Regency Hotel, 10-12 Scotts Rd., tel. 733–1188. Reservations advised. Dress: smart casual to elegant. AE, DC, MC, V.*

Tsui Hang Village. This well-reputed restaurant has reopened in Marina Square with a decor of green tiles, brick walls, and rooflike overhangs that give it a courtyard ambience. The

Singapore Dining

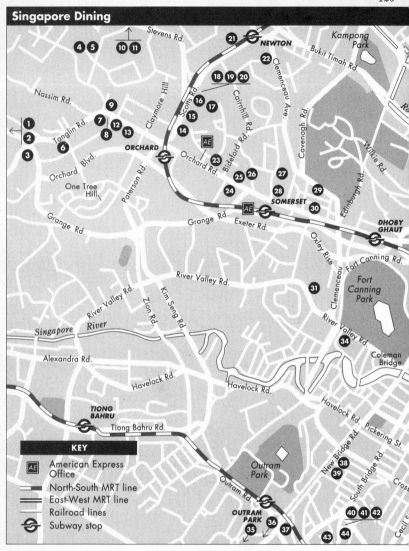

Alkaff Mansion, **35**
Annalakshmi, **45**
Aziza's, **27**
Banana Leaf
Apollo, **32**
Beng Hiang, **41**
Bintang Timur, **16**
Bombay
Meadowlands, **8**
Cairnhill Thai Seafood
Restaurant, **26**

Cherry Garden, **51**
Chiang Jian, **17**
Choon Seng, **22**
Compass Rose
Restaurant, **46**
Da Paolo, **44**
Dragon City, **10**
Fook Yuen, **23**
Golden Phoenix
Sichuan
Restaurant, **11**

Gordon Grill, **19**
Guan Hoe Soon, **56**
Hai Tien Lo, **53**
Harbour Grill, **13**
Her Sea Palace, **12**
Keday Kopi, **28**
Keyaki, **54**
La Brasserie, **3**
L'Aigle d'Or, **43**

Latour, **4**
Le Restaurant de
France, **30**
Li Bai, **21**
Long Beach Seafood
Restaurant, **58**
Long Jiang, **25**
Majestic
Restaurant, **37**
Marina Village, **49**

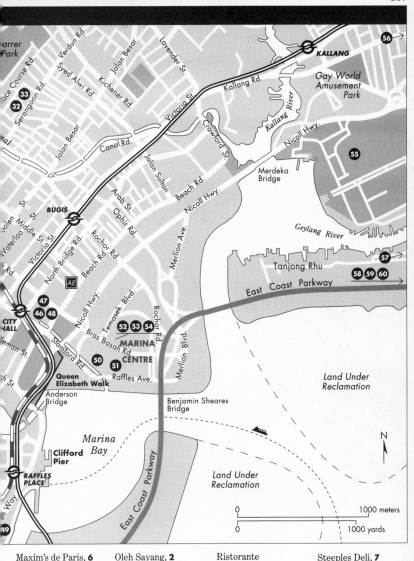

Maxim's de Paris, **6**
Min Jiang, **18**
Moi Kong, **40**
Moti Mahal, **42**
Muthu's Curry
Restaurant, **33**
Nadaman, **5**
New Nam Thong Tea
House, **38, 39**
Nonya and Baba, **31**

Oleh Sayang, **2**
Palm Beach
Seafood, **55**
Palm Grill, **47**
Peranakan Inn, **57**
Pete's Place, **15**
Pine Court, **24**
Prima Tower
Revolving
Restaurant, **36**

Ristorante
Bologna, **50**
Ristorante Italiano
Prego, **48**
Ruyi, **14**
Samy's Curry
Restaurant, **1**
Seafood International
Market and
Restaurant, **59**
Shima, **20**

Steeples Deli, **7**
Suntory, **9**
Tandoor, **29**
Tsui Hang Village, **52**
Tung Lok Shark's Fin
Restaurant, **34**
UDMC Seafood
Centre, **60**

braised superior shark's fin is among the best in town. Roast suckling pig and braised abalone are served here as well, but are usually reserved for banquet dining. The fresh seafood is flown in from Hong Kong. At lunch, try the inexpensive dim sum or one of the set menus. The deep-fried roast chicken pleases most palates. *6 Raffles Blvd., Marina Sq. (#02–142), tel. 338–6668. Reservations advised. Dress: smart casual. AE, DC, MC, V.*

Moderate **Majestic Restaurant.** The food at this restaurant, in a cloistered part of Chinatown on a street of gentlemen's clubs, is among the best for traditional Cantonese cooking. Rumor has it that the Wong family, who own the restaurant and the small hotel it sits in, made their fortune supplying meals to the millionaire's club next door. Famous dishes include suckling pig barbecued over glowing charcoal and braised superior shark's fin with chicken (each costs about S$100 and feeds 10); fried-shark's-fin-and-crabmeat omelet (wrap a spoonful in a lettuce leaf, fold the leaf over, and eat); and roast Cantonese chicken. The decor is premodern Chinese with hints of red; the seating's comfortable; the service is fast but without finesse. *31-37 Bukit Pasoh Rd., tel. 223–5111. No reservations. Dress: casual. AE, DC, V.*

Inexpensive **New Nam Thong Tea House.** Absolutely inelegant but totally authentic is this teahouse in Chinatown. Breakfast here between 5 and 9:30 for a view of real Singapore life. Older folk, mainly men, congregate daily to meet and gossip with friends and read the Chinese papers. Situated above an open-front shophouse, the teahouse is not air-conditioned and can be muggy, but it serves hearty, giant-size dim sum—*char siew bow* (steamed barbecued pork buns), *siew mai* (prawn-and-minced-pork dumplings), and other assorted dishes—for under S$2 a serving. Wash it all down with piping-hot Chinese tea. They don't understand English here, so just point. This is no tourist spot, but its popularity with the locals has prompted the owners to open a sister teahouse at 181 New Bridge Road. *8-10A Smith St., tel. 223–2817. No reservations. Dress: casual. No credit cards.*

Chinese: Hakka

Moderate **Moi Kong.** At this unpretentious and honest family eatery, try the prawns fried with red-wine lees, the steamed chicken with wine, or the *khong bak mui choy* (braised pork in dark soy sauce with a preserved salted green vegetable), delicious with rice. *22 Murray St., tel. 221–7758. No reservations. Dress: casual. AE, DC, V.*

Chinese: Hokkien

Moderate **Beng Hiang.** Like Hakka food, Hokkien cooking is peasant-style: hearty, rough, and delicious. *Kwa huay* (liver rolls) and *ngo hiang* (pork-and-prawn rolls) are very popular and are eaten dipped in sweet plum sauce. *Hay cho* (deep-fried prawn dumplings) are another Hokkien staple. Beng Hiang also serves *khong bak* (braised pig's feet) and what is reputedly the best roast suckling pig in Singapore. *20 Murray St., tel. 221–6695. No reservations. Dress: casual. No credit cards.*

You've Let Your Imagination Go, Now Get Up And Follow Your Dreams.

For The Vacation You're Dreaming Of, Call American Express® Travel Agency At 1-800-YES-AMEX.*

American Express will send more than your imagination soaring. We'll fly you, sail you, drive you to any Fodor's destination and beyond. Because American Express believes the best vacations happen from Europe to the Orient, Walt Disney® World to Hawaii and everywhere in between.

For dependable service, expert advice, and value wherever your dreams take you, call on American Express. After all, the best traveling companion is a trustworthy friend.

It's easy to recognize a good place when you see one.

American Express Cardmembers have been doing it for years.

The secret? Instead of just relying on what they see in the window, they look at the door. If there's an American Express Blue Box on it, they know they've found an establishment that cares about high standards.

Whether it's a place to eat, to sleep, to shop, or simply meet, they know they will be warmly welcomed.

So much so, they're rarely taken in by anything else.

Always a good sign.

Chinese: Hunanese

Expensive
★

Cherry Garden. The Cherry Garden restaurant is a beautiful setting for a meal: A wood-roofed pavilion with walls of antique Chinese brick encloses a landscaped courtyard. Artworks are tastefully chosen and displayed. The service is impeccable, and the food is a welcome change from the usual Cantonese fare. An unusual dish is the steamed rice in woven bamboo baskets. Also try the minced-pigeon broth with dry scallops steamed in a bamboo tube, or, in season, served in a fragrant baby melon; the superior Yunnan honey-glazed ham served between thin slices of steamed bread; or the camphor-smoked duck in a savory bean curd crust. *Oriental Hotel, 6 Raffles Blvd., Marina Square, tel. 338–0066. Reservations advised. Dress: smart casual to elegant. AE, DC, MC, V.*

Chinese: Pekingese

Expensive

Pine Court. Baked tench, marinated lamb, and fried dry scallops are just a few of the dishes that distinguish the cooking of the Pine Court. The restaurant's Peking duck is famed for its crisp, melt-in-your-mouth skin and delicate pancake wrapping. Dinner is the Pine Court's best meal; the more economical lunch (frequently a buffet) is less inspired. Refurbished in 1991, the Pine Court takes on a fresh look while the carved-wood wall panels create the ambience of a Chinese mansion; the service is fine and caring, by staff dressed in Chinese style. *Mandarin Hotel, 333 Orchard Rd., tel. 737–4411. Reservations advised. Dress: smart casual. AE, DC, MC, V.*

Moderate–
Expensive

Prima Tower Revolving Restaurant. Not far from the World Trade Centre is this restaurant atop a grain silo. The decor is luxurious but not outstanding, so concentrate on the spectacular view of Singapore harbor and Sentosa Island across the straits. The food has always been above par. House specialties are Peking duck, red fish on a hot plate, and grilled scallops with minced chicken. *201 Keppel Rd., tel. 221–5600. Reservations advised. Dress: smart casual. AE, DC, MC, V.*

Chinese: Shanghainese

Very Expensive

Chiang Jian. Meals in this stylish restaurant are served Western-style—portions are presented on dinner plates, and patrons do not serve themselves from a central platter. The kitchen staff was trained by the chef of Shanghai's leading restaurant, Yang Zhou. Recommended dishes are the chicken and goose surprise, fresh crabmeat in a yam basket, baby kale with scallops, lion's head in consommé, and sliced beef fillet stir-fried and served with leeks. Presentation is an art here. Even the chopsticks are gold-plated. Children are not welcome—the management wants to preserve the valuable furnishings and the serene atmosphere. If you must bring your child, he or she will add a cover of S$25. *Goodwood Park Hotel, 22 Scotts Rd., tel. 737–7411. Reservations advised. Dress: casual. AE, DC, MC, V.*

Chinese: Szechuan

Moderate–
Expensive
★

Dragon City. Singaporeans consider Dragon City the best place for Szechuan food. Set in a courtyard and entered through a flamboyant red moongate door, the restaurant is a large room that looks Chinese but is not particularly appealing. The food is where all the artistry is. Choose from such Szechuan staples as *kung po* chicken and prawns, in which the meat is deep-fried with whole dried chili peppers and coated with a sweet-and-sour sauce; or try the delicious minced-pork soup in a whole melon, steamed red fish with soybean crumbs, or smoked Szechuan duck. The service is fast. If you don't quite know how to order your meal, ask for Mr. Wang Ban Say, the restaurant's manager and one of the owners. *Novotel Orchid Inn, Plymouth Wing, 214 Dunearn Rd., tel. 254–7070. Reservations advised. Dress: smart casual. AE, DC, MC, V.*

Golden Phoenix Sichuan Restaurant. The first Szechuan restaurant to open in Singapore, the Golden Phoenix has a reputation for large portions. It is known for its braised pork, fresh abalone with vegetables, and Szechuan desserts. The look is rampantly Chinese, and the service is caring. *Hotel Equatorial, 429 Bukit Timah Rd., tel. 732–0431. Reservations advised. Dress: smart casual. AE, DC, MC, V.*

Long Jiang. Perhaps the greatest draw of this restaurant in the heart of the Orchard Road shopping area is the "all you can eat" offer. For a set price (which varies from S$17 to S$21, depending on the season), you can sample nearly 40 items on the menu, including hot-and-sour soup, shark's fin soup, smoked duck, and kung po chicken. It's not unlike most other Chinese restaurants in look, but the service is above average. *Crown Prince Hotel, 270 Orchard Rd., tel. 732–1111. Reservations advised. Dress: smart casual. AE, DC, MC, V.*

Moderate

Min Jiang. Housed in a Chinese pavilion on the grounds of the Goodwood Park, Min Jiang is always packed, thanks to its delicious food, fast service, and reasonable prices. The decor is very Chinese in a mellow, resplendent style. The camphor-smoked duck, kung po chicken, and long beans fried with minced pork are favorites. *Goodwood Park Hotel, 22 Scotts Rd., tel. 737–7411. Reservations advised. Dress: smart casual. AE, DC, MC, V.*

Continental

Very Expensive
★

Latour. Floor-to-ceiling windows provide a spectacular view of the palm-fringed swimming pool and the garden of the Shangri-La Hotel. Inside, an eclectic luxury reigns: salmon-pink walls, comfortable rattan chairs, batik paintings, and Austrian chandeliers, plus elegant crystal, china, and silver table settings. The food is French-based nouvelle cuisine. Thinly sliced beef marinated in lemon pepper à la Cipriani, cream of smoked salmon soup, fresh warm goose-liver salad enhanced with truffles, and deboned rack of lamb with herbed morello sauce are some of the star dishes. At lunch (about S$35 per person), appetizers and desserts are offered buffet-style while the main course is ordered à la carte from a small but well-chosen menu. The wine list is considered one of the best in town and includes a fine selection from France's Château Latour. *Shangri-La Singapore, 22 Orange Grove Rd., tel. 737–3644.*

Reservations required. Dress: smart casual to elegant; no jeans. AE, DC, MC, V.

Expensive **Compass Rose Restaurant.** The main attraction's the view from the 70th floor of the Westin Stamford: On a clear day, you can see Malaysia and some of the Indonesian islands. This elegant restaurant—spread out over three floors and decorated in subtle sunset shades of peach and purple—features a luxurious lounge (where high tea and drinks are served) as well as a more-formal dining room. "East meets West" is the dominant theme in such dishes as sautéed filet mignon wrapped in lotus leaf, lobster ravioli soup, and grilled king prawns. The presentation is painterly. There's always a line at night for seats in the lounge. *Westin Stamford Hotel, 2 Stamford Rd., tel. 338–8585. Reservations advised. Dress: smart casual; no shorts. AE, DC, MC, V.*

Gordon Grill. The Scottish country/hunting lodge look, with heavy draped curtains, is lightened with celadon and soft apple greens, light-wood chairs and accents, and glass panels etched with delicate drawings of Scottish lairds. The Goodwood Park's restaurant has changed decor and location within the hotel many times, but tradition is served up here very much as it always has been, including excellent roast beef, perfect steaks, and the best sherry trifle in town. This may be the best British fare in Southeast Asia. The service is also very good. You can go Scottish by ordering haggis with neeps and tatties and parcel of Scotch salmon. *Goodwood Park Hotel, 22 Scotts Rd., tel. 737–7411. Reservations advised. Dress: smart casual. AE, DC, MC, V.*

Harbour Grill. Dine here in luxurious comfort, surrounded by warmly masculine decor in deep reds and browns, and murals that capture Singapore's colorful history in the mid-19th century. The Harbour Grill introduced French nouvelle cuisine to Singapore in 1979; today, its cooking is what the chefs term *cuisine évolution*—a homey, down-to-earth style of cooking, using fresh ingredients and the latest technological inventions for the kitchen under the direction of Chef Thierry Merssonier. The nightly "Surprise Dinner" is very popular: They don't tell you what the seven courses are, you just wait and see what they bring. The steaks are very fine, as are the appetizers. Especially good choices are the pan-fried suprême of sea bass with oyster mushrooms, chives, tomatoes, red wine, and shallots; and the venison in a sauce of Noilly Prat, cognac, game stock, butter, and juniper, served with three purees: beetroot, celery, and broccoli. *Hilton Singapore, 581 Orchard Rd., tel. 737–2233. Reservations advised. Dress: smart casual to elegant. AE, DC, MC, V. No lunch weekends.*

L'Aigle d'Or. Glittering crystal contrasts with gaily decorated floral plates at this small, cheerful restaurant in the new Duxton Hotel (in the Tanjong Pagar area of Chinatown). A five-course *menu dégustation* for about S$70 may include chestnut soup, sautéed fresh foie gras, a delicate fillet of sea bass in a basil sauce, and a panfried medallion of veal. Desserts come in pairs; you'll rave about the chocolate cake in licorice sauce. *83 Duxton Rd., tel. 227–7678. Reservations advised. Dress: smart casual. AE, DC, MC, V.*

Marina Village. This is not one restaurant, but a newly constructed one-street village with 10 restaurants, a pub, and a disco. Each of the restaurants may be reached by dialing the village's central telephone number, 225–3055, and requesting the appropriate extension. Though there is one Cantonese restaurant, **City Qian Dong,** and a Malay open café, the emphasis is European with Greek (**Greece, My Love,** ext. 813), Swiss (**Tic Toc,** ext. 832), Danish (**H.C. Andersen,** ext. 826), Spanish (**Que? Manuel,** ext. 823), Italian (**Via Veneto,** ext. 819), German (**Bierstube,** ext. 834), and Moroccan (**Marrakech,** ext. 809) restaurants. All the restaurants take an intimate approach to dining, and the high prices (S$40–S$50 for an entrée) reflect it. The restaurant that wins most acclaim is the Marrakech—though at press time the owner (who is also the developer of Marina Village) was in the process of restructuring his financial obligations. If you make your way to Marina Village (a half-hourly evening shuttle bus runs back and forth between the Village and 11 of the major Singapore hotels) and then decide not to try any of the Village restaurants, walk along the bay front to **Garden Plaza,** a new, excellent, and vast collection of hawker stalls offering primarily Chinese food with an emphasis on seafood. *Marina Village, 31 Marine Park, Marina South, tel. 225–3055. Reservations not necessary. Dress: smart casual. AE, DC, MC, V. Open weekdays 7–11 PM, weekends 12:30 PM–3 AM.*

Palm Grill. This high-ceilinged restaurant brings back memories of the days of the transatlantic liners, when art nouveau, with its elaborate curves, ruled the waves. Carved-wood chairs and Chinese Coromandel screens add notes of Oriental richness, but the food is effervescently French, with a touch of nouvelle. An especially good start to a meal is the warm panfried goose liver on a bed of frisée. A popular dish is the steamed fillet of sole with eggplant: The fish is cooked slowly in stock, stuffed with *brandade* (a blend of potatoes, cream, olive oil, salt, and pepper), and steamed, then served with a white wine-based sauce. *Westin Plaza Hotel, 2 Stamford Rd., tel. 338–8585. Reservations required. Dress: smart casual. AE, DC, MC, V. No lunch Sat., closed Sun.*

French

Expensive–
Very Expensive
Le Restaurant de France. French master chef Louis Outhier is the consultant here and makes annual appearances. The cooking is light, creamy, and full of surprises thanks to the way Outhier combines new ingredients he finds in Singapore's markets. Le Restaurant offers sheer elegance, from the opulent and romantic decor—pink-on-pink tones, chandeliers, fabric-covered chairs, huge displays of lilies, and gleaming crystal—to the superbly discreet French style of service. On the terrace, you may dine beside a fountain under a trellis entwined with vines, with a view of the park beyond (actually, a mural by Count Bernard de Perthuis). *Meridien Singapore, 100 Orchard Rd., tel. 733–8855. Reservations advised. Dress: smart casual to elegant. AE, DC, MC, V. No lunch weekends.*

Maxim's de Paris. The turn-of-the-century decor—pink-shaded lamps, red velvet seats and banquettes, mahogany paneling, massive cut-glass mirrors, rococo paintings, and a faithful re-creation of the original Paris restaurant's stained-glass ceiling—strongly evokes the Belle Epoque. This is a restaurant *made* for romance. Dine on excellently prepared *côte de boeuf grillée, sauce vignerons* (grilled prime rib with red wine and grape sauce), or poached scallops in ginger-and-herbs sauce, as well as seasonal French delicacies. *Regent Hotel, 1*

Cuscaden Rd., tel. 733–8888. Reservations advised. Dress: smart casual to elegant. AE, DC, MC, V. No lunch weekends.

Moderate–
Expensive
★

La Brasserie. Often named as the favorite French restaurant in Singapore, this is an informal place, with garçons clad in traditional ankle-length aprons serving hearty traditional fare like French onion soup, *émincé de veau à la crème* (sliced veal with mushrooms in cream sauce), and fluffy lemon pancakes with vanilla ice cream. Here you'll dine on the spirit of Paris as well as the food: Red-checkered tablecloths, antique wrought-iron lamps, exuberant French art, lace curtains, gleaming copper pans, and two very attractive bar counters bring this brasserie to life. *Marco Polo Hotel, Tanglin Rd., tel. 474–7141. Reservations advised. Dress: smart casual. AE, DC, MC, V.*

Indian

Expensive
★

Tandoor. The food has a distinctly Kashmiri flavor at this luxurious restaurant, where Indian paintings, rust and terra-cotta colors, and Indian musicians at night create the ambience of the Moghul court. The clay oven, seen through glass panels across a lotus pond, dominates the room. After you place your order for tandoori chicken, lobster, fish, or shrimp—marinated in yogurt and spices, then roasted in the oven—sit back and watch the chef at work. Also cooked in the oven is the northern Indian leavened bread called *naan;* the garlic naan is justifiably famous. The tender spice-marinated roast leg of lamb is a favorite of the regulars. Spiced masala tea at the end of the meal seems to wash down the richness of the meal perfectly. Service is exceptionally attentive. *Holiday Inn Park View, 11 Cavenagh Rd., tel. 733–8333. Reservations advised. Dress: smart casual. AE, DC, MC, V.*

Moderate–
Expensive

Annalakshmi. "Earnest" and "honest" are compliments you can pay the owners of this Indian vegetarian restaurant run by a Hindu religious and cultural organization. The staff are all volunteers; the waitresses, some of whom are lawyers, float by in alluring saris. The Indian decor is lush, with carved-wood wall panels and chairs, Indian paintings, and fabric wall hangings studded with small mirrors. The paper-thin *dosai* pancakes are delicious in the special Sampoorna dinner, confined to only 30 servings per night and presented on silver. The selection often includes cabbage curry, potato roast, *channa dhal* (a sort of lentil stew), *kurma* (a mild vegetable curry with ground spices like cumin, coriander, cinnamon, and cardamom, cooked in soured milk or cream), *poori* (a puffy, ball-shaped bread), *samosa* (a deep-fried patty with a vegetable filling), and *jangri* (a cold dessert). The flavors are delicate, and spices are judiciously employed to enhance rather than mask the taste. Annalakshmi has been raising its prices rather dramatically recently. *Excelsior Hotel & Shopping Centre (#02-10), 5 Coleman St., tel. 339–9993. Reservations advised. Dress: smart casual. AE, DC, MC, V. Closed Thurs.*

Moti Mahal. This northern Indian restaurant in Food Alley, on the outskirts of Chinatown, started with a retired police officer who thought that his wife's home cooking would surely appeal to gourmets. He was right. Make a meal of butter chicken (a mild and creamy dish of boneless chicken in a tomato-based sauce), Punjabi dhal (a lentil stew from the Punjab), and prawn Jalfrazie (a dry and spicy dish, with capsicum slices, onions, tomatoes, cauliflower, and green peas). Sop up the curry gravies with some naan, hot from the tandoori oven. The restaurant has a red plush look with wall-to-wall carpet and Moghul murals. *18 Murray St., tel. 221-4338. Reservations advised. Dress: casual. AE, DC, MC, V for bills over S$30.*

Moderate **Bombay Meadowlands.** Locals are switching their allegiance
★ from Annalakshmi to this restaurant, now relocated from the Forum Galleria to Tanglin Road. The decor is still simple: A single flower decorates the white paper tablecloths and the walls are left unadorned. The superb, zesty food is southern Indian and vegetarian. The curries are not that hot but can be made hotter upon request. The breads, especially the dosa and the fluffy, bulbous Bhatura, are wonderful enough to make a meal on their own. *19 Tanglin Rd. (#B1-07), tel. 235-2712. Reservations optional. Dress: casual. AE, MC, V.*

Inexpensive **Banana Leaf Apollo.** Walls tiled up to waist level, Formica-
★ topped tables, a hodgepodge of colors—just general bad taste is what makes eating here such fun. It's so bad it's good. The food itself is fabulous, though you may end up crying yourself through the fiery, southern-Indian-style meals. Each person is given a large piece of banana leaf: Steaming-hot rice is spooned into the center; then two *papadam* (deep-fried lentil crackers) and two vegetables, with delicious spiced sauces, are arranged neatly around the rice. Order the fish-head curry if you're daring and have at least six people to share it with. Or try the dry mutton curry, chicken curry, fish cutlets, and fried cuttlefish. The food is displayed in chafing dishes in glass cabinets so you can peek before you order. The restaurant is very clean, the service fast and furious. *56/58 Race Course Rd., tel. 298-5054. No reservations. Dress: very casual. No credit cards.*
Muthu's Curry Restaurant. Curry aficionados argue endlessly over which sibling serves the better food, Muthu or his brother, who owns the Banana Leaf Apollo down the street (*see above*). The decor is similar, and Muthu's also has air-conditioning. *78 Race Course Rd., tel. 293-7029. No reservations. Dress: casual. AE, MC, V.*
Samy's Curry Restaurant. It's *très* chic to lunch at this restaurant on the grounds of the Ministry of Defense, not least because there's no way you can stumble upon it by chance—you have to be in the know. The old, no-fuss Civil Service clubhouse is a legacy of the British rule. The decor and service are equally no-fuss. The food—southern Indian curries that are chili-hot and spicy and served on banana leaves—is excellent. There's no air-conditioning, which means that you sweat it out in true colonial fashion. *Singapore Civil Service Club House, Blk. 25 Dempsey Rd., tel. 472-2080 or 296-9391. No reservations. Dress: casual. AE, DC, V. No dinner Thurs.*

Italian

Expensive **Ristorante Bologna.** The Bologna insists on making pastas fresh and on using fresh herbs in dishes like *spezzatino di sogliola ai peperoni e zucchini* (pan-fried strips of sole fillet with sweet bell pepper and zucchini) and *agnello al dragoncello* (roasted rack of lamb stuffed with snow peas and tarragon). Ingredients are flown in from Italy to ensure authenticity. Waiters in waistcoats provide impeccable service. The decor is light, airy, and luxurious; Renaissance-inspired murals adorn the walls, Carrera marble tiles the floor, and a cascading waterfall tops off the view. *Marina Mandarin Hotel, 6 Raffles Blvd., Marina Square, tel. 338–3388. No reservations. Dress: smart casual. AE, DC, MC, V.*

Moderate   **Da Paolo.** This exciting new Italian restaurant in the renovated district of Tanjong Pagar, Chinatown, is the beginning of a trend in Singapore—small, intimate establishments in contrast to splendid hotel dining rooms. Chef Paolo hails from Venice and cooks recipes from his home town in a small 11-table dining room on the second story of a shophouse. His wife, Judie, greets you in the downstairs bar and preps you on the specialties of the day. The antipasto buffet is a must, followed by *al pomodoro fresco e basilica* (pasta in a tomato, basil sauce) or the *gamberoni alla pado* (shrimp in a vodka basting), though the menu varies depending on the chef's inspiration that day. *66 Tanjong Pagar Rd., tel. 224–7081. Reservations advised. Dress: smart casual. AE, DC, MC. V. Closed Sat. lunch, Sun.*

★   **Pete's Place.** This is one of the city's most popular restaurants. The look is cozy Italian-country, with rustic brick walls and checkered tablecloths. The food is Italian-American, with staples like pizza and pastas. A salad bar with crisp, fresh vegetables, a wide array of dressings, and a large selection of breads add an extra touch of homeyness. There's also a light-lunch selection of soups and salads. The service is friendly, yet full of finesse, making this restaurant a fun, relaxed place. A plus is Pete's proximity to two of the best shopping centers—Scotts and Far East. *Hyatt Hotel, 10/12 Scotts Rd., tel. 733–1188. Reservations advised for dinner. Dress: casual. AE, DC, MC, V.*

Ristorante Italiano Prego. I can't quite decide whether I like the rampantly red-and-green decor, but there's no doubt about the pastas: They're the best in town, all made on the spot by the Italian chef. Center stage at this long, narrow restaurant is the pizza-and-pasta kitchen, glassed in on three sides so you can see what's going on. The spaghetti *con vongole* (with clams in a cheese sauce) is a particular favorite, as are the seafood stew and scaloppine. The chef is very proud of his zabaglione. The service can be annoyingly slow, and children are not encouraged. *Westin Stamford Hotel, 3rd floor, 2 Stamford Rd., tel. 338–8585, ext. 16310. Reservations required. Dress: smart casual. AE, DC, MC, V.*

Japanese

Expensive–   **Suntory.** Owned by the famous Japanese beer company, this is
Very Expensive   reputedly the most expensive Japanese restaurant in town. Choose from among all the different Japanese dining styles: There's a teppanyaki room, a sushi counter, shabu-shabu tables, tatami rooms, and a very attractive lounge. The decor is exquisite, the staff is well trained, and the food is excellent. *Delfi Orchard (#06-01/02), 402 Orchard Rd., tel. 732–5111. Reservations advised. Dress: smart casual. AE, DC, MC, V.*

Expensive   **Keyaki.** A Japanese farmhouse has been re-created in a formal Japanese garden, with a golden-carp pond, on the rooftop of the Pan Pacific Hotel. The waitresses dressed in kimonos, waiters in *happi* coats, and Japanese lacquerware and porcelain make you feel as though you're in Japan (despite the incongruous European-look wood chairs). The teppanyaki is said to be the best in Singapore, with excellent beef, scallops, salmon, large shrimps, and a distinctive Japanese fried garlic rice. *Pan Pacific Hotel, 7 Raffles Blvd., Marina Square, tel. 336–8111. Reservations advised. Dress: smart casual. AE, DC, V.*

★ **Nadaman.** There's nothing quite as exciting as watching a teppanyaki chef perform his culinary calisthenics at this 23rd-floor restaurant, which boasts the Singapore skyline as a backdrop. The Nadaman offers sushi, sashimi (the fresh lobster sashimi is excellent), teppanyaki, tempura, and kaiseki. Those on a budget should try one of the *bento* lunches—fixed-price meals (less than S$20) beautifully decorated in the Japanese manner and served in lacquer trays and boxes. The decor is distinctly Japanese, and the service is discreetly attentive. *Shangri-La Singapore, 24th floor, 22 Orange Grove Rd., tel. 737–3644. Reservations advised. Dress: smart casual. AE, DC, MC, V.*

Moderate–Expensive **Shima.** "German baronial" is perhaps the best way to describe the look of this Japanese restaurant. Teppanyaki, shabu-shabu, and yakiniku are the only items on the menu. You sit around a teppanyaki grill, watching the chef at work, or at the shabu-shabu and yakiniku tables, watching yourself cook. Copper chimneys remove the smoke and smell. The all-you-can-eat yakiniku lunch is one of the best buys in town. *Goodwood Park Hotel, 22 Scotts Rd., tel. 734–6281/2. Reservations advised; for buffet lunch, required. Dress: casual. AE, DC, MC, V.*

Malay

Expensive **Alkaff Mansion.** Once the estate of wealthy merchants, this 19th-century house on Mt. Faber Ridge opened as a restaurant in 1991. You can sit inside under twirling fans or out on a veranda decorated to reflect the diverse tastes of the old Arab traders. Downstairs there's a huge Malay-Indonesian dinner buffet; on the upstair's balconies, 10 sarong-clad waitresses serve a *rijsttafel* (a multicourse rice table). Western food is also offered, from the S$32 three-course luncheon to a more elaborate à la carte menu (from steaks to seafood bordelaise) at dinner. Overall, the delightful turn-of-the-century ambience (something hard to find in Singapore) and the presentation are more rewarding than the food. *10 Telok Blangah Green, tel. 278–6979. Reservations advised. Dress: smart casual. AE, DC, MC, V.*

Moderate **Aziza's.** Hazizah Ali has brought elegant Malay cooking out of the home and into her intimate street-front restaurant on the charming Emerald Hill Road, just up from Peranakan Place. It's the spicy cooking of the Malay Peninsula you get here—lots of lemon grass, galangal, shallots, pepper, coriander, cloves, and cinnamon. Try the beef *rendang* (stewed for hours in a mixture of spices and coconut milk), *gado gado* (a light salad with a spiced peanut sauce), or *bergedel* (Dutch-influenced potato cutlets). The oxtail soup is especially delicious. Ask for *nasi ambang* and you'll get festive rice with a sampling of dishes from the menu. The Orchard Road location and the friendly setting make this an easy place to experiment with Malay food. *36 Emerald Hill Rd., tel. 235–1130. Reservations advised for dinner. Dress: casual. AE, DC, MC, V.*

Inexpensive–Moderate **Bintang Timur.** This is a very pleasant restaurant done up in green and light wood, with a good view from picture windows.

It serves Malay food with a touch of Indonesian and Arab influences. Try the deep-fried satay *goreng*, the prawn satay, the fish-head curry (cooked Malay-style, with lots of fresh root spices, such as galangal and lemon grass), or the *ikan pepes* (flaked fish mixed with a ground hot-spice paste, wrapped in banana leaves, then grilled over charcoal). The tastes are rather sharp. *Far East Plaza (#02-08/13), ground floor, 14 Scotts Rd., tel. 235–4539. No reservations. Dress: casual. AE, DC, V.*

Nonya

Moderate **Nonya and Baba.** This restaurant serving the authentic food of the Babas is situated near the Tank Road Hindu Temple. It's intimate but not particularly well decorated. Habitués like it for the food and the basic comforts it provides. Try the *buak keluak ayam* (a spicy, sour gravy made with chicken and a black Indonesian nut that has a creamy texture and the smokiness of French truffles), *bakwan kepiting* (Chinese soup of crabmeat and pork dumplings), *babi pongtay* (pork stewed in soy sauce and onions), *satay ayam* (fried chicken satay), or *sambal* "lady's fingers" (okra with a spicy sauce). *262 River Valley Rd., tel. 734–1382/6. No reservations. Dress: casual. V.*

Inexpensive–Moderate **Guan Hoe Soon.** The heartland of the Baba culture is Katong, a suburb about 20 minutes by cab from the city center. The Guan Hoe Soon is air-conditioned, simple, and comfortable, with authentic Nonya food at a reasonable price. The specialty is the *otak otak* (charcoal-grilled fish quenelle mixed with spices and wrapped in banana leaves). Also taste the buak keluak ayam and the fried noodles. Next door is Peter Wee's absolutely "must visit" **Katong Antique House.** Inside this house, in the terrace style of the Babas, Peter has lovingly displayed his collection of antique Baba beaded slippers, embroidered blouses (called *kebayas*), Chinese export porcelain, carved-wood furniture inlaid with mother-of-pearl, embroidered wedding-bed hangings, and much more. *214 Joo Chiat Rd., tel. 344–2761. No reservations. Dress: casual. No credit cards. Closed Tues.*

Keday Kopi. This is the ground-floor restaurant in the preserve of Baba culture called Peranakan Place, a charming enclave with a palm-lined mall next door to the up-market Centrepoint shopping complex. The restaurant, with lots of carved-wood detail, is decorated to re-create the languid, easy Baba lifestyle at the turn of the century. The food itself is representative of the Nonya kitchen but is not the best example of it in town. A dish to savor here is the buak keluak ayam. Upstairs is a lounge with lively entertainment. *Peranakan Place, 80 Orchard Rd., tel. 732–6966. No reservations. Dress: casual. AE, DC, V.*

Oleh Sayang. Another charming part of Singapore, also away from the city center, is Holland Village, a labyrinth of streets with restaurants, coffee shops, bookshops, a market, and antiques stores. The Oleh Sayang is small, family-run, and casual-chic. The buak keluak ayam is a must, as are the babi pongtay, chicken curry, and prawns fried in tamarind paste. *25B Lorong Liput, Holland Village, tel. 468–9859. No reservations. Dress: casual. No credit cards. Closed Mon.*

Peranakan Inn. The frontage is charming; the interior is just serviceable, but comfortable. The food—also serviceable—includes fish-head curry, Nonya mee, *ayam siyow* (chicken stewed in soy sauce, coriander powder, and shallots), *udang* *kuah nanas* (prawns in a sour tamarind gravy), and pepper soup. *210 East Coast Rd., tel. 440–6194. No reservations. Dress: casual. No credit cards.*

Seafood

Moderate–Expensive
★

Long Beach Seafood Restaurant. The Long Beach is a 30-minute cab ride from town but is considered one of Singapore's finest seafood restaurants. The decor—pretty garish, with lots of plastic and clashing colors—is pure 1950s Singapore chic, complete with multicolored fairy lights strung outside. You eat either indoors (there's no air-conditioning) or out. If your tastebuds can withstand the hotness, try the pepper crabs—large Indonesian crabs chopped into pieces, then fried in a mixture of freshly ground black pepper, oyster sauce, and butter. Make up the rest of your meal with drunken prawns (live prawns mixed with cognac or Chinese wine, left for a few minutes to soak up the liquor, then lightly poached), barbecued fish, and stuffed deep-fried dough sticks called *you tiao. Bedok Rest House, 610 Bedok Rd., tel. 445–8833/344–7722. No reservations. Dress: casual. AE, DC, MC, V. Dinner only (5–12:15 weeknights, 5–1:15 weekends).*

Seafood International Market and Restaurant. It's considered chic to select your own food in this restaurant at the Big Splash complex. Dine in a garden under the stars on steamed sea bass, lemon chicken, drunken prawns, and black-pepper crabs. *902 East Coast Pkwy., tel. 345–1211. No reservations. Dress: casual. AE, DC, MC, V. No lunch weekdays.*

Moderate

Choon Seng. At this famous seafood restaurant you dine alfresco in unadulterated country surroundings. About a 40-minute cab ride from town, it is housed in an open-sided half-concrete, half-wood house with a zinc roof. Try the chili crabs, Indianstyle *mee goreng* (fried Chinese noodles with spices), steamed fish Teochew-style, deep-fried dough sticks stuffed with minced cuttlefish, and *chili kangkong* (a leafy green vegetable fried with a mixture of pounded chilies, shallots, and shrimp paste). A stall in front of the restaurant offers very good satay—order some as an appetizer. *892 Ponggol Rd., tel. 288–3472. No reservations. Dress: casual. No credit cards.*

Palm Beach Seafood. This restaurant used to be on the beach, with tables set under palm trees—hence the name. A few years ago, it was resettled in its new home: under the grandstand of the National Stadium. The food's still excellent, and every night people flock here for the famous chili crabs, prawns fried in black soy sauce, deep-fried crispy squid, and fried noodles. The decor is simple and the ambience is comfortable. *National Stadium, West Entrance, Stadium Dr., tel. 344–1474. No reservations. Dress: casual. No credit cards. Dinner only (6–1).*

UDMC Seafood Centre. You *must* visit this place at the East Coast Parkway, near the entrance to the lagoon, for a true picture of the way Singaporeans eat out, as well as real value for the money. Walk around the eight open-fronted restaurants before you decide where to eat. Chili crabs, steamed prawns, steamed fish, pepper crabs, fried noodles, and deep-fried squid are the specialties. *East Coast Pkwy. Tel.: Bedok Sea View, tel. 241–4173; Chin Wah Heng, tel. 444–7967; East Coast Park Live Seafood, tel. 448–2020; Golden Lagoon, tel. 448–1894; Jumbo, tel. 442–3435; Kheng Luck, tel. 444–5911; Red House,* *tel. 442–3112. No reservations. Dress: casual. AE, DC, MC, V. Dinner only (5–midnight).*

Thai

Moderate–
Expensive
★

Cairnhill Thai Seafood Restaurant. This pretty restaurant, with dark-wood accents, waitresses dressed in feminine Thai attire, and a fine view of the old-fashioned Cairnhill Hotel, made its name with its lunch and teatime buffets. The cooking is a mixture of authentic Thai and Teochew Chinese. Especially delicious are the *hor mok* (steamed quenelle of fish with spices and coconut milk in banana-leaf cups or in a whole young coconut), chili crabs, pineapple rice, and fried honey chicken. The same people own the Parkway Thai restaurants in Katong and in the Centrepoint Shopping Centre in Orchard Road. *Cairnhill Place (#07-03), 15 Cairnhill Rd., tel. 733–6666. No reservations. Dress: casual. MC, V.*

Her Sea Palace. A runaway success of the late 1980s, Her Sea has since changed ownership. However, the chef stayed on to serve Thai food with a Teochew Chinese touch. Dishes to savor are the thick soup of sliced fish maw (stomach lining) that has been dried and then deep-fried, mixed with lots of fresh crabmeat; pickled-olive rice; and Thai chili crabs, rich with coconut milk. The decor is pleasant, the service not possessed of much finesse; but the food is absolutely delicious. *Forum Galleria (#01-16), 583 Orchard Rd., tel. 732–5688. Reservations required. Dress: smart casual. DC, V.*

6 Lodging

A few years ago, Singapore had a surfeit of top-flight hotels. Occupancy ran at less than 40%; eager to offset some of their fixed costs, hotels heavily discounted rooms. Times have changed. With tourists and business travelers now flocking to Singapore in record numbers, hotels are recording 70% to 80% occupancy rates and are sometimes fully booked.

However, except perhaps during the busiest periods—in August and at Christmas—you should be able to get reservations at the hotel of your choice. This can be easily arranged through your travel agent, since most Singapore hotels are either part of an international chain or have representatives in the States. If you're willing to take the gamble and arrive without reservations, you are likely to find hotels willing to offer discounts. The Singapore Hotel Association maintains two reservations counters at Changi Airport and can set you up with a room—and often a discount if the hotels are having a slow period—upon your arrival. There is no fee for the booking.

Singapore's hotels are no longer inexpensive compared to New York's. The average tariff ranks just under Hong Kong's and above that of Jakarta, Bangkok, Manila, and Kuala Lumpur (in that order). At deluxe hotels, a superior double room runs more than S$400 a night. A room with a private bath in a modest hotel should cost no more than S$200. At budget hotels with shared bathroom facilities, the rates are under S$35. And if all you're looking for is a bunk, there are dormitory-type guest houses on Bencoolen Street where you can sleep for no more than S$15 a night.

Service in the deluxe properties is exemplary: The staff go to great lengths to meet guests' needs. (A 10% charge is added to your bill to cover service. Tipping is frowned upon, except for bellmen who bring luggage to the rooms.) Guest rooms are spacious and fitted out with the latest amenities, from bedside computer control panels to marble-tiled bathrooms with telephone extensions and speakers for the television—so you can listen to the news and answer the phone while relaxing in the tub. Many hotels offer business and fitness centers loaded with the latest technology and equipment.

All of the major hotels have several restaurants, each specializing in a different cuisine—European as well as Asian. While relatively expensive, these restaurants offer some of Singapore's best food, served in elegant surroundings. Hotel coffee shops generally offer a mix of Western and local foods, and many are open 24 hours a day.

Perhaps because Singapore's top hotels set such high standards, less-expensive properties appear to work harder. Indeed, a major reason why Singapore makes such a convenient and comfortable base from which to explore Southeast Asia is the overall high quality of its lodgings. And, with more than 70 hotels and 24,000 guest rooms to choose from, there's certain to be a place just right for you.

Most of the better hotels are new, but two notable exceptions have been witness to—and sometimes the scene of—a good chunk of Singapore's history: the Goodwood Park, which is 90 years old, and the Raffles Hotel, which has been around for 130 years. The Goodwood Park has been renovated to bring its facilities up to world-class standing; the Raffles has been completely gutted and resurrected as a theme-park version of its former self.

Among the newer hotels, three have opened on Marina Square, a minicity created by a vast reclamation project that pushed back the seafront. More than 200 shops and a multitude of restaurants surround these towering atrium hotels, of which the Oriental is in a class by itself, almost unrivaled in the world for service and elegance. Other modern hotels (some of which are a decade or two old by now) have undergone additions and renovations to keep up with the newcomers. The Shangri-La, for example, was built in 1971, but its new Valley Wing has some of the most luxurious accommodations that Singapore—perhaps the world—has to offer.

Conventions are big business in Singapore, and there are megahotels geared specifically to handling hundreds of delegates. The Westin Plaza and Westin Stamford in Raffles City together offer more than 2,000 guest rooms and a ballroom that can accommodate 5,000 people. In Marina Square, which was opened in 1986 with conventions in mind, the Pan Pacific has 800 rooms and a meeting hall for 1,000 delegates. In the same complex are the more upscale Marina Mandarin, with 640 rooms to satisfy higher-level delegates, and the Oriental, with 527 rooms suitable for the most persnickety CEOs.

Singapore's hotels have developed in clusters throughout the city. The best-known is around the popular tourist belt at the intersection of Orchard and Scotts roads. Another is around Raffles City, where the megalithic Westins stare down at the grande dame of Singapore's hotels, the Raffles. At the south end of the Shenton Way commercial district are a number of business-oriented hotels, while to the west of Chinatown and the south of the Singapore River another cluster has sprung up. The newest hotel area is Marina Square, where three hotels and a vast shopping-mall complex have established an independent hub within the city. The hotels in Marina Square and at the Orchard and Scotts roads intersection do reflect the high price of the real estate on which they stand. But even within these clusters prices vary, and at their fringes you will find good, moderately priced hotels.

Your choice of hotel location may be influenced by your reason for visiting Singapore. Certainly the Orchard and Scotts roads area favors the shopper and evening reveler. Marina Square would be the logical choice for those attending conventions in the complex or who like the openness of space the area offers. For those doing business in the financial district, a hotel close to Shenton Way is ideal; likewise, hotels along the Singapore River are convenient for anyone making trips to the industrial city of Jurong. But location should not be overemphasized. Singapore is a relatively compact city, and taxis and public transportation, especially the new subway, make travel between one area and another a matter of minutes. Orchard Road, in the northern part of the city, is less than 10 minutes by subway from Shenton Way, to the south. Furthermore, no hotel is more than a 30-minute cab ride from Changi Airport.

All hotels listed, unless otherwise noted, have rooms with private baths. All deluxe hotels have International Direct Dial (IDD) telephones with bathroom extensions, color televisions with Teletext for world news and information, and minibars.

Highly recommended lodgings are indicated by a star ★.

Category	Cost*
Very Expensive	over S$400 (US$235)
Expensive	S$300–S$400 (US$176–US$235)
Moderate	S$200–S$300 (US$118–US$176)
Inexpensive	S$100–S$200 (US$59–US$118)
Budget	under S$100 (US$59)

All prices are for a standard double room, excluding 4% tax and a 10% service charge.

Very Expensive

★ **Goodwood Park.** Ideally located just off Scotts Road and within minutes of Orchard Road, the Goodwood Park began life in 1900 as a club for German expatriates. Since then it has hosted the likes of the Duke of Windsor, Edward Heath, and Noël Coward and was the setting for a performance by the great Anna Pavlova. Today it may be overshadowed by the glitz of the high rises, but for those who appreciate personal service and a refined atmosphere, this one stands alone. Guests are remembered and greeted by name, high tea is accompanied by a string quartet, and guest rooms are furnished in the style of a country house. Service tends to vary and can be condescending to those who don't appreciate tradition. After a two-year renovation, all the guest rooms now offer the latest in amenities. For long-term guests, there are the newly refurbished split-level Parklane suites, each with a separate bedroom and a living-dining room. Restaurants include the Gordon Grill, the Garden Seafood Restaurant, the Min Jiang, and the Chiang Jian (*see* Chapter 5) as well as a coffee lounge that has been given a new look with French windows and a terrace. *22 Scotts Rd., Singapore 0922, tel. 737–7411, fax 732–8558. 235 rooms, including 64 suites. Facilities: 24-hr coffee shop, lounge for afternoon tea and light meals, 24-hr room service, beauty salon, business center with lap-top computers, baby-sitting, tour desk, 3 outdoor pools, 5 function rooms. AE, DC, MC, V.*

Hyatt Regency. In 1990, the Hyatt restructured and refurbished its hotel, converting half its accommodations to suites. These Regency Suites consist of 421 one-, two-, and three-room apartments equipped with telecommunications equipment, dual-line telephones, Reuters services, separate guest bathrooms, and individual work areas. The suites are priced approximately 30% higher than the remaining 317 standard rooms, which are adequate, though on the small side. A tropical garden with 16 miniwaterfalls and the new Canopy Bar, which overhangs Scotts Road and serves afternoon tea and evening cocktails, have been added to the hotel. Restaurants include Pete's Place and the elegant Ruyi (*see* Chapter 5), as well as Nutmegs, for steaks and seafood; Plums, a 24-hour café-restaurant-lounge; and Brannigan's, a popular watering hole. *10-12 Scotts Rd., Singapore 0922, tel. 733–1188, fax 732–1696. 738 rooms. Facilities: 24-hr coffee shop, 24-hr room service, fitness center with sauna and massage, 24-hr business center, beauty*

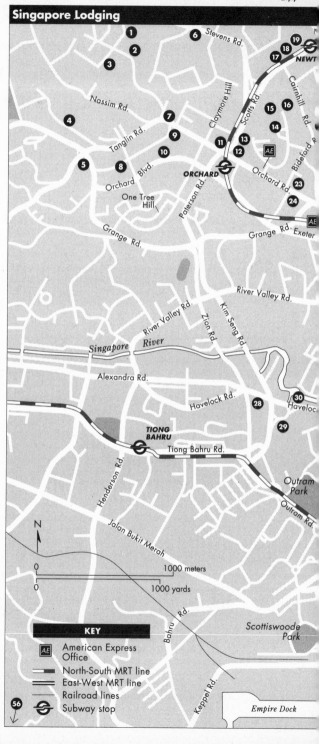

Singapore Lodging

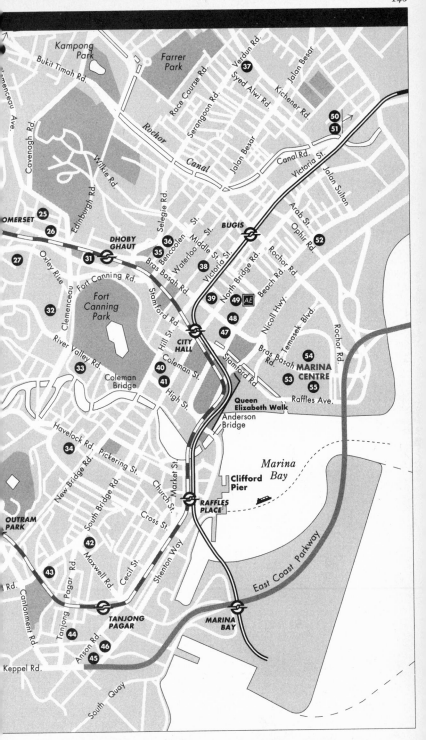

salon, outdoor pool, tennis and squash courts. AE, DC, MC, V.

Mandarin Hotel. Centrally located on Orchard Road, the Mandarin—opened in 1969, with later additions—boasts a main lobby of translucent white-and-black Italian marble, with a huge mural, *87 Taoist Immortals,* based on an 8th-century Chinese scroll. Guest rooms on the upper floors command fabulous views of the harbor, the city, and Malaysia beyond. The best rooms in the main tower now include in-room safes, VCRs, and push-button bedside controls. Each bathroom has a tub and separate shower, as well as twin wash basins. The many restaurants at the Mandarin include the Pine Court (*see* Chapter 5); the Top of the M for Continental (the only revolving restaurant in Southeast Asia); Stables Grill for steaks and prime rib; the New Tsurunoya for Japanese specialties; the 24-hour Chatterbox coffee house for Western food; and hawker-stand Chinese food. *333 Orchard Rd., Singapore 0923, tel. 737–4411, fax 732–2361. 1,208 rooms. Facilities: 24-hr coffee shop, 24-hr room service, Kasbah nightclub, disco, business center, fitness center with sauna and massage, beauty salon, outdoor pool, tennis and squash courts, minigolf course, shops, travel desk (Singapore Airlines, Qantas, and KLM offices on the premises). AE, DC, MC, V.*

★ **The Oriental.** Within this pyramid-shaped Marina Square hotel, architect John Portman has created a 21-story atrium with interior balconies that are stepped inward as they ascend. Through the center of the atrium, glass elevators glide from floor to floor. Since the entrance to the hotel is at street level and the reception floor is on the fourth level, with the banqueting and function rooms in between, the lobby area is free from the bustle of transients. The Oriental offers subdued, modern elegance. It is smaller than many of the other modern deluxe hotels in Singapore; this permits the staff to give personalized attention to each guest, making the service the best in Singapore. All the rooms are decorated in soft hues of peach and green; hand-woven carpets and paintings of old Singapore add to the feeling of understated elegance. The Italian-marble-tiled bathrooms offer separate tubs and showers, a telephone extension, radio and television speakers, and an array of toiletries, including terry-cloth bathrobes. One-bedroom suites have elegant sitting rooms and a separate guest washroom. The Cherry Garden (*see* Chapter 5) serves some of the best Hunanese food in Singapore. Fourchettes offers elegant surroundings and haute Continental cuisine. Regional and more casual dining is offered at the Café Palm and the Oriental Pool Terrace and Bar, which specializes in grilled dishes and seafood steamboat. The Captain's Bar, decorated with portraits of famous Singaporean sea traders, serves a roast beef luncheon, and international entertainers perform there in the evening. Recently introduced is high tea at the Café Palm, where Chinese, Nonya, Malay, and Western delicacies are served with a variety of teas. *6 Raffles Blvd., #01-200, Singapore 0103, tel. 338–0066, fax 339–9537. 640 rooms. Facilities: 24-hr room service, outdoor pool, jogging track, tennis and squash courts, fitness center with sauna and massage, travel desk, arrangements for golf, business center, banquet and function rooms. AE, DC, MC, V.*

Raffles Hotel. The Sarkies brothers opened Raffles in 1887, and embellished by the visits of Conrad, Kipling, and Maugham, the hotel became the belle of the East during its heyday in the '20s and '30s. After World War II it fell on hard times. True to form, Singapore has taken the noble old and spent millions (S$160 million in this case) to make it fit a desired self-image. In the process, the charm of the original has been sanitized out of recognition. The new Raffles is a glistening showpiece, especially from the outside; inside, it's sterile (*see* Tour 1: Colonial Singapore, *above*). The polished marble lobby seems cold. All guest suites have teak floors, 4.3-meter (14-foot) ceilings, overhead fans, central air-conditioning, and '20s-style furnishings that can be a little stiff. The rectangular layout, with a small living room facing directly into the bedroom and the bathroom beyond, is awkward. For this you pay S$750 (S$650 if you'll accept a suite facing the busy street), when S$100 less will pay for a suite at one of Singapore's truly superb deluxe hotels. *1 Beach Rd., Singapore 0718, tel. 337–1886, fax 339–7650. 104 suites. Facilities: several restaurants, 24-hour room service, outdoor pool, small fitness and business centers, shopping arcade. AE, DC, MC, V.*

★ **Shangri-La.** This hotel has consistently ranked as one of the top three in Singapore since it opened in 1971. The most attractive rooms are in the newer Valley Wing, with its own entrance, check-in counter, concierge, and boardrooms. These guest rooms are exceptionally spacious, and the bathrooms are delightfully indulgent, with huge tubs, separate showers, and terry-cloth bathrobes. Rooms in the main building have been upgraded with warm beige and blue fabrics and furniture of maple, cherry wood, and rattan. The main lobby, dominated by a world time-zone map, has been sparklingly redesigned. Set amid 15 acres of gardens in a residential area at the top of Orchard Road, the Shangri-La is a pleasant 10-minute walk from the shopping areas; taxis are always on call for those in a hurry. The Coffee Garden, designed after an English conservatory, has recently opened to offer light meals and a luncheon buffet; the Waterfall Café now serves breakfast and snacks throughout the day in a delightful outside setting. Among the hotel's more formal haute cuisine restaurants are the Shang Palace, noted for its dim sum lunches and fine Cantonese cuisine, and the Japanese Nadaman (*see* Chapter 5). *22 Orange Grove Rd., Singapore 1025, tel. 737–3644, fax 733–7220. 821 rooms (136 in the Valley Wing). Facilities: 24-hr room service, tennis and squash courts, fitness center, indoor and outdoor pools, poolside bar, putting green, live evening entertainment (jazz and contemporary music), disco, 24-hr business center, shuttle service to Shenton Way, meeting and banquet rooms. AE, DC, MC, V.*

Expensive

Amara Hotel. Situated at the south end of the business district, near the railway station, this 18-story hotel is convenient for the business traveler who prefers to be close to the commercial and port facilities. The hotel itself is characterless, but it is part of a vibrant shopping-and-entertainment complex, and close to the redevelopment of Tanjong Pagar in Chinatown. *Tanjong Pagar Rd., Singapore 0208, tel. 224–4488, fax 224–3910. 337 rooms. Facilities: restaurants, coffee shop, squash and tennis courts, fitness center, pool, jogging track, karaoke nightclub, children's play area. AE, DC, MC, V.*

ANA Singapore. This 14-story hotel, in a residential area near the Botanical Gardens and the embassies, opened in 1978 and is owned by All Nippon Airways hotel division. It offers a full range of modern facilities; the antique tapestries and wood-paneled walls in its lobby create a less ostentatious ambience than the building's glistening facade would suggest. The Hubertus Grill offers Continental cuisine, seafood, and prime rib. The Unkai features Japanese food. *16 Nassim Hill, Singapore 1025, tel. 732–1222, fax 235–1516. 462 rooms, including 17 suites. Facilities: coffee shop, 24-hr room service, disco, outdoor pool, poolside snack bar, business center, fitness center, shops, tour desk. AE, DC, MC, V.*

The Beaufort. This resort hotel on Sentosa Island made its debut in 1992. While it is aimed at tourists, it seems more suited to business seminars than short-stay visitors who want to shop and explore the republic. The best feature is the swimming pool overlooking the Malacca Straits, flanked by an open-air seafood restaurant that's a romantic spot for dinner. (The main dining room, serving Asian and Western fare, enjoys a similar view with air-conditioning.) The rooms—down concrete corridors, past pond-filled courtyards—don't share these fine views; instead they look onto tropical parkland. Standard rooms (called deluxe) aren't very large, except for the bathrooms. The pastel furnishings are undistinctive. The Garden Rooms offer larger bedrooms and work areas. There are also four luxurious two-bedroom villas, each with its own pool. *Sentosa Island, Singapore 0409, tel. 275–0331, fax 275–0228. 175 rooms, 34 suites, 4 villas. Facilities: 3 restaurants, outdoor pool, 2 tennis and 2 squash courts, fitness center, golf nearby. AE, DC, MC, V.*

Boulevard Hotel. It's at the top end of Orchard Road, away from the main thoroughfare but within easy walking distance of the Singapore Handicraft Centre and the main Orchard Road area. Both of its wings have been refurbished. The airy atrium lobby is dominated by a floor-to-ceiling sculpture. The emphasis is on the traveling executive. Guest rooms include large work desks, minibars, IDD telephones, and pantries with coffee- and tea-making facilities. Rooms come in three sizes: deluxe (with a corner pantry), executive (a work desk area), and standard. *200 Orchard Blvd., Singapore 1024, tel. 737–2911, fax 737–8449. 528 rooms. Facilities: 3 restaurants (American, Cantonese, Northern Indian), 24-hr coffee shop, 24-hr room service, fitness center, 2 outdoor pools, business center, hairdresser, drugstore, disco, tour desk, shops. AE, DC, MC, V.*

★ **The Dynasty.** The 33-story, pagoda-inspired Dynasty is a striking landmark dominating Singapore's "million-dollar corner"—the Orchard and Scotts roads intersection. Depending on your taste, the three-story lobby in rich, deep red—the Chinese color for good fortune—is either opulent or garish. Notice especially the 153-bulb crystal chandelier and 24 remarkable carved-teak wall panels, each 1.2 meters wide and 12.2 meters high (4 feet wide and 40 feet high). Guest rooms, refurbished in 1991, take a more Western approach with light gray carpets, pink vinyl wallpaper, pink-gray upholstery, and ample wood for a feeling of warmth. The marble-floored bathrooms have been enlarged to have a separate shower and mirrors fitted with de-misters. The furnishings in the opulent Imperial Suite are museum-quality antiques, and the stage-set bathroom fulfills fantasies. The Tang Court restaurant serves Cantonese cuisine in a comfortable and formal setting; the new Truffles restaurant, under the consultancy of two-star Michelin chef R. Mazère, is gradually coming into its own for gourmet dining. A terrace pool and garden, with trickling waters, palms, and bamboo, suggest an imperial Chinese courtyard. *320 Orchard Rd., Singapore 0923, tel. 734–9900, fax 733–5251. 400 rooms, including 21 suites. Facilities: 24-hr coffee shop, 24-hr room service, business center, fitness center, Twilight disco, outdoor pool with poolside bar, ballroom, function rooms. AE, DC, MC, V.*

Hilton International. It may be short on glitter and dazzle, but the rooms have all the standard amenities of a modern deluxe property, and the rates are highly competitive. The rooms at the back used to have an uninterrupted view, but the new Four Seasons hotel now stands alongside the Hilton so you may prefer the street side, unless you like to sleep with the sliding window open—a nice feature of the Hilton and a rarity among Singapore hotels, which usually rely solely upon air-conditioning for ventilation. The most prestigious lodgings are the Givenchy suites, each individually designed by Hubert de Givenchy and serviced by a personal valet. The hotel's strong suit is its shopping arcades, which have some of Singapore's most exclusive boutiques. The Hilton has a fortunate location: The attractions of Orchard and Scotts roads are minutes away. Within the hotel are the Inn of Happiness for Cantonese cuisine, the Tradewinds for rooftop and poolside dining, and the Harbour Grill (*see* Chapter 5) for seafood and French cuisine. *581 Orchard Rd., Singapore 0923, tel. 737–2233, fax 732–2917. 435 rooms. Facilities: 4 restaurants, 2 bars, 24-hr room service; rooftop outdoor pool; health club with sauna, steambath, whirlpool, and massage; shopping arcade; business center; large ballroom; 10 function rooms. AE, DC, MC, V.*

Hotel New Otani. Its orange-brick facade set against the greenery of Fort Canning Park, this Japanese-owned hotel is slightly off by itself on the north bank of the Singapore River. Part of the Liang Court complex, which houses more than 40 specialty shops as well as the large Japanese department store Daimaru, the New Otani attracts many Japanese travelers. A large refurbishing project was completed in 1990. Rooms come equipped with coffee-, tea-, and soup-making facilities, and the marble-tiled bathrooms have tubs and separate showers. The hotel's location is best suited to business travelers wishing to be close to Shenton Way. *177A River Valley Rd., Singapore 0617, tel. 338–3333, fax 339–2854. 408 rooms. Facilities: Chinese and Japanese restaurants, Trader Vic's cocktail bar, rooftop pool, fitness and business centers, function rooms. AE, DC, MC, V.*

Marina Mandarin. As at the other hotels on Marina Square, the John Portman–designed atrium is the Marina Mandarin's focal point: It narrows as it ascends 21 floors to a tinted skylight. The lobby area is relatively peaceful. Guest rooms are modern and smart, decorated in pastels, with twin washbasins in the bathrooms and tea- and coffee-making facilities. Rooms overlooking the harbor have the best views. Rooms on the concierge floor— the Marina Club—cost approximately 25% more and have additional amenities, such as terry-cloth bathrobes, butler service, and complimentary breakfasts and cocktails. Another floor is designed for the business person who does not need the extras of the concierge floor but wants hotel services streamlined for efficiency. The House of Blossoms has an excellent Cantonese lunch and dinner. The Ristorante Bologna (*see* Chapter 5) serves northern Italian cuisine and fresh seafood. The Cricketeer pub is pleasant for evening drinks or an English buffet lunch. *6 Raffles Blvd. #01-100, Singapore 0103, tel. 338–3388, fax 339–4977. 640 rooms. Facilities: 24-hr coffee shop, 24-*

hr room service, no-smoking floor, split-level disco, outdoor pool, tennis and squash courts, fitness center with sauna and massage, business center, shops. AE, DC, MC, V.

Meridien Singapore Orchard. On Orchard Road, slightly away from the center of activity, this French hotel is part of a shopping complex that includes the department store Printemps. Rumors persist that it may receive a much-needed face-lift soon. The reception area is a large atrium lobby reminiscent of a train station. Guest rooms are decorated in salmon, pink, and blue, with silkscreened murals. Rooms on the concierge level— the seventh-floor Le Club Président—have extra amenities. On the other floors, the nicer rooms are those with private balconies loaded with potted plants. Le Restaurant de France (*see* Chapter 5) offers some of the finest French cuisine in Singapore. There is also the Brasserie Georges for relaxed dining on local and French food, and the Spice Garden for Cantonese cuisine. *100 Orchard Rd., Singapore 0923, tel. 733–8855, fax 732–0540. 419 rooms. Facilities: 24-hr coffee shop, outdoor pool, poolside Indonesian restaurant, 24-hr room service, business center, fitness center, shopping arcade. AE, DC, MC, V.*

Omni Marco Polo. Set on 4 acres in a high-rent residential district and a 15-minute walk from the Scotts and Orchard road intersection, this hotel is set apart from the center of action. The new configuration of the lounge area has alleviated the rush of guests and their baggage; now there's a restful sitting area to the left of reception. The guest rooms in the Continental Wing have been refurbished with Chippendale reproductions and marble-tiled bathrooms. These rooms have also been equipped with room safes, writing desks, and hand-held controls for television and lights. There are three restaurants: the smart, formal Le Duc, with haute Continental cuisine; the cheerful Brasserie, with bistro-style cooking; and the coffee shop, serving local cuisine. At night, a basement bar turns into a private-membership disco open to hotel guests. Perhaps because the British and Australian High Commissions are right across the road, guests are frequently from the Commonwealth. *Tanglin Rd., Singapore 1024, tel. 474–7141 or 800/223–5652, fax 471–0521. 603 rooms, including 30 suites. Facilities: lobby lounge and bar, disco, hair dryers, minibars, coffee- and tea-making facilities, 24-hr room service, landscaped outdoor pool, fitness center, business center, function rooms. AE, DC, MC, V.*

Pan Pacific. Of the three Marina Square hotels, this one is the largest and least expensive. It caters to group tours and large conventions, though the range of rooms and restaurants can also accommodate the needs and expense account of the junior executive as well as senior management. Perhaps because of its size and openness, it has a transient and impersonal feel. The hotel has a rooftop Chinese restaurant, Japanese and Polynesian restaurants, and a grill room as well as six other food and beverage outlet spots. All the guest rooms have marble-lined bathrooms with tubs, separate showers, and hair dryers. Upper-floor guest rooms have the better views and more amenities (minibars and bathrobes). The Pacific Floor offers butler service and complimentary breakfast and cocktails. *7 Raffles Blvd., Singapore 0103, tel. 336–8111, fax 339–1861. 800 suites and rooms. Facilities: 4 restaurants, 24-hr coffee shop, outdoor pool, pool bar, tennis courts, shops, fitness center, 24-hr business center, banquet and meeting rooms. AE, DC, MC, V.*

The Regent. The ambience is relaxed and comfortable, with soft tones, Oriental carpets, wood panels, and flower beds. In the center, glass-enclosed elevators bob up and down the spacious atrium lobby rather obtrusively, but guests can relax in the quiet tea and lobby lounges. The second-floor cocktail lounge, The Bar, has a clublike atmosphere with leather chairs, brass fittings, and polished wood paneling. All the guest rooms feature the pastels favored by so many hotels. Guests have the option of one king-size or two queen-size beds. All the rooms have writing desks and marble bathrooms; rooms on the terrace east and west sides have balconies overlooking green spaces. The hotel's four restaurants are the Tea Garden, for informal Continental and Asian dining and buffet breakfasts; the Steak Corner, serving U.S. prime beef; the Summer Palace, offering Cantonese cuisine prepared by Hong Kong chefs; and Maxim's de Paris (*see* Chapter 5), for French cuisine in an opulent Belle Epoque setting. The Regent is a good 10-minute walk from the busy Scotts and Orchard roads intersection and so appeals more to those who seek a quiet haven and don't mind taxis. *1 Cuscaden Rd., Singapore 1024, tel. 733–8888 or 800/ 545–4000, fax 732–8838. 441 rooms, including 44 suites. Facilities: large outdoor pool; fitness center with sauna, steam room, hydro-pool, massage; business center; 24-hr room service. AE, DC, MC, V.*

Royal Holiday Inn Crowne Plaza. This Orchard Road–area Holiday Inn has an expansive lobby with Italian marble floors, Burmese teak wall paneling, stained-glass skylights, and hand-woven tapestries. The coffee shop–lounge to the left of the lobby bustles with activity until 1 AM, and tour groups line up at the reception counters on the right. An "executive club" floor has its own private lounge for complimentary breakfast and evening cocktails. Rooms are compact, decorated in light colors and serviced with high-tech control buttons and large private safes. A new Muslim restaurant, the Sukmaindra, offers Halal Malay and Indonesian fare; the Meisan offers Szechuan cooking; and the Baron's Table provides a combination of German and French dining. The Bar offers rather noisy live entertainment, including karaoke on weekends. The hotel's prime asset remains its location at the junction of Scotts and Orchard roads. *25 Scotts Rd., Singapore 0922, tel. 737–7966, fax 737–6646. 493 rooms. Facilities: 24-hr room service, rooftop pool, miniature golf course, fitness center, 24-hr business center, travel agency, shops. AE, DC, MC, V.*

★ **Sheraton Towers.** Perhaps because the general manager, Carl Kono, makes a special effort to take care of his staff, service at this hotel, which opened in 1985, is a key attraction. For example, guests are asked upon arrival if they'd like their suits pressed at no charge, and complimentary early morning coffee or tea is delivered to your room with your wake-up call. Also complimentary are in-house movies, breakfast, and evening cocktails. The pastel-decorated guest rooms have all the deluxe amenities, including a small sitting area with sofa and easy chairs. (Room No. 1816 is particularly pleasant.) The hotel's dramatic visual is the cascading waterfall—the rocks are fiberglass—seen through a 9-meter (30-foot) glass panel from the Terrazza restaurant (especially welcoming for a superb high tea). Other restaurants are Domus for Italian cuisine and Li Bai (*see* Chapter 5) for refined Cantonese. The hawker stalls at Newton Circus are just a short distance away. There is a large, comfortable lounge with live music in the evening. *39 Scotts Rd., Singapore 0922, tel. 737–6888, fax 737–1072. 406 rooms.*

Facilities: 24-hr coffee lounge, 24-hr room service, health center with sauna and massage, outdoor pool, poolside snack bar, business center, disco, ballroom, function rooms. AE, DC, MC, V.

Westin Plaza and **Westin Stamford.** Of these twin hotels in the mammoth Raffles City complex, the Plaza is the smaller and higher-priced and caters to the business executive, while the Stamford, the tallest hotel in the world, attracts package-tour travelers and convention delegates. Combined, the hotels offer more than 2,000 uniform guest rooms. They are certainly not intimate, custom-service hotels. Located next to the Raffles Hotel between Marina Square and the bottom of Orchard Road (10 minutes by taxi or five by subway from the Orchard and Scotts roads intersection), these hotels have formed a hub of their own, with 100 or more shops (including a department store), convention facilities, and 16 restaurants and lounges, of which the best known is the Compass Rose (*see* Chapter 5). Also within the complex is a disco, a fitness center, two outdoor pools, six tennis courts, and three squash courts. For business meetings and banquets, there are convention rooms, including one of the largest column-free meeting rooms in the world, and a ballroom that can accommodate 3,000. *2 Stamford Rd., Singapore 0617, tel. 338–8585, fax 338–2862. Stamford, 1,257 rooms; Plaza, 796 rooms. Facilities: see above. AE, DC, MC, V.*

Moderate

Allson. This 20-year-old hotel has been given a face-lift. The rooms in the newer wing on the Excellence Floor are more spacious and more expensive. All rooms have rosewood furnishings, minibars, coffee- and tea-making facilities, air-conditioning, and IDD phones. The published room rates are lower than at similar hotels, such as the nearby Carlton. The hotel's location near Raffles City Tower puts it close to Marina Square, the colonial historic district, Little India, Bugis Street, and the Arab District, but it is a 10-minute subway or bus ride to the bustle of Orchard Road. *101 Victoria St., Singapore 0718, tel. 336–0811, fax 339–7019. 500 rooms. Facilities: Chinese restaurant, 24-hr coffee shop, Japanese and Thai café, disco, outdoor pool and poolside café, fitness center, business center, shops, free shuttle to business district and Chinatown. AE, DC, MC, V.*

Apollo Singapore. Located to the south of the Singapore River and to the west of Chinatown and the business district, this decade-old, semicircular, 19-story hotel is more suited to business travelers than to tourists. The lobby and all the rooms have been refurbished. As the Tanjong Pagar section of Chinatown develops, so does the appeal of Apollo, with its modern, clean, and cheerful rooms and its new fitness center. There are Chinese, Indonesian, and Japanese restaurants, a coffee shop serving Nonya food and a Tamalak (local cuisine) buffet at lunch, and evening entertainment. A daytime shuttle bus runs hourly between the hotel and Orchard Road. *405 Havelock Rd., Singapore 0316, tel. 733–2081, fax 733–1588. 317 rooms. Facilities: 24-hr coffee shop, disco, fitness center, banquet rooms. AE, DC, MC, V.*

★ **Carlton Hotel.** Near Raffles City, between Orchard Road and the financial district of Shenton Way, this stark, pristine hotel has a more relaxed feeling than when it first opened in 1989.

The lobby is still an open forum echoing the footsteps of guests coming and going, but the lounges to the side are quiet enclaves where you can sit and have afternoon tea. All the amenities of this hotel are up-to-date and modern, and compared with the prices of other hotels in its class, this one's tariff is reasonable. The upper five stories are concierge floors, with express check-in and complimentary breakfast and evening cocktails. *76 Bras Basah Rd., Singapore 0718, tel. 338–8333, fax 339–6866. 420 rooms, including 53 suites. Facilities: 2 gourmet restaurants (Cantonese and Continental), 24-hr coffee shop, wine bar, lounge bar, outdoor pool with poolside grill and bar, 24-hr room service, fitness center, business center, function rooms. AE, DC, MC, V.*

The Concorde. Once called the Glass Hotel for its glazed exterior, this 27-story structure lies just south of the Singapore River and west of the business district. A glass canopy curves down from the ninth story over the entrance, which faces southeast for good fortune. The main action takes place around the dining and entertainment facilities on the fourth floor. Guest rooms feature modern decor and autumn hues plus all the standard modern amenities. On the three executive floors, the tariff includes complimentary breakfast and cocktails. In addition to a French and Japanese restaurant, there is a Chinese theater restaurant that seats 800. *317 Outram Rd., Singapore 0316, tel. 733–0188, fax 733–0989. 509 rooms (4 Japanese-style). Facilities: outdoor pool and children's pool on landscaped rooftop, fitness center with sauna, steam bath, and massage, tennis court, business center, 600-person ballroom that can be divided into several banquet-meeting rooms, shopping annex. AE, MC, V.*

Crown Prince Hotel. This Japanese-chain hotel has a large, sparse lobby decorated with Italian marble and glass chandeliers. For drama, the elevators are glassed in and run along the outside of the building, which allows guests to check out the traffic congestion on Orchard Road. Guest rooms are neat, trim, and decorated in pastel colors; amenities include televisions with Teletext. The Cafe de Prince serves local and Western food; the Long Jiang offers Szechuan food from a set menu; and the Sushi Kaiseki Nogawa, Japanese. The general ambience is one of efficiency rather than warmth. Many of the hotel's clients are Japanese. *270 Orchard Rd., Singapore 0923, tel. 732–1111, fax 732–7018. 303 rooms, including 6 corner executive suites with steam baths. Facilities: outdoor pool, business center, 24-hr room service, 3 function rooms, banquet hall. AE, DC, MC, V.*

Dai-Ichi. This 29-story Japanese-owned hotel is designed for the business person who desires proximity to the business district and does not want to be tempted by the bright lights of Orchard Road. Guest rooms are small, neat, and functional; two are in tatami (Japanese) style. With most of the clientele from Japan, the hotel's main restaurant is the Kuramaya, with Kaiseki cuisine. There is also a Continental restaurant. *81 Anson Rd., Singapore 0207, tel. 224–1133, fax 222–0749. 420 rooms. Facilities: 24-hr coffee shop, outdoor pool, business center, fitness center with sauna and massage, free shuttle service to Orchard Rd. AE, MC, V.*

The Duxton Hotel. In a city of high-rise accommodations, Singapore's first boutique hotel—eight smartly converted shophouses in the Tanjong Pagar district of Chinatown—is a breath of fresh air: intimate and smart. It's furnished with colonial reproductions. The standard rooms, at the back of the building, are small; you may prefer spending the extra S$50 for one of the small duplex suites. Since windows aren't double-glazed, there is some street noise (including a few alley cats). Breakfast is included, and afternoon tea is served in the lounge. The excellent French restaurant, L'Aigle d'Or (*see* Chapter 5), is off the lobby. *83 Duxton Rd., Singapore 0208, tel. 227–7678, fax 227–1232. 48 rooms. Facilities: restaurant, secretarial service. AE, DC, MC, V.*

Furama Hotel. On the doorstep of Chinatown and within a 10-minute walk of Singapore's commercial district, the Furama is a modern, curvilinear building that stands out amid the surrounding Chinese shophouses. The guest rooms are well worn and tend to fall below the level of cleanliness of most Singapore hotels. Daily guided walking tours through Chinatown are offered. *10 Eu Tong Sen St., Singapore 0105, tel. 533–3888, fax 534–1489. 354 rooms. Facilities: Cantonese and Japanese restaurants, beauty parlor, drugstore, lobby bar, outdoor pool with snack bar, sauna, steam bath, secretarial services, function rooms. AE, DC, MC, V.*

Hotel Meridien Changi. Located 10 minutes from the airport, this hotel has no particular merit except for those who are in transit and do not have the time to stay overnight in downtown Singapore. *1 Netheravon Rd., Singapore 1750, tel. 542–7700, fax 542–5295. 280 rooms. Facilities: French restaurant, coffee shop, outdoor pool, business center, drugstore, baby-sitting, fitness center; access to tennis, squash, golf, and water sports; free shuttle to airport and downtown; free bicycle rental. AE, DC, MC, V.*

Imperial Hotel. Set on a small hill between Orchard Road and Shenton Way, the Imperial offers guest rooms decorated with pastel colors and mirrored walls. Air-conditioning is individually controlled, and the rooms have minibars, free videos, and large windows with expansive views of Singapore. The hotel also offers the Hill-Top Lounge, a bar area with live entertainment in the evenings, backgammon and chess during the day. *1 Jalam Rumbia, Singapore 0923, tel. 737–1666, fax 757–4761. 600 rooms, including 42 suites. Facilities: 3 restaurants (French, Cantonese, and northern Indian), 24-hr coffee shop, disco, landscaped outdoor pool, business center, banquet facilities. AC, DC, MC, V.*

★ **Ladyhill Hotel.** Unlike most other Singapore hotels, which cater to both business travelers and tourists, Ladyhill emphasizes home comforts and relaxation. Located in a residential area a good 10-minute walk uphill from Orchard Road, the hotel consists of a main building and a series of cottages surrounding a pool. In the main building are the intimate Swiss-style restaurant Le Chalet, a cozy split-level bar with a Filipino band in the evenings, and some guest rooms. The recent refurbishing of the guest rooms (in warm earthtones and pastels) and lobby and lounge has made the Ladyhill even more inviting. "Superior" rooms in the cottages around the pool are spacious enough that an extra bed may be added for children. Usually in the evening there is a poolside barbecue. *1 Ladyhill Rd., Singapore 1025, tel. 737–2111, fax 737–4606. 171 rooms. Facilities: coffee shop, outdoor pool, bar/cocktail lounge with live band, 2 small conference rooms. AE, V.*

Melia Scotts. Next door to the Sheraton Towers and not far from Newton Circus is this modern, oblong-shaped hotel with a cold and sterile atmosphere. Guest rooms have IDD telephones, individually controlled air-conditioning, and minibars. The property's market appears to be package-tour groups from Australia. The MRT station next door provides quick access to the whole island. *45 Scotts Rd., Singapore 0922, tel. 732–5885, fax 732–1332. 245 rooms. Facilities: formal restaurant, coffee shop, 24-hr room service, rooftop bar, outdoor pool, business center, function rooms. AE, V.*

Orchard Hotel. Close to the bustle of Orchard Road, several embassies, and the Botanical Gardens, this hotel is a popular central base. The small lobby and public areas can become a mob scene of groups arriving and departing, but once over that hurdle the hotel offers comfortable, functional rooms decorated in light pastels. The 1992 Claymore Wing, a 17-story tower extension, added 300 rooms, making this one of the largest hotels in Singapore. The new rooms are slightly larger and have built-in safes and bathrooms with separate glass-enclosed showers. Rooms in the Orchard Wing, now being refurbished, cost S$30 less. The top four Claymore floors form the Harvesters' Club, which has separate check-in facilities and complimentary breakfast and evening cocktails. The Louis Restaurant serves Continental cuisine; the Hua Ting offers Cantonese and Shanghainese cooking both in a formal setting; Ficus Cafe is open 24 hours for light meals; the outdoor Orchard Terrace is for casual dining; and a downstairs pub offers evening music. *442 Orchard Rd., Singapore 0923, tel. 734-7766, fax 733–5482. 699 rooms. Facilities: 4 restaurants, terrace pool and poolside bar, business center, 24-hr room service, tour desk. AE, DC, MC, V.*

Plaza Hotel. This Little Araby hotel recently renovated its rooms to include IDD telephones, refrigerators, coffee- and tea-making facilities, hair dryers, and sensor-touch bedside control panels. With a full house, the hotel can be quite lively. Service is friendly, if a bit laid back. Its three restaurants offer Cantonese and Thai cuisine, Western and regional fare, and spicy Oriental-style steaks. There is live entertainment in the evenings and a jumping disco. *7500A Beach Rd., Singapore 0719, tel. 298–0011, fax 296–3600. 350 rooms. Facilities: disco and 2 bars with live entertainment, rooftop pool, badminton and squash courts, fitness center with steam bath, business center, free shuttle to city center. AE, MC, V.*

York Hotel. While *near* bustling Orchard Road, the York—situated in a quiet enclave—offers a privacy that is not always available in the hotels actually *on* it. The hotel is divided into two parts: The tower has only suites; the poolside wing has split-level cabanas and "superior" rooms surrounding a garden. Aside from the White Rose Cafe, which serves Asian and Western fare, the York has the Balalaika Room, which offers Russian specialties. Extensive renovations have given the lobby areas a classic European design; now the rooms are being redecorated and refurnished to include two queen-size beds. *21 Mt. Elizabeth, Singapore 0923, tel. 737–0511, fax 732–1217. 400 rooms. Facilities: bar, 24-hr room service, beauty salon, outdoor pool, fitness center with sauna, small shopping arcade. AE, DC, MC, V.*

Inexpensive

★ **Cairnhill Hotel.** Once an apartment block, this hotel is a 10-minute walk from Orchard Road. While the building is not particularly attractive, its location on a hill does allow many of its rooms a good view of downtown Singapore. Amenities range from a small pool to an executive business center. Its restaurant serves Pekingese and Szechuan food, as well as regional fare. *19 Cairnhill Circle, Singapore 0922, tel. 734–6622, fax 235–5598. 220 rooms. Facilities: 24-hr coffee shop, business center, fitness center, pool with drink service, shopping arcade, small function room. AE, V.*

Excelsior Hotel. Close to its sister hotel, the older Peninsula, and a few blocks from Raffles City, the Excelsior is economical for central Singapore. Across the street are nearly 1,000 shops. The centrally air-conditioned rooms are reasonably large and well maintained and have IDD telephones and coded safes. *5 Coleman St., Singapore 0617, tel. 338–7733, fax 339–3847. 300 rooms. Facilities: restaurants (Chinese, Indian, Japanese, Western), piano bar, disco, outdoor pool, tour desk. AE, MC, V.*

Hotel Equatorial. Situated in a residential area a good 10-minute drive from Orchard Road, the Equatorial offers reasonably priced air-conditioned rooms equipped with IDD telephones, minibars, and televisions with Teletext. *429 Bukit Timah Rd., Singapore 1025, tel. 732–0431, fax 737–9426. 224 rooms. Facilities: 3 restaurants (Swiss, Szechuan, Japanese), coffee shop, outdoor pool, poolside café, free shuttle bus to Orchard Rd. V.*

Hotel Grand Central. Within easy strolling distance of Orchard Road's popular shopping centers, this hotel offers clean, air-conditioned rooms with IDD telephones and minifridges. Its extensive convention facilities mean that numerous name-tagged delegates wander around the lobby, and their presence seems to attract unattached ladies. In addition to the Omei Sichuan, there are Italian and Mongolian restaurants. *32 Orchard Rd., Singapore 0922, tel. 737–9944, fax 733–3175. 365 rooms. Facilities: coffee shop, outdoor pool, poolside bar, 24-hr room service, fitness center with sauna and massage, shopping arcade. MC, V.*

Hotel Royal. Near Newton Circus and a 20-minute walk from Orchard Road, this modest hotel has recently updated its rooms to include IDD telephones, air-conditioning, individual safes, and minibars. On the premises is an International Forwarding Service, which can be useful for anyone wishing to send excess baggage back home. *36 Newton Rd., Singapore 1130, tel. 253–4411, fax 253–8668. 331 rooms. Facilities: 3 restaurants (Chinese, Continental, Japanese), 24-hr coffee shop (decorated with old trishaws), outdoor pool, sauna, massage. AE, MC, V.*

The Inn of the Sixth Happiness. The stretch of shophouses on Erskine Street at the top end of Tajong Pagar in Chinatown has been converted into a hotel that pays tribute to Singapore's Chinese heritage with original Chinese paintings, rosewood furniture, and antiques from the mainland. Standard rooms aren't overdecorated, but they're spacious; all rooms tend to be a little dark. But the price makes this hotel the best value in the Inexpensive or even the Moderate category. The management is friendly and gracious. The Mandarin Ducks Suite (S$300) deserves special mention for its wedding bed from the early Ching Dynasty, with some 236 intricately carved human figures adorning its inner and outer canopy, and the huge tub in its bathroom—a two-person delight. *33–35 Erskine Rd., Singapore 0106, tel. 223–3266, fax 223–7951. 35 rooms, 9 suites. Facilities: restaurant, coffee shop, pub, nightclub. AE, DC, MC, V.*

New Park Hotel. Formerly the President Merlin Hotel, this 19-story, six-year-old hotel on the northern edge of Little India is a good 10-minute taxi ride to Orchard Road (the hotel offers a free shuttle bus) and another 10 minutes to the city's commercial center and Chinatown. The air-conditioned rooms are clean and fairly spacious, and the new management is planning a general upgrade. The Huang Palace offers Chinese fare, and the Terrace Garden Coffee House has regional and Continental food. There is live entertainment every night in the lounge. *181 Kitchener Rd., Singapore 0820, tel. 291–5533, fax 297–2827. 525 rooms. Facilities: 24-hr room service, shopping arcade. AE, V.*

Peninsula Hotel. Near the Padang and between the fashionable areas of Orchard Road and Singapore's commercial district, this hotel offers the basic creature comforts. The fairly spacious guest rooms are clean—the best are on the newly refurbished 17th floor—though one may have to tolerate water stains in the bathtub. All rooms have televisions with Teletext, minibars, and self-coded safes. The lobby area is small, serving only as a place where guests register or gain access to the entertainment and dining rooms. *3 Coleman St., Singapore 0617, tel. 337–2200, fax 339–3580. 315 rooms, including 4 suites. Facilities: 24-hr coffee shop, cocktail lounge, nightclub with floor shows and hostesses, outdoor pool, fitness center with sauna and massage, 24-hr room service. AE, MC, V.*

★ **RELC International House.** This is less a hotel than an international conference center often used by Singapore's university for seminars. However, the upper floors of the building are bargain guest rooms: large, centrally air-conditioned, and furnished with the basic comforts. The wide windows throw in welcome daylight, and though the bathrooms have rather sloppy plaster repair work, they are clean and functional. The building is in a residential neighborhood, up a hill beyond the Shangri-La Hotel; it's a stiff 10-minute walk to the Orchard and Scotts roads intersection. Because of its good value, it is often completely booked, so reservations are strongly advised. *30 Orange Grove Rd., Singapore 1024, tel. 737–9044, fax 733–9976. 128 rooms. Facilities: coffee shop, laundry facilities. No credit cards.*

River View Hotel. This new high-rise hotel is located on the south bank of the Singapore River and is about 10 minutes by taxi from both the commercial center and Orchard Road. Rooms are equipped with modern amenities, including minibars and telephone extensions in the bathrooms. Expect some changes to occur over the next few years as the new manager, Roberto Pregarz, once of Raffles Hotel, takes the helm. *382 Havelock Rd., Singapore 0316, tel. 732–9922, fax 732–1034. 476 rooms. Facilities: Japanese and Continental restaurants, 24-hr coffee shop, 24-hr room service, pool area with bar, fitness center, business center, disco, function rooms with audiovisual setups. AE, DC, MC, V.*

Seaview Hotel. Off the East Coast Parkway, midway between Changi Airport and Singapore city, this hotel is more convenient for travelers in transit than for visitors. Guest rooms come with the basic amenities. There are restaurants, nightclubs, and shops on the premises and in the area. The nearby East Coast Park offers golf, tennis, cycling, and water-sports facilities. *Amber Close, Singapore 1543, tel. 345–2222, fax 345–1741. 435 rooms. Facilities: 24-hr coffee shop, 24-hr room* *service, live evening entertainment at the lounge bar, outdoor pool, disco. MC, V.*

Budget

Hotel Asia. Next to the Sheraton Towers and between Orchard Road and Newton Circus, the Hotel Asia is a modest economy hotel. Guest rooms have air-conditioning but few other luxuries. The Tsui Hang Village restaurant serves Cantonese cuisine. *37 Scotts Rd., Singapore 0922, tel. 737–8388, fax 733–3563. 146 rooms. Facilities: 24-hr coffee shop, cocktail lounge. MC, V.*

Hotel Bencoolen. On the commercial street that leads from Orchard Road to Little India, this hotel has recently been refurbished to add a fresher feel to its air-conditioned rooms, which include IDD phones. Usually one can negotiate a discount on the room tariff, making the Bencoolen an especially good value. A rooftop restaurant serves Chinese and Continental fare. *47 Bencoolen St., Singapore 0718, tel. 336–0822, fax 336–4384. 69 rooms. Facilities: restaurant, rooftop garden. MC, V.*

Metropole Hotel. This is a very modest and basic hotel near Raffles City. The rooms are very simply furnished, and the only luxuries are air-conditioning and television. *41 Seah St., Singapore 0718, tel. 336–3611, fax 339–3610. 54 rooms. Facilities: Chinese restaurant, coffee shop, room service until 11 PM. No credit cards.*

Metropolitan YMCA, International Centre. At this older of the two Singapore Ys, at the end of Shenton Way in the central business district, most of the rooms are singles and for men only—a single female will be given a double and charged at a single rate. Bathrooms are shared, except for the double rooms (which are a bargain at S$50). All rooms have air-conditioning but no telephones. *70 Palmer Rd., Singapore 0207, tel. 224–4666. 52 rooms, including 16 doubles. Facilities: restaurant. No credit cards.*

Metropolitan YMCA, Tanglin Centre. A 10-minute walk to Orchard Road, this Y has rooms with air-conditioning and private baths. There are even a few suites. The budget restaurant offers wholesome English breakfasts for only a few Singapore dollars, as well as Chinese, Malay, Nonya, and Western meals. *Tanglin Centre, 60 Stevens Rd., Singapore 1025, tel. 737–7755, fax 235–5528. 88 rooms. Facilities: outdoor pool, gym, 2 squash courts, coffee house, 7 conference rooms. No credit cards.*

★ **Mitre Hotel.** Overhead fans whirl in sparsely furnished bedrooms; downstairs, in the lounge–lobby bar, old-timers ruminate on how life used to be. If you are looking for shades of Sidney Greenstreet, staff who can manage Pidgin English at best, and a Conradesque atmosphere, this small hotel is for you. It does not have modern amenities, nor is it listed with the Singapore Tourist Promotion Office, so you will likely be the only Westerner in residence. *145 Killiney Rd., Singapore 0923, tel. 737–3811. 25 rooms with shared bath. Facilities: Count only on breakfast and drinks at the bar. No credit cards.*

Queen's Hotel. In a quiet area off Orchard Road, this hotel is a friendly, homey place. The rooms are quite modest but do have air-conditioning and television. In the "deluxe" four-story wing, the rooms even boast refrigerators; since these rooms are newer, they're worth the extra S$10. *24 Mt. Elizabeth, Sin-*

*gapore 0922, tel. 737-6088. 61 rooms. Facilities: coffee shop,
outdoor pool, sauna, massage. MC, V.*

Strand Hotel. This hotel's simple, clean rooms have IDD telephones and color televisions with in-house videos. The location,
between Raffles City and Orchard Road, is central, though a
10-minute walk is required to reach either. *25 Bencoolen St.,
Singapore 0718, tel. 338-1866, fax 336-3149. 130 rooms. Facilities: coffee shop, lounge bar. No credit cards.*

YMCA International House. This well-run YMCA at the bottom
end of Orchard Road offers hotellike accommodations, with
double (S$70) and single (S$45) rooms, plus dormitories for
budget travelers (S$20). (S$5 will buy you temporary YMCA
membership.) All rooms have private baths, color TVs, and direct-dial phones. In addition to an impressive gym, there are a
rooftop pool and squash and badminton courts. And there's a
McDonald's at the entrance. *1 Orchard Rd., Singapore 0923,
tel. 336-6000. 60 rooms. Facilities: pool, gym, 2 squash courts.
AE, DC, MC, V.*

7 The Arts and Nightlife

BOO.

Sprint's WorldTraveler FŌNCARD. The easy way to call from around the world.

Imagine trying to place a call in another country: You have to deal with foreign currency. Alien operators. And phones that look like they're from another planet.

Talk about frightening.

Now imagine making the same call with a Sprint WorldTraveler FŌNCARD™:

To begin with, you'll reach an English-speaking operator just by dialing one easy, toll-free access code. An access code, by the way, that's right on your calling card.

Not only that, you won't have any trouble remembering your card number. Because it's based on your home phone number.

Now what could be easier than that? So call today and find out how you can get a WorldTraveler FŌNCARD.

Because we may not be able to do anything about the phones you'll have to call from. But at least it won't be a ghastly experience.

1·800·347·8989

No matter what your travel style, the best trips start with **Fodor's**

Fodor's 1993

affordable
GREAT
BRITAIN

How to see the best for less

Fodor's

Bed &
Breakfasts,
Country
Inns,
and Other
Weekend
Pleasures

NEW
ENGLAND

THE WALL STREET JOURNAL
GUIDES TO BUSINESS TRAVEL

USA &
CANADA

The first guides to take
business travel seriously

Fodor's 1993

affordable
GERMANY

How to see the best for less

Fodor's

GREAT AMERICAN
VACATIONS

50 AFFORDABLE
HEALTH-CONSCIOUS TRIPS
TO THE COUNTRY'S BEST-LOVED
TRAVEL DESTINATIONS

"The King of Guidebooks" —*Newsweek*

Fodor's 93

San Francisco
*And the Best of
the Wine Country*

23 pages of maps

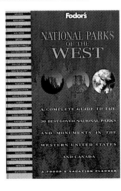

Fodor's

NATIONAL PARKS
OF THE
WEST

A COMPLETE GUIDE TO THE
30 BEST-LOVED NATIONAL PARKS
AND MONUMENTS IN THE
WESTERN UNITED STATES
AND CANADA

A FODOR'S VACATION PLANNER

"The King of Guidebooks" —*Newsweek* ★★★★

Fodor's 93

Spain
*Including Mallorca,
Ibiza and the
Canary Islands*

Fodor's

HEALTHY
ESCAPES

SPAS • FITNESS RESORTS • CRUISES

Fodor's

Canada's
Great
Country
Inns
*The Best in
Food and
Lodging*
by Anita
Stewart

"The King of Guidebooks" —*Newsweek* ★★★★

Fodor's 93

Caribbean
*A Complete Guide to
27 Island Destinations*

Fodor's

TRAVEL GUIDES
The name that means smart travel
Available at bookstores everywhere.
See back pages for complete title listing.

Perhaps because eating out consumes so much of Singaporeans' time and money, there is less variety in other forms of entertainment. Still, there's enough to keep visitors busy. The Singapore Tourist Promotion Board (STPB) has listings of events scheduled for the current month. You can also find the schedules of major performances in the local English-language newspaper, the *Straits Times*, or in the free monthly *Arts Diary* brochure (available at most hotel reception desks).

The Arts

Chinese, Indian, and Malay cultural events are limited to sporadic performances and to festivals (check with the STPB to see whether any are scheduled during your stay), but some commercial shows drawing on Asian culture are given nightly for tourists *(see* Cultural Shows, *below).* Indian music, drama, and dance performances are staged during some of the major festivals at the more important temples, including the Sri Mariamman Temple on South Bridge Road and the Chettiar Temple on Tank Road. Themes are from the ancient epics— tales of gods, demons, and heroes.

Singapore is weakest in the area of serious international theater and classical concerts. The best of what there is may be found at the **Victoria Theatre and Memorial Hall,** in two adjoining Victorian buildings at the Padang. This is the home of the 85-member **Singapore Symphony Orchestra,** which was founded in 1979 and has built an excellent reputation for its wide repertoire, including popular classics as well as works by local and Asian composers. Also presented here from time to time are Chinese opera and Indian classical dance, as well as performances by Singapore's various theatrical and operatic societies. Several times a year, festivals featuring music and dance groups from throughout Southeast Asia are held in these auditoriums.

Concerts

The **Singapore Symphony Orchestra** gives concerts on Friday and Saturday evenings twice a month at the Victoria Theatre *(see above).* Tickets cost S$4–S$15 and may be reserved by telephone between noon and 8 PM (tel. 339–6120; American Express or Visa accepted).

Three times a year, the 70-member **Chinese Orchestra of the Singapore Broadcasting Corporation** performs Chinese classical music, also at the Victoria (tel. 338–1230 or 256–0401, ext. 2732). Tickets: S$3–S$5.

Theater

Theatreworks (tel. 280–0188) is a professional drama company focusing on contemporary works. **Act 3** (tel. 734–9090) concentrates on children's plays. **Stars** (tel. 468–9145) is a community theater that offers performances of family shows, such as American musicals and Christmas specials, as well as classic and modern dramas. **Hi! Theatre** (tel. 468–1945) is Singapore's theater of the deaf; its mask, mime, black-light, and sign-language performances appeal as much to the hearing as to the nonhearing.

Dance

Performances are given throughout the year by the **Singapore Ballet Academy** (tel. 737–5772) and by the **Sylvia McCully** dance group (tel. 457–6995), who perform a combination of ballet and jazz.

Cultural Shows

"ASEAN Night" at the Mandarin Hotel offers traditional songs and dances from the various countries of ASEAN (the Association of South East Asian Nations): Singapore, Indonesia, Malaysia, Thailand, and the Philippines. The shows are held at poolside, and dinner is available during performances. *333 Orchard Rd., tel. 737–4411. Tues.–Sun. Dinner starts at 7, the show at 7:45. Cost: dinner and show, S$44.10; show only, S$22.60.*

The **"Cultural Wedding Show"** is a 45-minute re-creation of a Peranakan wedding ceremony. The presentation is part of a three-hour immersion in the culture of Straits-born Chinese that includes a tour of Peranakan Place's Show House Museum and dinner at Bibi's restaurant, serving Nonya food. *Bibi's, Peranakan Place, 180 Orchard Rd., tel. 732–6966. Weeknights 6:30 PM. Cost: S$36 adults, S$18 children.*

"Instant Asia" is a 45-minute revue of Chinese, Indian, and Malay dance. The show begins with the clash of cymbals and gongs and the beat of drums that accompany a traditional Chinese lion dance. The subsequent "Harvest Dance" sets quite a different mood as a Malay troupe performs, gracefully moving with lighted candles in each hand. Indian dancers then take the stage, telling stories in mime while snake charmers play their flutes. At the end of the show, members of the audience are invited onto the stage to participate—perhaps to dangle a python around their necks or join the dancers in mime. The show is cliché and commercial, but fun if you've never seen this kind of thing before. *Singa Inn Seafood Restaurant, 920 East Coast Pkwy., tel. 345–1111. Weeknights at 7:30 PM. Free to diners. Daytime version performed at Cockpit Hotel, tel. 345–1111. Show at 11:45 AM. Admission: S$5 adults, S$2 children.*

"Malam Singapura" is the Hyatt Regency's colorful 45-minute show of song and dance (mostly Malay) performed at poolside with or without dinner. *10–12 Scotts Rd., tel. 733–1188. Nightly. Dinner starts at 7, the show at 8. Cost: dinner and show, S$38; show only, S$18.*

Raffles Jubilee Hall, a 392-seat Victorian theater, presents an audiovisual history of Raffles against the backdrop of Singapore. There are five shows daily, at 10, 11, 1, 2, and 3 (S$5 adults, S$3 children). At noon, 20 local artists put on the 25-minute multi-ethnic "Life and Times of Singapore" (S$10).

Chinese Opera

Chinese operas—called *wayangs*—are fascinating and far more worthwhile than any of the commercial cultural shows. Usually they are performed on temporary stages set up near temples, in market areas, or outside apartment complexes. Wayangs are staged all year, but are more frequently seen in

August and September, during the Festival of the Hungry Ghosts. (The STPB has the dates and times of performances.)

The wayangs, based on legends, are full of action. Gongs and drums beat, maidens weep, devils leap, and heros reap the praise of an enthusiastic audience. The characters are weirdly made up—take a look behind the stage and watch the actors apply their makeup—and gorgeously costumed. With Chinese programming on television mostly in Mandarin, street wayangs—spoken in dialect, though totally different from the conversational dialect—have become popular with the older generation, who rarely have a chance to be entertained in their own language.

Do try to seek out a wayang. It is an experience you will not quickly forget. And don't be bashful about asking a fellow spectator who the characters portrayed on stage are.

Nightlife

Music clubs, offering everything from serious listening to jazz to the thumping and flashing of discos, are becoming more popular as Singaporeans take up the Western custom of dating. The increasingly popular *karaoke* ("empty orchestra") bars, where guests take microphones and sing along to the music track of a video, offer chronic bathroom singers the opportunity to go public.

Nightclubs with floor shows are also popular, and the feeling seems to be that the bigger the place is, the better—some accommodate as many as 500 guests. Often these clubs have hostesses (affectionately called public relations officers, or PRO's) available for company. Depending on the establishment, companionship is remunerated by either a flat hourly fee (the term used is "to book the hostess") or a gratuity given at the end of the evening.

At nightclubs or music bar/lounges, there is usually a cover charge or first-drink charge (cover plus one free drink) of about S$15 weeknights and S$25 weekends. At the nightclubs where there are floor shows and hostesses, the common practice is to buy a bottle of brandy—Chinese consider brandy a high-status drink, whereas whiskey is "bad smelling and shows poor taste." A bottle of brandy may cost as much as S$300. You are advised to let your "hostess" drink from your bottle, rather than order her own.

Risqué nightlife disappeared long ago from Singapore. Prostitution is not exactly legal, but certain areas, such as Geylang, do have red-light districts. However, the fear of AIDS has made Westerners suspect, and when they're not downright unwelcome, they must pay a higher price. The bars along Keppel Road are not recommended. Ladies have been known to slip sleeping draughts into men's drinks. A sleeping customer does not miss his wallet until he wakes up.

Dance and Theater Nightclubs

The most popular nightclubs among Singaporeans are those with floor shows and hostesses. You are not under any obligation to select a hostess, however. The cost of going to these clubs is in the bottle of brandy you are expected to buy (if you don't mind losing face, you can forgo the brandy and order whatever you want from the bar). There are also "dinner theater" evenings held from time to time at the Hilton, Hyatt, and Shangri-La hotels. Dinner and a show at the **Shangri-La,** which often has some good comics, runs about S$85.

Apollo Theatre Restaurant and Nightclub. This club is very popular with Chinese businessmen, who come here to be entertained by a steady stream of Chinese singers and hostesses and to enjoy the cuisine (Hunanese). *Apollo Singapore Hotel, 405 Havelock Rd., 17th floor, tel. 235–7977. Brandy: S$270. Hourly hostess fee: S$25. Open nightly 8–2.*

Golden Million. Here you can either dine or just listen to Hong Kong bands play a mixture of Mandarin, Cantonese, and Western music. The decor is rich and expansive, with lots of gold and red to give a feeling of extravagance. This was one of the clubs that started the hostess concept; it has become well established among Chinese and Singaporean businessmen. *Peninsula Hotel, 3 Coleman St., 5th floor, tel. 336–6993. Brandy: S$250. Hourly hostess fee: S$25. Open nightly 8–2.*

Grand Palace. Performers from Hong Kong, Taiwan, and occasionally Europe entertain at this lush and ornate club. A video screen keeps your eyes occupied between shows. *1 Grange Rd., tel. 737–8922. Brandy: S$260 and up. Hourly hostess fee: S$25. Open nightly 9–3.*

Kasbah. The decor is Moroccan in this long-established, tiered nightclub where, on occasion, good artists from abroad entertain. Dancing is both fast and slow, and the music allows for conversation. The crowd, too, is more subdued and "properly" dressed. *Mandarin Hotel, Orchard Rd., tel. 737–4411. First drink: S$16 Sun.–Thurs., S$22 Fri. and Sat. Open nightly 9–2.*

Lido Palace Niteclub. Promoting itself as the "palace of many pleasures," this lavish establishment offers Chinese cabaret, a band, DJ-spun disco music, hostesses, karaoke, and, for those who wish to dine, Cantonese cuisine. *Concorde Hotel, 317 Outram Rd., 5th floor, tel. 732–8855. First drink: S$30. Shows at 9:30 PM and 12:30 AM. Open nightly 9–3.*

Marco Polo. A four-piece band plays popular dance music to which diners can take a turn on the floor between courses in the formal and elegant split-level Le Duc Continental restaurant in the Omni Marco Polo Hotel. Either side of center stage, some of the dining tables are discreetly positioned in alcoves, while others overlook the dance floor. *Tanglin Rd., tel. 464–7141. Dinner for 2: approximately S$70. Open nightly 8–11.*

Neptune. This sumptuous two-story establishment, designed as an Oriental pavilion, is reputed to be the largest nightclub in Southeast Asia. Cantonese food is served, and there is a gallery for nondiners. Local, Taiwanese, and Filipino singers entertain in English and Chinese; occasionally a European dance troupe is added to the lineup. The Neptune is most fun if you are in a group. Operated by the Mandarin Hotel, it is often booked for private functions, so call ahead to be sure it is open to the public. *Overseas Union House, Collyer Quay, tel. 224–3922; for show information and reservations, tel. 737–4411. Cover charge: S$8. Dinner: S$15. Open nightly 8–2.*

Discos and Dance Clubs

The distinction between a disco and a place with live music and a dance floor has become blurred. At all the following establishments, the decibel levels allow for only snatches of conversation.

Black Velvet. This is one of the oldest discos, and still retains its popularity among all generations. *Century Park Sheraton Hotel, Nassim Hill, tel. 732–1222. First drink: S$12.50. Open nightly 9–2.*

Caesars. The decor and the waitresses dressed in lissome togas give this disco an air of decadent splendor. DJ-spun music plus imported live bands make it a hot venue for entertainment. *Orchard Towers front block (#02-36), 400 Orchard Rd., tel. 235–2840. First drink: S$15 Sun.–Thurs., S$24 Fri. and Sat. Open Sun.–Thurs. 8–2, Fri. and Sat. 8–3.*

Celebrities. Having moved from Centrepoint to Orchard Towers, this establishment is now considered a sophisticated night spot. Dance music spun by a DJ is interspersed with live pop music; one of the key attractions is the all-girl band Heaven Knows. There is ample room to drink at the 150-foot-long bar. *Orchard Towers rear block (#B1-41), 400 Orchard Rd., tel. 734–5221. First drink: S$12 Sun.–Thurs., S$15 Fri., S$20 Sat. Open Sun.–Thurs. 8–2, Fri. and Sat. 8–3.*

Chinoiserie. This is currently the in place for Yuppies. Outside, lines of people wait to enter and be entertained by a variety of musical groups. *Hyatt Hotel, 10–12 Scotts Rd., tel. 733–1188. First drink: S$20 Sun.–Thurs., S$30 Fri., Sat. Open nightly 8–3.*

East-West Express. This is both a restaurant and a disco. A changing menu each month reflects the cuisines of various countries, and the decor adapts to suit the cuisine. After about 10:15 PM, disco dancing becomes the focus of attention. *121 Marina Square (#03-119), tel. 339–1618. Cover: S$11 Mon.–Thurs., S$16 Fri., S$20 Sat. Open Mon.–Sat. 6–2.*

Rainbow. This place has been around for some time and draws a young crowd to hear Filipino show bands and local heavy-metal bands play music from the top 40. *Ming Arcade, 21 Cuscaden Rd., tel. 333–7140. Minimum 2-drink charge: S$20. Open Sun.–Thurs. 8–2, Fri. and Sat. 8–3.*

Rumours. One of the largest discos in Singapore, this is a current favorite among the younger crowd. The two-level glass dance floor is designed to make you feel as though you are dancing in space; the play of mirrors adds to the distortion. *Forum Galleria (#03-08), 483 Orchard Rd., tel. 732–8181. First drink: S$15 Sun.–Thurs., S$20 Fri. and Sat. Open Sun.–Thurs. 8–2, Fri. and Sat. 8–3.*

TGIF. This establishment is strictly for drinking from lunchtime to 7:30, whereupon it turns into a disco. However, the action rarely begins before 10. Dinner is also served, if you like to eat amid flashing lights. *Far East Plaza, 14 Scotts Rd., tel. 235–6181. First drink: S$7. Open daily noon–2 AM.*

Top Ten. This old, converted cinema has a decor of cityscapes, including the Manhattan skyline, as well as a four-tier bar, a dance floor, and a stage. Imported bands alternate with disco music. There is a popular "happy hour" in the lobby bar between 5 and 9 PM. *Orchard Towers (#04-35/36), 400 Orchard Rd., tel. 732–3077. First drink: S$15 Sun.–Thurs., S$25 Fri. and Sat. Open nightly 9–3.*

The Warehouse. In this new club, made from two former river-side warehouses, there is enough room for 500 disco fanatics and the largest video screen in Singapore. This is a popular night spot, especially for the younger crowd. *Next to the River View Hotel, 332 Havelock Rd., tel. 732–9922. Cover: S$12 Sun.–Thurs. (includes 1 drink), S$24 Fri. and Sat. (includes 2 drinks). Open Sun.–Thurs. 8–2, Fri. and Sat. 8–3.*

Xanadu. The reputation of the Shangri-La Hotel and the intricate, high-tech lighting system of this disco bring in a steady, sophisticated crowd, plus hotel guests. The newest gadgetry is a "changing environment." With the pull of a switch, the American Western scene (complete with square dancing) of a moment ago becomes a tropical island night for smooching. Gimmicky perhaps, but it works; each time the switch is pulled (twice an evening), to the amused surprise of the clientele, the ambience at this popular Yuppie nightclub changes. *Shangri-La Hotel, 22 Orange Grove Rd., tel. 737–3644. First drink: S$18 Sun.–Thurs., S$24 Fri. and Sat. Open nightly 9–3.*

Pubs and Beer Gardens

Brannigans. This is one of Singapore's most popular watering holes. It is often used as a convenient meeting spot before an evening of revelry or as a friendly place for an evening nightcap. *Hyatt Regency, 10–12 Scotts Rd., tel. 733–1188. Open daily 11 AM–1 AM.*

The Coolies' Pub. The Inn of the Sixth Happiness in Tajong Pagar has devoted the top floors of four shophouses to this friendly, casual café, where light music is offered most evenings. *Eskine Rd., tel. 223–3266. Drinks from S$8. Open nightly 7–midnight.*

Dickens Tavern. At this mixture of a pub and a lounge, regulars listen to bands while being served by friendly waitresses (not hostesses). It's a good place to visit if you do not want to have a raucous and expensive evening. *Parkway Parade #04-01, 80 Marina Parade Rd., tel. 440–0215. No cover. Drinks: from S$7. Open nightly 8–2.*

Hard Rock Café. Hamburgers and light fare are served at this pub/café and a live band plays in the evenings. The mood is casual, young, and festive, and similar to the mood at other Hard Rock cafés with a bar, booth tables, and souvenir shops. *#02-01, 50 Cuscaden Rd., tel. 235–5232. Cover: S$12 (includes one drink). Drinks: from S$8. Open nightly 6–1.*

Jim's Pub. Try this cozy bar, owned and managed by pianist Jimmy Chan, for an evening of light music from a vocalist or instrumentalist. *Hotel Negara, 15 Claymore Dr., tel. 737–0811. Beer runs S$3 a glass. Open nightly 7–1.*

Jazz

Captain's Bar. For a sophisticated evening of jazz and rhythm and blues, this bar-lounge is elegant and comfortable. *Oriental Hotel, Marina Square, tel. 338–0066. Drinks: from S$12. Open nightly 9–1.*

Club 3992. Owned by the same people who own Caesars, this club is keeping a high jazz profile with international artists. *Orchard Towers, 400 Orchard Rd., tel. 235–2840. Drinks: from S$10. Open nightly 9–2.*

Saxophone. At this club, which offers both jazz and popular rock, the volume is loud and the space is compact, with standing room only. However, there is a terrace outside where you can sit and still hear the music. After seven years in business, the customers keep coming, so the sound must be right. *23 Cuppage Terr., tel. 235–8385. Drinks: about S$10. Open nightly 6–1.*

Somerset Bar. The New Orleans–style jazz played here has attracted a loyal following. With a larger space than the Saxophone, it offers room to sit and relax, making it more popular with the older crowd. *Westin Plaza, 4 Stamford Rd., 3rd floor, tel. 338–8585. Drinks: from S$10. Open nightly 5–2.*

Country-and-Western

Golden Peacock Lounge. This has long been a favorite of those who enjoy country music. The star attraction is Matthew Tan, Singapore's own singing cowboy, who has a vintage country twang. *Shangri-La Hotel, 22 Orange Grove Rd., tel. 737–3644. Drinks from S$15. Open nightly 8–2.*

Rock

Anywhere. Crowds gather, especially on weekends, in this smoke-filled room to hear the music of the local rock band Tania. *Tanglin Shopping Centre (#04-08), 19 Tanglin Rd., tel. 734–8233. First drink: S$12 Sun.–Thurs., S$18 Fri. and Sat. Open Sun.–Thurs. 8–2, Fri. and Sat. 8–3.*

Karaoke Bars

Dai-Ichi Karaoke. Up onto a revolving platform patrons climb, to sing along with videos and lyrics flashed on a screen. Understanding Mandarin helps one appreciate the vocalists. *Dai-Ichi Hotel, 81 Anson Rd., tel. 222–8931. Drinks: from S$9. Open nightly 8–2.*

Park Avenue. Formerly the Peppermint Park, this is a large, cavernous karaoke lounge, with imitation facades of old houses decorating the walls. Different sections permit different kinds of crooning, from French love songs in a library setting to John Denver in a Western landscape. *80 Marina Parade (#04-08), tel. 440–9998. Drinks: from S$15. Open nightly 8–2.*

8 Excursions to Malaysia and Indonesia

Peninsular Malaysia

This excursion into southern peninsular Malaysia (as West Malaysia, the 11 Malaysian states that, with southern Thailand, make up the Malay Peninsula, is called) takes you to some of the beautiful beaches of the east coast and to the beach resort island of Tioman in the South China Sea. Crossing the peninsula from east to west, we pass the hilltown resort of Genting Highlands, then continue on to Malaysia's capital, Kuala Lumpur (called KL), and the west coast. North of Kuala Lumpur are several resort islands, of which the best known is Penang, but this excursion instead heads south, toward the historic city of Malacca, where the Portuguese established the first European settlement. From there we return to Singapore.

The excursion can be taken either as a whole, which would require a minimum of four days, or broken up into shorter legs to suit your interests. The Malay town of Johore Bahru (called JB), just across the causeway from Singapore, makes for an easy afternoon excursion; for S$.80, bus No. 170 from the Queen Street terminal will take you there in 45 minutes. The formalities for crossing the Singapore–Malaysia border are simple and straightforward, requiring no more than filling out an Immigration card and having your passport stamped. Traveling as part of any of the guided tours available through most hotels is even easier, since the tour leader books you through as a group and you are escorted through special gates (cutting down time waiting in lines).

Essential Information

Tourist Information
Free maps and information are available at the Singapore office of the **Tourist Development Corporation of Malaysia** (#01-03 Ocean Bldg., 10 Collyer Quay, tel. 532–6321). For those heading to Sarawak rather than peninsular Malaysia, there is the **Sarawak Tourism Centre** (268 Orchard Road, #08-07, Yen San Building, Singapore 0923, tel. 736–1602) with maps, brochures, and an unhelpful staff. In the United States, contact the **Malaysia Tourist Information Center** (818 W. 7th St., Los Angeles, CA 90017, tel. 213/689–9702).

Passports and Visas
Passports but no visas are required for citizens of Great Britain, Canada, or the United States wishing to enter Malaysia for less than three months.

Staying Healthy
Yellow fever vaccinations are required of anyone coming from an infected area. The water in Kuala Lumpur is perfectly drinkable, but it may be wise to drink bottled water in the countryside.

When to Go
The monsoon months—November–January on the east coast, May–August on the west—can be very wet. However, even then the sun pokes through the clouds most days. Temperatures are 70°F–90°F year-round, and the humidity is always high. March and April are the ideal travel times.

Currency
At press time, the Malaysian ringgit, known as a Malay dollar, was worth US$.39 and M$2.50=US$1; M$1=23 pence and £1=M$4.33.

Guided Tours
Scenic Travel (110 Killiney Rd., #01-02, tel. 02/733–8688) is one Singapore company offering excursions into peninsular Malay-

sia. Among its choices are three-day, two-night excursions to either Kuantan (including a visit to Cherating village, a kampong that sells beautiful pandan and mengjuang mats, hats, baskets, etc.) or Malacca. For other companies, *see* Guided Tours in Chapter 1, Essential Information.

Getting to and Around Peninsular Malaysia

By Plane **Singapore Airlines** (in Singapore, tel. 223–8888; in KL, tel. 03/292–3122) and **Malaysia Airlines** (in Singapore, tel. 336–6777; in KL, tel. 03/746–3000) have frequent service between Singapore and Kuala Lumpur's Subang Airport; they also serve many other destinations on the peninsula, including Johore Bahru, Kuantan, and Penang. **Pelangi Air** (tel. 03/746–3000) has 45-minute flights from Singapore to Malacca, and **Trade Winds** (c/o Malaysia Airlines, tel. 336–6777) flies to Tioman Island. Sample times and prices from Singapore: to Kuala Lumpur, 50 minutes, S$130 (S$90 if you go standby); to Kuantan, 45 minutes, S$120. From JB to KL or to Kuantan, the fare is M$77, so you might consider crossing the causeway by bus and flying out of JB if you're interested in saving money. To Tioman Island, the fare from Singapore is S$99.

By Car A hired car is the most convenient way of seeing West Malaysia. Roads are congested but well paved and well signposted. Driving here is more freewheeling than in Singapore—watch carefully for erratic movements on the part of Malay drivers. To rent a car you need a valid driving license, a passport, and a credit card for deposits and charges. One-way drop-offs are permitted, usually with a small surcharge. Check the brakes before you drive away, and make sure there's an inflated spare tire and a jack. And driving is on the left side of the road.

In Malaysia, typical rental rates are M$115 a day or M$594 a week, with unlimited mileage. A collision/damage waiver (CDW) insurance premium of M$10 a day will cover you for the initial M$2,000 not covered by the insurance included in the basic charge. Singapore rates are at least 60% higher because of the surcharge imposed for taking the car out of Singapore. For rental agencies in Singapore, *see* Getting Around Singapore by Car in Chapter 1. In Johore Bahru, try **Sintat/Thrifty** (tel. 07/332313) or **Calio Car Rentals and Tours** (tel. 07/233–325). Wearing seat belts is required (fine is M$200) and remember that traffic gives way to the right on rotaries.

By Taxi Shared taxis, a popular form of transportation between cities, are usually available at bus stations. Private taxis can cost up to four times more. A private ride from Johore Bahru to Mersing can cost M$10; from Mersing to Kuantan, M$15; from Kuantan to Kuala Lumpur, M$23; from Kuala Lumpur to Malacca, M$15; and from Malacca to Johore Bahru, M$14.

By Train **Malaysian Railways** operates six trains a day from Singapore's Keppel Station (tel. 222–5165). These trains go up Malaysia's west coast to Kuala Lumpur and beyond—one goes all the way to Bangkok, departing at 10 PM and arriving in Bangkok 35 hours later, for a cost of S$121 second class and S$237 first class. From Johore Bahru to Kuala Lumpur, the trip takes six hours and costs M$27.

By Bus Buses leave Johore Bahru's Bangunan Mara Terminal for numerous points on the peninsula. One company is **National Express** (tel. 07/234–494). Sample fares: to KL, M$15; to Malacca, M$10. Bus service is fast and efficient; departures are frequent. Both air-conditioned and non-air-conditioned buses are available. To reach Johore Bahru for S$.80 by bus from Singapore, take No. 170 from Bukit Timah Road (off Newton Circus).

Exploring Peninsular Malaysia

Numbers in the margin correspond to points of interest on the Peninsular Malaysia map.

Johore Bahru At the end of the causeway from Singapore, the town of **Johore**
❶ **Bahru,** an old royal and administrative capital, begins. The apparent lack of town planning stands in sharp contrast to the orderliness of Singapore. There are no center and no right angles; streets follow no grid or other logical plan but run into one another higgledy-piggledy. The pace, too, is noticeably different: Here, watches seem to have no minute hands.

The town's major sight is the **Istana Besar,** the old palace of the sultans of Johore. This neoclassical, rather institutional-looking building, erected in 1866, has been converted into a museum; it holds the hunting trophies of the late sultan as well as ceremonial regalia and ancient weapons. (The new sultan's palace, the **Istana Bukit Serene,** was built in 1933 and is noted for its gardens, which are popular with joggers.) The **Sultan Abu Bakar Mosque,** built in 1900 in European Victorian style, is one of Malaysia's most beautiful, with sparkling white towers and domes surrounding the main prayer hall. It can accommodate more than 2,000 worshipers. At the cemetery on Jalan Muhamadiah, the **Royal Mausoleum** has been the final resting place to the Johore royal family since they left Singapore. Visitors may not enter the mausoleum, but a number of impressive Muslim tombs surround it. Also in Johore Bahru are handicraft centers, such as Sri Ayu Batik Industries (136 Jln. Perwira Satu), where demonstrations of batik making and songket weaving are given.

Tioman Island For the first hour out of Johore, the road (follow signs) is congested with traffic and busy towns. After 45 kilometers there is
❷ a junction. The right fork goes to **Desaru.** For a decade this has been a beach resort for Singaporeans, and now the area is undergoing a large-scale expansion program to provide four golf courses, more water sports facilities, an additional 4,000 holiday homes, and more hotels along its 17-kilometer (10.5-mile) stretch of jungle-fringed beach. (*See* Beaches and Water Parks in Chapter 4.) Taking the left fork for Mersing, the road cuts through thick jungle growth. Scampering monkeys keep you alert. After about three hours (161 kilometers, or 100 miles),
❸ you reach **Mersing,** a low-key market town that has its roots as a fishing village and is the gateway to Tioman Island.

Boats are scheduled to leave Mersing harbor for the two-hour trip to Tioman every day around noon, though because they are dependent on the tides, the actual departure time varies. If you plan to stay at the Tioman Island Resort, you can arrange your passage with the hotel's reservation center near the dock. (The resort is the island's only hotel, but there are numerous inexpensive guest houses that always seem to have rooms.) Otherwise, arrange to have one of the boat owners who approach you at the dock take you over. The cost is M$30 one way. Because the boats must wait for the morning tides to make the return from Tioman, a day excursion is not possible; you must stay overnight. *Note:* If you miss the boats and need to stay the night in Mersing, there is a modern, moderately priced 34-

Peninsular Malaysia

THAILAND

Kangar

Langkawi Island

Kota Bharu

George Town
Penang Island

Butterworth

South China Sea

Taiping

MALAYSIA

Kuala Trengganu

Ipoh

Cameron Highlands

Telok Anson

Kuala Lipis

⑧ Chendor Beach
Pancing Caves
⑦ Cherating
⑨
⑥ Kuantan

Fraser's Hill

S. Pahang

⑤ Pekan

Kuala Lumpur
⑪ — ㊶

⑩
Genting Highlands

Klang

NEGRI SEMBILAN

Tioman Island
④

Seremban ㊷
Sri Menanti ㊸
Port Dickson ㊹
Gemas
Segamat

③ **Mersing**

Pengkalan Kempas ㊺
Malacca ㊻

Keluang

Strait of Malacca

Dumai

Johore Bahru ① **Desaru**
②

SINGAPORE ★ *Strait*
Singapore **Batam**
Bintan

S U M A T R A

Pakanbaru

INDONESIA

0   100 miles
0   150 km

N

KEY
— Rail Lines

room hotel just outside town (**Merlin Inn,** 1st mile, Endau Rd., tel. 07/791–311). **Tradewinds Charter Service**'s daily shuttle flight to Tioman Island leaves Singapore's Seletar Airport at 10:45 AM (cost M$90). You can also reach Tioman by a 200-passenger, twin-hulled ferry, the *Island Pearl,* making the four-hour run between March and October and operated by the Tioman Island Resort Office. Meals and bar service are available. Reservations and information may be obtained in Singapore at #11–09 Orchard Towers, 400 Orchard Rd., tel. 733–5488, and tickets purchased at Finger Pier, Singapore, where the catamaran departs at 7:40 AM.

❹ Tioman Island was Bali Hai in the movie *South Pacific.* Enough said? This lush tropical island hasn't changed much since then, except for the tourists, and it is large enough to absorb them. Sunbathe on the sandy coves, swim in the clear waters, try the 18-hole golf course, or take walks through the jungle-clad hills (some as high as 1,037 meters, or 3,400 feet). Plenty of water sports are available; brightly colored fish and coral make for enjoyable snorkeling. Boats and bicycles—your transportation around the island—are available for rent from the Tioman Island Resort Hotel, which is currently being expanded.

Travel north from Mersing via the shore route, which passes a number of traditional kampongs. These small villages of wood houses, sometimes built on stilts, are good places to stop for light refreshment on the 177-kilometer (110-mile) trip to Kuantan. The fishing villages are especially colorful.

❺ The only major town en route is **Pekan,** 70 kilometers (43 miles) south of Kuantan, the home of the sultan. You can see his modern palace, with its manicured lawns and, of course, its polo field, but only from outside the gates. Don't bypass this town, as the signposts invite; drive through the center instead. Built on the western shore of a river, it is delightfully old-fashioned, with two-story shophouses lining the main street. At the **Silk Weaving Centre** at Pulau Keladi, traditional Pahang silk is woven into intricate designs.

Kuantan Now the major beach resort on Malaysia's east coast, **Kuantan**
❻ offers numerous small hotels and resorts, such as the Hyatt. The first hotel area begins just north of the city at the crescent-shaped sandy bay of Telak Champedak. To get there, take Jalan Telok Sisek, just past the Hotel Suraya—you'll see signs for the Merlin Inn Resort. This small community consists of several hotels (including the Hyatt Kuantan), four or five restaurants and bars, discos, and a small but attractive curving beach. Sunbathers come for the company of other vacationers rather than solitude. If you prefer privacy, continue a few miles north. Here, smaller hotels dot a long stretch of virtually untrodden sands.

Cherating Another half hour north is the peaceful village of **Cherating,**
❼ which has become a rustic haven of beachcombing along miles of white, clean beaches, fanned by gentle breezes through the coconut trees. Club Med has staked its claim on a fine stretch of beach here, responding to the spirit of the place with its Malay-style bungalows built on stilts.

Turtle-watching—one of the east coast's most popular attractions—begins at Cherating and continues north (the best view-
❽ ing place is said to be **Chendor Beach,** an hour north of Kuantan). Most nights between May and September (peak

month is August), enormous leatherback turtles slowly make their way ashore to lay as many as 200 eggs each. Signs at the hotels will tell when and where to go, and the crowds do gather to watch as the 1,000-pound turtles laboriously dig their "nests" before settling down to their real work.

Several excursions inland to the jungled hills and small Malay kampongs can be arranged out of Kuantan. One is to the **❾ Pancing Caves** (or, more correctly, **Gua Charah**), 25 kilometers (15 miles) to the west. First you pass rubber and oil-palm plantations. To reach the caves you must climb 220 steps. Buddhists still live here, and there are many altars. Don't miss the cave with the reclining Buddha some 9 meters (30 feet) long, carved by a Thai Buddhist monk who devoted his life to the task.

Should you have the time, the premier resort on the east coast of Malaysia is 100-room **Tanjong Jara Beach Hotel** (13 km, or 8 mi, off Jalan Dungun, Dungun, Terengganu, tel. 09/841–801), 60 kilometers (37 miles) south of Kuala Terengganu. Built on stilts with magnificent woodwork, the Malaysian building blends into the landscaped tropical gardens and, while having the ambience of the palatial 19th century, offers all the amenities of the 20th.

To the West Coast From Kuantan to Kuala Lumpur, it is an easy four-hour drive across central Malaysia over thickly forested hills. As you near the capital, the views over the mountains become more dramat**❿** ic. You may want to make a 20-minute detour to **Genting Highlands,** a 1,711-meter-high (5,614-foot-high) hill resort popular with Southeast Asians. It is very much a family resort, with an artificial lake full of paddleboats, an amusement park for the young, and a gambling casino—the only one in Malaysia—for adults. (For information, contact Genting Highlands Tours and Promotions, 9th floor, Wisma Genting, Jalan Sultan Ismail, 50250 Kuala Lumpur, tel. 03/261–3833.) While the views from Genting Highlands are dramatic and the air is a cool contrast to the humidity and heat of the lowlands, the resort is modern and probably not what the overseas visitor has come to Asia to see. It's a steep descent into Kuala Lumpur. Should you wish to visit from Kuala Lumpur, the hour's journey by shared taxi costs M$20. If, however, you wish to enjoy the cool climates of a hill station, consider going to the **Cameron Highlands,** a two-hour drive north of Kuala Lumpur. Stay at **Ye Olde Smokehouse** (Tanah Rata, Cameron Highlands, tel. 05/941–214) for the nostalgic atmosphere of this colonial-built hill station and the many marked hiking trails. If you require modern luxury, there's a new condo-hotel complex nearby.

Kuala Lumpur The following walking tour of **Kuala Lumpur** covers the area **⓫** known as the Golden Triangle—from the National Museum to the Pertama Complex to Sungei Wang Plaza to Pudu and back to the Dewan Bandaraya. The walk can be completed in a couple of hours, but it will take much longer to explore and experience the activities of the city you will encounter. Sightseeing on foot requires a map, comfortable walking shoes, and loose, light clothing (cotton breathes and keeps you cooler than synthetics). When you need maps, brochures, or help in figuring out how to get somewhere, the guides at the Kuala Lumpur Visitors' Centre will be ready to help, and the center is the best place to orient yourself to the city's layout. The low cost of taxis—M$.70 for the first 1.6 kilometers or M$6 an hour, plus 20%

surcharge for air-conditioned cabs—makes them the best way to hop between sites.

Numbers in the margin correspond to points of interest on the Kuala Lumpur map. Note: The Friday prayer break usually lasts from 12:15 to 2:45.

⑫ The national museum, **Muzim Negara,** is just a short walk from the Visitors' Centre. Behind the museum, in the scenic **Lake Gardens** park, you can find city dwellers relaxing and picnicking. Boating on the lake is popular (M$4 for an hour's boat rental), and at night Lake Gardens becomes a lover's lane. In the northern portion of the area stands the **National Monument,** a bronze sculpture dedicated to the nation's war dead. Nearby is the modern **Parliament** complex, with its 18-story office tower. When Parliament is in session, visitors can go into the gallery, provided they make arrangements in advance (inquire at the Visitors' Centre) and are properly attired.

A number of exhibits are located behind Muzim Negara. The transportation shed houses an example of every form of transport in the country. You'll also see a model tin dredge, which represents one of Malaysia's main industries. Don't miss the Malay-style house, Istana Satu ("first palace").

The museum building itself is modeled after an old-style Malay village house, enlarged to institutional size; the two mosaic murals on its facade depict significant elements in the country's history and culture. The cultural gallery, to the left as you enter, emphasizes traditional Malay folk culture. At the far end of the gallery, a model Nonya home shows classical Chinese furniture, exquisite antique carved canopy beds, and a table and chair set with inlaid pearl.

Across the lobby, the historical gallery has more models of regional-style homes; a collection of ceramic pottery, gold and silver items, and other artifacts; and traditional costumes (now seen only at festivals or on hotel doormen). Exhibits trace the stages of British colonization from the old East India Company in the late 18th century to its withdrawal in the mid-20th century. Photos and text outline the Japanese occupation during World War II and Malaysia's move toward federation status in 1948 and independence in 1957.

The natural history exhibit upstairs shows the country's indigenous animals. The other upstairs gallery, more like a trade show, deals with the national obsession with sports and recreation. *Jln. Damansara, tel. 03/238-1067. Admission free. Open daily 9–6 (except during Friday prayers, 12:15–2:45).*

⑬ The four-story building next door was the old Majestic Hotel until it was converted into the **National Art Gallery** in 1984. The large permanent collection suggests the country's pluralistic style and its palette, its vistas, and its issues of concern. One recognizes quickly that the local artists reflect a refined sensibility while working in contemporary modes: conceptual pieces, pop images, bold sculptures, humorous graphics, landscapes, and realism. *Jln. Hishamuddin, tel. 03/230-0157. Admission free. Open daily 10–6 (except during Friday prayers).*

⑭ The imposing Moorish structures next door and across the street are the **main railway station** (tel. 03/274-7435) and the administrative offices of **KTM** (Kereta-api Tanah Melayu), the national rail system. Built early in this century, the Islam-

176

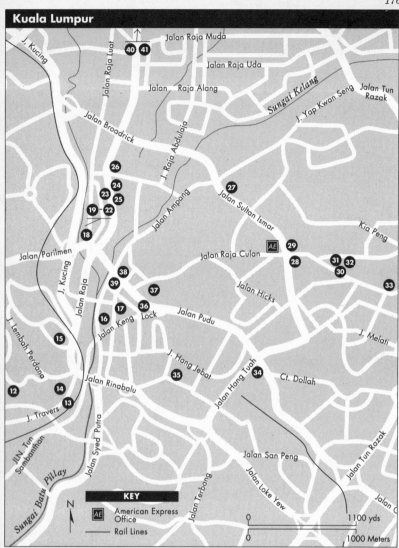

Kuala Lumpur

Anak Ku, **29**
Bank Bumiputra, **38**
Batik Malaysia
Berhad, **39**
Batu Caves, **40**
Central Market, **17**
Coliseum Theatre, **23**
Concorde Hotel, **27**
Crafts Museum, **31**
Fu Kwee Siang, **33**
International Crafts
Museum, **32**

Karyaneka Handicraft
Centre, **30**
Kompleks
Dayabumi, **16**
Main railway
station, **14**
Masjid India, **22**
Masjid Jamek
Bandaraya, **21**
Maybank Building, **37**
Mun Loong
department store, **24**

Muzim Negara, **12**
National Art
Gallery, **13**
National Mosque, **15**
Pertama Kompleks, **26**
Pudu Prison, **34**
Puduraya, **36**
St. Mary's Anglican
Church, **20**
Selangor Club, **18**
Selangor Pewter
Factory, **41**

Selangor Pewter
showroom, **25**
Shahzan Tower, **28**
Stadium Negara, **35**
Sultan Abdul Samad
Building, **19**

ic-influenced buildings were designed by a British architect to reflect the Ottoman and Mogul glory of the 13th and 14th centuries. The KTM building blends Gothic and Greek designs and features the wide verandas common in tropical climates.

⑮ Up Jalan Sultan Hishamuddin is the **National Mosque,** or Masjid Negara. Its contemporary architecture features a 240-foot minaret spire, convoluted purple roof, and geometric grillwork. The main dome is designed as an 18-pointed star, representing the 13 states in Malaysia and the Five Pillars of Islam. The entrance is on the left, up Jalan Lembah Perdana. The mosque complex houses a meeting hall, ceremonial rooms, offices, a library, and a mausoleum, and can accommodate 10,000 worshipers. *Open Sat.–Thurs. 9–6, Fri. 2:45–6.*

On the main road, notice the hibiscus bushes that bloom all year long—the hibiscus is the national flower. At Jalan Cenderasari, walk under the road via the pedestrian walkway to the impressive Dayabumi complex.

⑯ Kompleks Dayabumi, constructed in 1984, has three parts: the main post office building, the gleaming white office tower with its Islamic motif, and the plaza that connects the two. In the **post office,** just around the corner from the main lobby, the tiny **stamp museum,** Galeri Setem, will be opened for viewing on request. A huge fountain stands at the center of the two-level plaza area. From the upper level, you can get a close-up view of the commercial district dominated by banks, with the Bangkok Bank building at the center. Another landmark on the horizon is an Indian Hindu temple, **Sri Mahamariamman.** The ornate structure, with its numerous deities created from tiles, gold, and precious stones, is worth exploring on a side trip.

On the town side of the plaza, cross the pedestrian bridge to the
⑰ Central Market, a lively bazaar in the heart of the city. The renovated art deco building served as the city's produce market until it was converted into a series of stalls and shops in 1986, and today the 50-year-old market, painted apricot and baby blue, serves as the commercial, cultural, and recreational hub of downtown. Some 250 tenants, mostly retail shops and stalls, do business within the two-story, block-long market. This is a great place to sample dishes you have never tried before, whether it's Chinese dim sum or *laksa,* a noodle dish with fish paste. At night, there are cultural performances given outside on the riverside, and the Central Market becomes a popular gathering spot for inexpensive dining. (The small Riverbank Restaurant offers light Continental fare and live jazz.)

You can exit where you came into the market, or you can leave by the door into Leboh Pasar Besar ("big market"). Cross the river again and walk up a block to the corner, where you will see
⑱ the padang (playing field) of the **Selangor Club,** a private club housed in a rambling Tudor-style building. The padang now covers an underground car park for the central business district. A new garden proclaims the area as Merdeka Square, commemorating national independence.

⑲ Built in 1897, the massive **Sultan Abdul Samad Building,** with its Moorish arches, copper domes, and clocktower, is considered the center of the old city. Within it, the Dewan Bandaraya, or state secretariat, houses the judicial department and high courts. Preservationists fought to have the stylish brick building restored in the early 1980s, and it now also accommodates a small crafts museum, a branch of the national handicrafts center, on the corner of Jalan Tun Perak.

Three major religious centers surround the Samad Building. ❷⓿ Near the entrance to the Selangor Club is the pristine little **St. Mary's Anglican Church,** with its red-tile roof and manicured grounds. Services are now held in Tamil as well as in English.

❷① Behind the building, the **Masjid Jamek Bandaraya** is situated on a point where the Klang and Gombak rivers flow together. The two minarets of this traditional-style mosque are only slightly taller than the coconut palm trees on the grounds.

❷② The third site is **Masjid India,** an Indian Muslim mosque near the Gombak River a half block off both Jalan Tun Perak and Jalan Tuanku Abdul Rahman. A modern structure, this mosque is the linchpin of the Little India district, where the attractions include street vendors who sell the local concoctions *ubat* (medicine) and *jamu* (cosmetics).

As you head north up Jalan Tuanku Abdul Rahman (Batu Road), notice the few remaining turn-of-the-century, two-story shophouses with their decorative flourishes along the top near the roofline, located adjacent to high-rise sliver buildings. Walking here is exciting because the streets are often crowded, and there are lots of steps to negotiate and lots of things to look at in the shops. But be careful: The pavement is often uneven, broken, and treacherous.

❷③ At the **Coliseum Theatre,** a cinema showcasing the Malaysian and Indonesian film industries, there are *tandas* (public toilets) in the parking lot near the traffic signal. You'll also see a number of fast-food outlets of American-based chains.

Across the road, on Jalan Bunus, lots of little shops and vendors ❷④ compete with the modern and bustling **Mun Loong department store,** which carries such international goods as polyester dress shirts and French perfumes. A convenient bank of telephones is located just outside the Mun Loong entrance.

Time Out The **Coliseum Cafe** (No. 100, tel. 03/292–6270), built in 1921, is known for serving the best steak in town. Among the regulars are a number of journalists, including the local columnist Johan and a cartoonist nicknamed Lat; when the mood becomes boisterous, just before the 10 AM closing, you can bet Lat is leading the singing.

Saturday nights this street is closed off for a *pasar malam,* a night market that begins at about 6 and ends at about 11. Here you'll find many goods, from bootleg tapes of the latest music to homemade sweets.

Walking north on Batu Road, keep in mind that midnight the street life changes dramatically, as *pondans* (transvestites) chat up men who cruise by in cars. In the daytime, shopping families fill the streets in front of the Globe Silk Store, while a troupe of blind musicians with bongo drums and electric piano entertains passersby.

Turn off Batu Road, up Jalan Bunus Enam, and have a look at the scarfs in the stalls. Just past the alley on the corner, the open-air **Restoran Lebat** is where folks on their way to work pause for a breakfast of *roti canai,* a fried bread dipped in curry sauce.

Time Out Across the street is the **Restoran Alisan,** which is ringed by hawkers' stalls. Street food is a main event in Malaysia, and locals share tables when it's crowded. You don't need to know what the dishes are; look at what others are eating, and if it looks good, point and order. One favorite is the *popiah,* a soft spring roll filled with vegetables. The *meehom* or *kweh teow* (grilled fish and fried noodles) are especially tasty and cheap. The shop owner sells only drinks and dessert, so when you order two or three different dishes, you have to pay each provider. Be cautious with the *nasi kandar,* a local favorite, for the chilies rule the spicy prawns and fish-head curry.

Farther along Batu Road, look in at the **Peiping Lace Shop** (No. 217), which features Chinese linens, lace, jewelry, and ceramics. **China Arts** next door is a branch of Peiping Lace that sells furniture; the rambling shop is filled with decorative coromandel screens, carved writing desks, teak and camphor chests, and antique vases.

㉕ The **Selangor Pewter showroom** (No. 231) has a full range of pewter products, which have been made in Malaysia for more than 100 years. Most designs are simple and of world-class quality; a few items are pure kitsch. In the back of the shop you can see a demonstration of the process of pewter making: the casting, soldering, and polishing.

At the meeting of Jalan Dang Wangi and Jalan Tuanku Abdul Rahman, the Odeon Theatre occupies one corner and the huge **㉖** **Pertama Kompleks** another.

Turn left onto Jalan Ampang, where the auto dealership shows various models of the Proton Saga. Turn right at the next corner and you'll see the **Concorde Hotel** (formerly the Merlin). **㉗** The Concorde's coffee shop and lobby lounge are popular meeting spots, and in front of the hotel, in the early morning hours, a makeshift stand hawks Malaysia's favorite breakfast dish, *nasi lemak*—a bundle of rice with salt fish, curry chicken, peanuts, slices of cucumber, and boiled egg—for one ringgit.

The next stretch of Kuala Lumpur's "gold coast," with its highrise luxury hotels and modern skyscraper offices, argues convincingly that Malaysia is a nation emerging into modernity.

Time Out At the **Shangri-La** hotel (11 Jalan Sultan Ismail, tel. 03/232-2388), the garden terrace with its fountain and its tropical landscaping is a pleasant place to enjoy a cup of tea and read a newspaper. On the other side of the main lobby, the **Gourmet Corner** deli has cold cuts, pastries, and chocolates.

Caution: Travelers should watch their handbags and shoulder bags in this district. Snatch thieves on motorcycles are known to ride up alongside strollers, snatch their goods, and buzz off. Police advise walkers to carry bags under the arm, on the side away from the street, to forestall such incidents.

At the corner of Jalan Sultan Ismail and Raja Chulan, the new **㉘** star in the firmament is the **Shahzan Tower,** a 40-story luxury apartment building with a distinctive step design.

Turn right on Jalan Raja Chulan. In the next block you'll see a row of outdoor food stalls along Jalan Kia Peng, just behind the Hilton Hotel in the car park. Locals insist that this hawker **㉙** area, **Anak Ku,** is among the best in the city. First-time visitors to Asia might be alarmed at the standards of cleanliness. As a general rule, food handlers are inspected by health enforcement officers, but it's best to patronize popular places: Consumers everywhere tend to boycott stalls that have a reputation for poor hygiene. Because Muslims do not eat pork, the word "ham" is offensive, so Malaysians call hamburgers simply "burgers" or sometimes "beef burgers."

30 The **Karyaneka Handicraft Centre** on Jalan Raja Chulan is a campus of museums and specialty shops that sell regional arts and crafts. On entering, you'll notice that each of the 13 little houses is labeled with the name of a Malaysian state. Inside, as might be expected, goods from that area are on display and demonstrations are regularly conducted by local artisans. The main building of the center, shaped like a traditional Malay house, stocks goods from the entire country.

Behind the center, across a little stream, are two small muse-
31 ums. The **Crafts Museum** shows changing exhibits of the work
32 of Malaysian artisans. The **International Crafts Museum** nearby has a modest collection of work from other parts of the world, especially Asia, Africa, and Europe. The **botanical gardens** that border the little stream offer a quiet spot to rest and reflect.

As you leave the center, turn left and head for the next block, which is Jalan Bukit Bintang, and then turn right. A couple of blocks along on the left you'll find the **Kuala Lumpur Shopping Centre** and, across the street, the new **Regent Hotel** (tel. 03/242–5588), excellent for afternoon tea served among a cavalcade of flowers by Kuala Lumpur's most beautiful waitresses.

The next intersection, perhaps the busiest in the city, requires caution; traffic moves in every direction, so you should take care to cross with the lights. Two shopping complexes here, the **Bukit Bintang Plaza** in front and the **Sungai Wang Centre** behind it, form one of the largest shopping areas in the city. Among the tenants are fast-food restaurants, boutiques, bookshops, and the Metrojaya and Parkson department stores, possibly the city's finest.

Outside, just across from the taxi stand, are racks of a strange green produce that more resembles a porcupine than a fruit. The Malaysian durian, the "king of fruits," grows in the jungle and is prized highly by city dwellers. But be prepared: The smell of a durian is not sweet, even though its taste is.

Jalan Bukit Bintang is a jumble of modest hotels, goldsmiths
33 and other shops, and finance companies. **Fu Kwee Siang** specializes in dried and minced pork and stocks Asian dried fruits, cookies, and candies, all displayed decoratively in huge glass jars with red plastic tops. Salesgirls will sell you small amounts so that you can sample the dried nutmeg, the mango, or—for the more adventurous—the roast cuttlefish and the dried pork floss. This taste experience should not be missed.

Head east up Jalan Pudu one block, past the cheap hotels and motorcycle repair shops. On the corner at Jalan Imbi stands the
34 **Pudu Prison** with its beautifully painted tropical landscape wall—topped with barbed wire. The mural, painted by inmates, is the longest in the world, according to the *Guinness Book of World Records*. You'll also note a warning that death is

the mandatory sentence for drug trafficking in Malaysia, and the news reports will confirm that the law is enforced.

Turn around and head back down Jalan Pudu. This road passes a series of private hospitals and the Selangor Chinese Recreation Club, with its modest Tudor-style clubhouse and playing
㉟ field. At Jalan Pudu Lama you can see the dome of **Stadium Negara,** an indoor arena said to be the largest such structure in Southeast Asia. The building is used for concerts, conventions, and trade fairs as well as sports events. On the sidewalk near the Voon Radio shop a Chinese fortune teller works from a little table. Since he speaks only Chinese, you may have to bring along an interpreter if you want a reading.

㊱ The **Puduraya** bus station has all the rough-and-tumble of a big-city bus station, with touts calling out the names of towns and offering express bus and taxi service to those destinations. The area has a severe litter problem; the government has been imposing fines on offenders, but habits are slow to change.

㊲ On the imposing hill just ahead is the new **Maybank Building,** designed to resemble the handle of a *kris* (a Malay knife). Up the escalators, you can enter and walk around the soaring five-story bank lobby during banking hours. Of special interest is the **Numismatic Museum** in 1 South East, which exhibits Malaysian bills and coins from the past, offers information on the nation's major commodities, and adjoins a gallery that shows contemporary art. *Tel. 03/280–8833, ext. 2023. Museum admission free. Open daily 10–6.*

Beyond Leboh Ampang you'll come again to the Klang River.
㊳ To your right is the **Bank Bumiputra,** built in the shape of a kampong house, with its tower next door. Trading corporations that deal in natural rubber are located in this area.

On the other side of Jalan Tun Perak you'll see Wisma Batik,
㊴ with the **Batik Malaysia Berhad** (BMB) situated on the first and second floors. This shop has a wide selection of batik fabrics, shirts, dresses, and handicrafts upstairs. Hock Lee's pastry shop has freshly cut orchids for sale; the tiny, delicate flowers are as common here as marigolds are in the United States. At the next intersection the loop of our tour is completed.

㊵ About 11 kilometers (7 miles) due north of the city are the **Batu Caves,** vast caverns in a limestone outcrop. The caves are approached by a flight of 272 steps, but the steep climb is worthwhile. A wide path with an iron railing leads through the recesses of the cavern. Stalagmites, such as the fancifully named Onyx Rock, have been tinted over the years by internal chemical processes and now can be viewed in all their glory. It is here, during January or February, that the spectacular but gory Thaipusam festival (*see* Festivals and Seasonal Events in Chapter 1) takes place in its most elaborate form. In the main cave is a Hindu Temple dedicated to Lord Subramaniam. Behind the Dark Cave lies a third cave called the Art Gallery, displaying colorful and elaborate sculptures of figures from Hindu mythology. The caves are staggering in their beauty and immensity: The Dark Cave is 366 meters (1,200 feet) long and reaches a height of 122 meters (400 feet). To reach them, take a taxi (about M$25) or a local bus from Pudu Raya Bus Terminal.

A number of local companies offer sightseeing tours of Kuala Lumpur and excursions into the nearby countryside. The **Tour-**

ist **Development Corporation** (26th floor, Menara Dato Onn, Putra World Trade Centre, Jalan Tun Ismail, tel. 03/293–5188) has a list of licensed tour operators, and brochures are available in hotel lobbies and at travel agencies.

④ One very popular excursion 5 miles to the northeast of Kuala Lumpur is the **Selangor Pewter Factory,** the world's largest. In its showroom you can see how pewter is made. A duty-free shop sells the finished products.

Negri Sembilan *Numbers in the margin correspond to points of interest on the Peninsular Malaysia map.*

It is a journey, mostly by express road, of 155 kilometers (97 miles) from KL south to Malacca, by either car, bus, or shared taxi. On the way, you'll pass through an area called **Negri Sembilan** ("Nine States"). Negri Sembilan is unique in Malaysia, for it's an internal union of ancient states, and it is a matriarchy—tribal lines descend from women rather than from men.

④ **Seremban,** its capital, is a pleasant city with attractive botanical gardens. An old Malay palace has been moved to the gardens and serves as a museum; there also is a reconstructed Malay house, an example of early Minangkabau (or Sumatran) architecture. The people of this area are related to the inhabitants of west Sumatra; homes in both places have the same buffalo-horn-shape peaked roofs.

④ At **Sri Menanti,** a few miles west of Seremban, is the sultan's headquarters, where both a new and an old *istana* (palace), the latter in Sumatran style, as well as an ancient royal burial ground may be visited. The drive to Sri Menanti takes you through the hill country, where bougainvillea and hibiscus

④ abound. **Port Dickson,** on the coast, is a seaside resort area, where casuarina trees line the shore. Near the Malacca border,

④ south of Port Dickson, is **Pengkalan Kempas.** Here are three famous stones, inscribed in cuneiform, that remain an archaeological mystery, and the **tomb of Sheik Ahmad,** dated 1467.

Malacca **Malacca,** once the most important trading port in Southeast

④ Asia, is now a relatively sleepy backwater. Created as the capital of a Malay sultanate, it was captured in 1511 by the Portuguese, who built fortifications and held it until 1641, when the Dutch invaded and took possession. The British took over in Victorian times and remained in control until Malay independence was declared in 1957. In this, Malaysia's most historic town, you'll find impressive buildings and ruins dating from all these periods of colonial rule. Coming direct from Kuala Lumpur, the fare by shared taxi is M$13. From Johore Bahru the fare is M$17. Should you need a guide, contact Robert Tan Sin Nyen (256-D Jln. Parameswara, Malacca, tel. 06/244857).

One of the oldest of Malacca's Portuguese ruins, dating from 1521, is **St. Paul's Church,** atop Residency Hill. The statue at the summit commemorates St. Francis Xavier, who was buried here before being moved to his permanent resting spot in Goa, India, where he began his missionary career. The **Church of St. Peter**—built in 1710 and now the church of the Portuguese Mission under the jurisdiction of the bishop of Macau—is interesting for its mix of Occidental and Oriental architecture. It is about a half mile east of the city center, on Jalan Bendahare. The only surviving part of the Portuguese fortress **A Famosa** is the Porta de Santiago entrance gate, which has become the symbol of the state of Malacca. Near the gate, the **Muzium**

Budaya, a museum with collections on Muslim culture and royalty is housed in a re-creation of a traditional wood palace.

The Dutch influence in Malacca is more prevalent. **Christ Church** was built in 1753 of salmon-pink bricks brought from Zeeland (Netherlands) and faced in red laterite. Across the street is the **Stadthuys,** the oldest remaining Dutch architecture in the Orient. This complex of buildings was erected between 1641 and 1660 and used until recently for government offices. It is being restored and converted into a museum. The Stadthuys is good and solid, in true Dutch style: Note the thick masonry walls, the heavy hardwood doors, and the windows with wrought-iron hinges.

Malacca's history, of course, predates the arrival of the Western colonialists. Six centuries ago, a Ming emperor's envoy from China set up the first trade arrangements in this ancient Malay capital; a daughter of the emperor was sent to Malacca as wife to Sultan Mansor Shah. She and her 500 ladies-in-waiting set up housekeeping on **Bukit China** (Chinese Hill). The early Chinese traders and notables who lived and died in Malacca were buried on this hill, and their 17,000 graves remain, making Bukit China the largest Chinese cemetery outside China.

The **Chinese quarter**—narrow streets lined with traditional shophouses, ancient temples, and clan houses (note the interesting carved doors)—reflects the long Chinese presence. **Cheng Hoon Teng Temple** is one of the city's oldest Chinese temples. You'll recognize it by its ceremonial masts, which tower over roofs of the surrounding old houses, and by the porcelain and glass animals and flowers that decorate its eaves. Built in the Nanking style, the temple embraces three doctrines: Buddhist, Taoist, and Confucian. You can tell the monks apart by their robes; the Taoists expose their right shoulder. On your way out, you can buy sandalwood (the scent that permeates the temple) as well as papier-mâché houses and cars and symbolic money ("hell money"), used to burn as offerings during funeral ceremonies.

Close by on Temple Street are the papier-mâché doll makers, who fashion legendary figures from Chinese mythology. Wander on, turning right onto Jalan Hang Lekiu and right again onto Jalan Hang Jelat, and you'll find good pork satay at No. 83 and several coffee shops selling wonderful noodles.

From Jalan Hang Jebat take a left onto Jalan Kubu, then another left onto Jalan Tun Tan Cheng Lock. This street was once called "Millionaires Row" for its glorious mansions, built by the Dutch and then taken over by wealthy Babas in the 19th century.

Before leaving Malacca, stop off at the **Sultan's Well,** at the foot of Bukit China. Tossing a coin into the well—a custom that dates to the founding of Malacca by Raja Iskandar Shah in the 14th century—is said to ensure your return to Malacca.

The ferry from Malacca to **Dumai** on Sumatra (Indonesia) takes four hours and departs (usually) Thursday at 10 AM. You'll need a visa to enter Indonesia. You can also spend the day picnicking on the little tropical isle of **Pulau Besar,** 4.8 kilometers (3 miles) off the mainland in the Straits of Malacca. A boat service from Umbai Jetty costs M$4 per person; or you can charter a boat for around M$35.

Those returning to Singapore might first pay homage to the man who made the island republic possible. **Tranquerah Mosque,** a 150-year-old building of Sumatran design, is the tomb of the Sultan of Johore who signed over Singapore to Raffles in 1819.

The 245-kilometer (153-mile) journey back to Singapore is along a crowded road and takes at least four hours. Malacca does not have a railway station, but there are frequent air-conditioned buses to Johore Bahru and Singapore (cost: M$11).

Dining

The center for dining in Malaysia is its capital city. Though it isn't by the sea, centrally located Kuala Lumpur still reaps its benefits, and seafood washed down with ice-cold beer is the rage with city folk. Thai as well as Japanese food has made its mark. Nonya food (the cuisine of the Straits-born Chinese), which is a combination of Malay, Chinese, and Thai, is gaining in popularity; the cooking methods are traditional and laborious, but fine cuisine is the reward.

Three styles of Indian cooking can be found in KL—southern Indian, Mughal, and Indian Muslim, the last a blend of southern Indian and Malay. Eating Indian rice and curry with your hands on a banana leaf is an experience to be savored.

Continental-style dining has found favor with an increasingly affluent city population. Such restaurants are mostly found in the four- or five-star hotels. There are also places such as the Coliseum for traditional steaks with a sizzle.

Venture out of KL into Petaling Jaya, 12 kilometers (7 miles) to the southwest (20 minutes by cab), for some of the finest restaurants for Chinese and other cuisines. Eating out in both Kuala Lumpur and Petaling Jaya is an informal affair. Jackets and ties are hardly worn, except perhaps in a formal restaurant at a five-star hotel.

Credit cards are accepted in most but not all restaurants, which are usually open for lunch from 11:30 AM to 2:30 PM and for dinner from 6:30 to 11, depending on business. Seafood restaurants are usually open from 5 PM to 3 AM.

In the more expensive restaurants, a service charge of 10% and a sales tax of 5% are added to the bill. Tipping is not necessary and is entirely up to you.

Highly recommended restaurants are indicated by a star ★.

Category	Cost*
Very Expensive	over M$100 (US$40)
Expensive	M$60–M$100 (US$24–US$60)
Moderate	M$30–M$60 (US$12–US$24)
Inexpensive	under M$30 (US$12)

per person, without tax, service, or drinks

Johore Bahru   **Jaws 5.** Overlooking the straits between Malaysia and Singa-
Moderate   pore, this casual restaurant offers a range of seafood and Cantonese dishes. Lunchtime is quiet, but at night the place takes

on a party atmosphere. Try for a table on the veranda—it's quieter there, and the views over the water are splendid. *Jalan Skudar, tel. 07/236–062. Dress: casual. No reservations. No credit cards.*

Kuala Lumpur
Expensive
★

Lai Ching Yuen. Master chef Choi Wai Ki came from Hong Kong to establish Kuala Lumpur's foremost Cantonese restaurant. The extensive menu draws on shark's fin, bird's nest, abalone, pigeon, chicken, and duck, as well as barbecue specialties; the drunken prawns are superb. The dining room is designed as two Chinese pavilions, with illuminated glass etchings, modern Chinese art, silver panels, a Burmese teak ceiling, and silver-and-jade table settings creating an elegant ambience. Traditional music on Malay instruments accompanies dinner. *The Regent, 126 Jln. Bukit Bintang, tel. 03/241–8000. Reservations suggested. Jacket and tie required. AE, DC, MC, V.*

Moderate
★

Coliseum Cafe. The aroma of countless sizzling steaks—the house specialty—clings to the walls of this old café, established before World War II. Enter through the swing door and hang your jacket and hat on the antique coat hanger. A nostalgic British colonial ambience prevails. The waiters still dress in starched white jackets, though the latter are a bit frayed at the seams. Steaks are served with brussels sprouts, chips, and salad. Crab baked with cheese is another favorite. On Sunday the curry tiffin lunch is not to be missed. *98 Jalan Tuanku Abdul Rahman, tel. 03/292–6270. Dress: informal. Reservations advised. No credit cards.*

Restoran Makanan Laut Selayang. Dine under the stars on a clear night or inside the zinc-roofed building in an air-conditioned room that seats 30 at three tables. The black chicken soup steamed in a coconut is quite wonderful. Also good are the deep-fried soft-shell crabs or the prawns fried with butter, milk, and chili. For those into exotica, there are steamed river frogs and soups of squirrel, pigeon, or turtle. For a taste of luxury, try the *fatt thieu cheong* ("monk jumps over the wall"), a soup of shark's fin, sea cucumber, dried scallops, mushrooms, and herbs; this must be ordered in advance. *Lot 11, 7½-mile Selayang, tel. 03/627–7015. Dress: informal. AE, V.*

★

Yazmin. It's housed in a sparkling white colonial bungalow on shady, sprawling grounds. A cozy kampong-style terrace extension of dark timber and attap at the side offers a buffet lunch and dinner to guests who can also watch traditional Malay dances at night. Within the house guests dine in a large, airy hall upstairs, whose windows overlook a wonderful bamboo grove at the front. Evocative black-and-white pictures taken by a sultan grace the walls. Its hostess and owner is Raja Yazmin, a Malay princess. Especially recommended are the *rendang tok* (tender beef chunks simmered in spices and coconut), *roti canai* (unleavened bread), and *rendang pedas udang* (prawns cooked in coconut cream, chili, lemon grass, and turmeric leaves). There is a high tea daily and a Sunday brunch. *No. 6 Jalan Kia Peng, tel. 03/241–5655. Dress: informal. Reservations advised. AE, DC, MC, V. Closed for 4 days at the end of Ramadan.*

Inexpensive

Kedai Makanan Yut Kee. This 60-year-old family-run coffee shop–restaurant is one of the few that have not been pulled down in the name of progress. Large and airy but rather noisy from the city traffic, the place boasts marble-top tables and old customers who insist on their favorite seats. Recommended are *roti babi* (a sandwich with pork filling dipped in egg and deep fried) and *asam* prawns, hot, sour, and fragrant with spices. The local black coffee is the best around, and the kaya Swiss roll makes a fine dessert. Open 7 AM–6 PM. *35 Jalan Dang Wangi, tel. 03/298–8108. Dress: informal. No reservations. No credit cards. Closed Mon.*

Kuantan
Expensive
Hugo's. In a soft candlelit setting, with rattan chairs, taupe linens, and sparkling crystal and silver, the new French cuisine is well prepared and attentively served. *Hyatt Kuantan, Telok Chempedak, tel. 09/525–211. Jacket and tie suggested. Reservations suggested. AE, DC, MC, V.*

Inexpensive
Segara. A buffet of Oriental and European specialties is served here in an open, airy atmosphere with simple light-wood tables and cane chairs. A wall of windows overlooks the beach. *Ramada Hotel, 152 Sungai Karang, tel. 09/587–544. Dress: casual. No reservations. AE, DC, MC, V.*

Lodging

The following is a sampling of the hotels available along the route of this excursion. (*Note:* "Asian toilets" refers to the primitive type with no seat.)

Highly recommended hotels are indicated by a star ★.

Category	Cost*
Very Expensive	over M$300 (US$120)
Expensive	M$220–M$300 (US$88–US$120)
Moderate	M$150–M$220 (US$60–US$88)
Inexpensive	M$75–M$150 (US$30–US$60)
Budget	under M$75 (US$30)

**All prices are for a standard double room with bath, excluding 10% service charge and 5% government tax.*

Cherating
Very Expensive
Club Med Cherating. This traditional Malaysian-style Club Med village is set on its own bay, surrounded by 200 acres of parkland. Accommodation is in twin-bedded bungalows with air-conditioning and showers. As with all Club Meds, the package is inclusive, with full sporting facilities, arts-and-crafts workshops, and buffet-style dining. The resort has just been refurbished and weatherproofed for year-round activity. *26080 Kuantan, tel. 09/591–131 or 800/258–2633, fax 03/503–624. 300 rooms. Facilities: 6 floodlit tennis courts, 3 squash courts, Hobie Cats, Caravels, Windsurfers, outdoor pool, archery, yoga, bodybuilding and fitness room, aerobics, boutique, restaurants (Malaysian, European, Chinese, Japanese, Indian cuisine), Mini Club (for children 4–9), Kid's Club (children 10 and 11).*

Moderate
Cherating Holiday Villa. With close connections to the Holiday Inn in Kuala Lumpur, this hotel hosts many tourist groups from the capital. A spot of paint and other refurbishing would be nice, but the atmosphere is jovial and hospitable. The focus of attention is the pool by day and the café-type restaurant at night. Since the hotel is not in the town but off by itself, a car is essential. Motellike guest rooms, which overlook the swim-

ming pool, are air-conditioned and have color TV, tea- and coffee-making facilities, and refrigerators. *Lot 1303, Mukim Sungei Karang, Cherating, 26080 Kuantan, tel. 09/508–900 (in KL, 03/243–4623), fax 09/507–078. 94 rooms. Facilities: restaurant (Continental), tennis court, squash court, outdoor pool, gym. AE.*

Budget **Cherating Beach Mini-Hotel.** The reason for staying in Cherating is to be a beachcomber, and this small hotel allows that. The rooms are small and sparsely furnished, but the beach is at the front door. The staff are wonderfully low-key and friendly, and the restaurant does its best to cook up European food (though it's better at Malay food). *Batu 28 Kg. Cherating, Jalan Kemaman, 26080 Kuantan, Pahang Darul Makmur, tel. 09/592–527. 35 rooms, most with shower and toilet. Facilities: small restaurant. No credit cards.*

Kampung Inn. The inn consists of a number of small A-frame chalets and cottages scattered in a compound 180 meters (200 yards) from a pleasant beach. At the shore is the restaurant, which becomes the social center at night. Take a "budget room" for less than US$4 or splurge on a larger room with an attached bathroom for US$15. *Jalan Cherating, 26080 Kuantan, Pahang Darul Makmur, tel. 09/501–739. 40 rooms, some with shower and Asian toilet. Facilities: small restaurant with barbecue dinners in the evening. No credit cards.*

Desaru
Expensive–
Very Expensive

Desaru View Hotel. At this full-service luxury resort hotel set in seaside gardens, all rooms have balconies and views of the South China Sea, plus air-conditioning, color TV and video, and minibar. A wide variety of facilities—including the longest swimming pool in Malaysia—are available, and pickup in Singapore can be arranged. *Box 71, 81907 Kota Tinggi, Johor, tel. 07/821–221 (in Singapore, tel. 250–3155), fax 07/821–237. 134 rooms. Facilities: 4 restaurants (Malay, Japanese, Chinese seafood, and Western cuisine), pool, tennis courts, 18-hole golf course, minigolf, own stable of horses, equipment for all water sports, bicycles, bar/disco, swim-up bar, games room, shopping arcade, meeting and conference rooms (for 50–100 people), organized tours. AE, MC, V.*

Moderate–
Expensive

Desaru Golf Hotel. This medium-class hotel is family oriented and set in a two-story building with double-peaked roof. Not all guest rooms have sea views. *Tanjung Penawar, Kota Tinggi, tel. 07/838–101. 100 rooms. Facilities: restaurant, casual lounge serving Malay and Western dishes, children's playground, convention facilities for 200–500, 18-hole golf course designed by Robert Trent Jones II, scuba instruction available. AE, MC, V.*

Desaru Holiday Chalets. Standard-, deluxe-, and family-class units with double-peaked roofs are available at this chalet village across from the Desaru Golf Hotel. *Tanjung Penawar, Kota Tinggi, tel. 07/821–211, fax 07/821–937. 35 chalets. Facilities: garden restaurant serving seafood, coffee shop, banquet hall with meeting facilities. AE, MC, V.*

Johore Bahru
Very Expensive

Puteri Pan Pacific. This 500-room hotel opened in 1991 adjacent to the Kotaraya Complex—the city's newest and most prestigious office and shopping mall. The design makes use of round, timber-clad columns and colorful batiks in an open court lobby. Guest rooms, decorated in popular pastel colors, are fully equipped with modern amenities. The Newsroom Café features local and international foods; the Selasih offers traditional Malay cuisine; the Hai Tien Lo presents Cantonese food in elegant surroundings; and the Poolside Terrace has evening barbecues. *Jalan Salim, Box 293, 80000 Johore Bahru, tel. 07/236-922, fax 07/236-622. 500 rooms. Facilities: 5 restaurants, 24-hr room service, outdoor pool with bar, business center, in-room safes, shuttle service to Senai airport, banquet rooms. AE, DC, MC, V.*

Kuala Lumpur
Very Expensive

Carcosa Seri Negara. This is KL's most prestigious address and the priciest—the least expensive room is US$317. Situated on 40 acres of landscaped gardens, the hotel has been converted from the former British Governor's House, with only 16 suites split between the two handsome late-19th-century mansions. The ambience is elegant colonial, with furnishings in Regency style. Every guest gets a personal butler. The sports center, with a small pool, sauna, and gym, is genteel, and dining is a jeweled occasion. *Taman Tasik Perdana, 50480 Kuala Lumpur, tel. 03/230-6766, fax 03/282-7888. 16 suites. Facilities: restaurant, tea salons, outdoor pool, 2 tennis courts, gym, business center, small banquet rooms. AE, DC, MC, V.*

Kuala Lumpur Hilton. KL's first high-rise luxury hotel still maintains its world-class standards for service and quality. Conveniently located in the Golden Triangle, the hotel offers bird's-eye vistas of the city from its 36th-floor Paddock Room. The pastel-decorated rooms have a bay window and sitting area, plus a desk. The Aviary Bar, just off the lobby, is a popular meeting lounge, and the Melaka Grill features gourmet dining. The hotel's cosmopolitan reputation is enhanced by an English pub and Chinese, Japanese, and Korean restaurants. *Box 10577, Jalan Sultan Ismail, 50718 Kuala Lumpur, tel. 03/242-2122, fax 03/244-2157. 581 rooms, including executive suites. Facilities: 24-hr coffee shop, shopping arcade, squash and tennis courts, fitness center, pool, conference facilities, business center. AE, DC, MC, V.*

★ **The Regent.** At KL's leading hotel, a quiet grace permeates the public areas: The marble floors and pillars glisten, and light floods in through the high glass front. Color is everywhere, with flower-filled terraces staggered up from the main lobby. Guest rooms are furnished in soft, elegant hues; the king-size beds come with six fluffy pillows. There is a desk with a two-line telephone in the triangular bay formed by two windows at right angles; the unusual design fills the rooms with light and provides wide-angled views. Bathrooms have huge tubs and separate showers, terry-cloth robes, and an extravagant array of toiletries. The staff is wonderfully attentive. There are three formal restaurants—Chinese, Japanese, and Continental—and a Brasserie. *126 Jln. Bukit Bintang, tel. 03/241-8000 or 800/545-4000, fax 03/242-1441. 454 rooms. Facilities: pool, 3 restaurants, tea lounge, coffee shop, business center, meeting rooms. AE, DC, MC, V.*

Shangri-La. The smartest and plushest hotel in Kuala Lumpur is the Shangri-La, centrally located in the business and shopping district. The atrium lobby sparkles with freshness. Guest rooms are spacious, decorated in warm pastels, and equipped with every convenience. Though the size of the hotel causes a certain impersonality, service is attentive and efficient. *11 Jln. Sultan Ismail, 50250 Kuala Lumpur, tel. 03/232-2388, fax 03/230-1514. 722 rooms. Facilities: Chinese and Continental restaurants, English pub, coffee shop, 24-hr room service, laundry service, outdoor pool with poolside bar, tennis and squash* courts, fitness center, 24-hr business center, function rooms, disco with music videos, travel desk. AE, DC, MC, V.

Moderate **Concorde Hotel.** Once the government-owned Merlin Hotel, this large, centrally located building has been completely—and impersonally—refurbished. But the rooms are bright and fresh and the price is right. Pay more for the concierge floor and you'll enjoy more personalized service, including complimentary breakfasts. The large lobby is often filled with tour groups. *2 Jln. Sultan Ismail, 50250 Kuala Lumpur, tel. 03/ 244–2200, fax 03/244–1628. 600 rooms, including suites and 3 concierge floors. Facilities: 3 restaurants (Malay, Continental, Chinese), coffee shop, pool, fitness center, car park. AE, DC, MC, V.*

Holiday Inn City Centre. Located on the banks of the Gombak River, a good 10-minute walk from the city's main shopping and entertainment area, this inn has suffered from the passage of many tour groups, and a thorough refurbishing is needed. However, for basic Holiday Inn–style amenities at a reasonable price, the hotel delivers. *12 Jalan Raja Laut, Box 11586, 50750 Kuala Lumpur, tel. 03/293–9233 or 800/HOLIDAY, fax 03/293– 9634. 250 rooms. Facilities: Chinese restaurant, coffee shop with Continental food, outdoor pool and snack bar, fitness center, business center, squash court, doctor on call, travel desk. AE, DC, MC, V.*

Inexpensive **Lodge Hotel.** Across from the Hilton in the Golden Triangle, this hotel offers basic air-conditioned accommodation. Everything is a little shabby—carpets have stains and bathrooms need some plaster repair—but the rooms are clean and service is friendly. *Jln. Sultan Ismail, 50250 Kuala Lumpur, tel. 03/ 242–0122, fax 03/241–6819. 50 rooms. Facilities: 24-hr coffee shop, bar, small outdoor pool. DC, V.*

Kuantan **Hyatt Kuantan.** The low-rise hotel opened in 1980, and though *Expensive* the architects were Malaysian and the lobby uses Malaysian ★ redwood, the design gives one a feeling of déjà vu. However, it takes full advantage of the sea breezes and is surrounded by lush cultivated gardens. The more expensive guest rooms facing the sea on the Regency Floor are considerably better in both decor and view than those facing the back of the building. The Kampong Café, built on stilts on the beach, is a romantic spot. *Telok Chempedak, Box 250, 25730 Kuantan, Pahang Darul Makmur, tel. 09/525–211, fax 09/507–577. 185 rooms. Facilities: formal European restaurant, open-air coffee shop, 24-hr room service, outdoor pool with swim-up bar, floodlit tennis and squash courts, fitness center and sauna, water sports, disco; golf nearby. AE, V.*

Inexpensive **Tanjung Gelang Motel.** This small Chinese-owned motel has simple cottages facing the beach. There are no frills, just the basics and a small restaurant, but the Coral Bay Resort (formerly the Ramada) and all its facilities are right next door. To reach this motel from Kuantan, you do need a car. *15 km Jalan Kemaman, 26100 Kuantan, Pahang Darul Makmur, tel. and fax 09/587–254. 40 rooms. Facilities: restaurant. No credit cards.*

Budget **Hotel Kuantan.** Rooms at this hotel across from the Hyatt (and the beach) contain nothing more than a bed, a small table and chair, and an overhead fan. Some rooms do have air-conditioning, and most have an Asian-style private bathroom. The hotel also has a sitting area where guests get together to swap travel tales. *Telok Chempedak Beach, Kuantan, Pahang Darul Makmur, tel. 09/24755. 37 rooms. No credit cards.*

Malacca **Ramada Renaissance.** This 24-story Ramada operates smooth-
Expensive ly for both the businessman and the tourist. The guest rooms
★ are bright, decorated in pastel colors, and equipped with IDD phones, color TV and video, and refrigerator; those overlooking the gardens and shore are obviously more pleasant than those at the back. In addition to the Renaissance floor, with concierge services, there are two nonsmoking floors. In the evening there is usually live entertainment in the Famosa Lounge, and throughout the year the hotel offers various festivities. *Jalam Bendahara, Box 105, 75100 Melaka, tel. 06/ 248–888, fax 06/249–269. 295 rooms. Facilities: Chinese and Continental restaurants, 24-hr coffee shop, 24-hr room service, laundry service, outdoor pool, poolside bar, squash courts, fitness center, business center, function rooms, doctor on call, nightclub, travel desk. AE, DC, MC, V.*

Moderate **City Bayview.** Opened in 1987, this modern 14-story high rise stands in contrast to the older buildings of Malacca. The look of the hotel is strictly functional, with no personality, but the rooms, with motellike furniture and IDD phones, are clean and satisfactory. *Jalan Bendahara, 75100 Melaka, tel. 06/239–888, fax 06/236–699. 181 rooms. Facilities: Chinese and European restaurants, coffee shop, 24-hr room service, outdoor pool, fitness center, business center, laundry service, function rooms, doctor on call, nightclub. AE, DC, MC, V.*

Budget **Majestic Hotel.** If you are looking for a local hotel where you can settle in to write the novel about colonial Malaya, the Majestic has the right ambience. Across from the Melaka River and situated in its own courtyard, the hotel has large, airy public rooms with slow-turning fans. Guest rooms are Spartan, with little more than a bed, a table, and a chair; a few have tired air-conditioning instead of fans. *188 Bunga Raya Rd., 75100 Melaka, tel. 06/222–387. 20 rooms, some with bath. Facilities: restaurant for breakfast. No credit cards.*

Tioman Island **Tioman Island Resort.** This resort—the island's only lodging
Moderate– alternative to guest houses—offers four different levels of ac-
Expensive commodations, which reflect the size of the room and the amenities. The superior rooms are small chalets, and both they and the deluxe rooms have refrigerators and IDD phones. All rooms are air-conditioned and come with their own bathroom, and all guests have access to the sports facilities. The resort is family-oriented, casual and low-key—you are here for the hotel's setting rather than for luxury amenities. However, expansion projects were under way at press time to add upmarket chalets modeled after a Malay house, a plan that will offer spacious rooms with air-conditioning as well as overhead fans. Also, two new restaurants are planned. An additional nine holes are being added to the golf course, and the water sports facilities have been improved. *Pulau Tioman, Pahang, Box 4, 86807 Mersing, Johor, tel. 09/445–445, fax 09/445–718. (Reservations may be made in Singapore, tel. 09/445–444 or, in Kuala Lumpur, tel. 03/242–9611.) 400 rooms. Facilities: restaurant (Chinese, Continental, and Malay foods), cocktail lounge, outdoor pool, snorkeling and scuba diving, Jet Skiing, windsurfing, bicycles, games room, TV lounge, 9-hole golf*

course (currently being extended to 18 holes), horseback rid-ing, tennis, glass-bottom boat, gift shop. AE, MC, V.

Bintan Island

From the tallest buildings in Singapore, you can see the nearby islands of Indonesia. In 30 minutes, you can cross the straits on a hydrofoil ferry south to the Bataam Islands. Bataam is under-going a vast development project that includes a duty-free in-dustrial zone and a tourist complex. However, while it may appeal to Singaporeans looking for cheaper shopping, its inter-est for the long-haul traveler is limited. Lying to its east is the more interesting island of **Bintan,** which is also slated for devel-opment, but primarily for tourists. Every morning two ferries make the 90-minute trip (S$51 one-way) from Finger Pier at Singapore's World Trade Centre and return in the late after-noon.

Bintan's main town is **Tanjong Pinang,** where the primary ac-tivity is shopping at Pasar Pelantar Dua. You can rent a motor boat at the pier to take you up the Snake River through the mangrove swamps to the oldest Chinese temple in Riau; as the boatman poles his way up the small tributary choked with man-groves, it's thrilling to come upon the isolated 300-year-old temple with its murals of hell. You'll be back in time for lunch; try the **Flipper Restaurant** just off Tanjong Pinang's main street, Jalan Merdeka.

If you're staying overnight, the best hotel in Tanjong Pinang is the **Riau Holidays Inn** (53 Jln. Pelanta Dua, tel. 0771/22573; in Singapore, 737–5735), though the rooms are depressing and a little smelly. But the bar lounge, which is built on stilts and looks out over the port, is a good local hangout. To get to the beach you'll need to take a taxi 40 kilometers (24 miles) to the east coast, where the best resort hotel (though not luxurious) is the **Trikora Country Club** (Trikora Beach Resort, no phone; reservations in Singapore, tel. 221–9655). It has just nine rooms, each a small chalet with a balcony overlooking the beach, and it's a true hideaway until the big developers arrive in a couple of years.

For tourist, passport and visa, health, and currency informa-tion, *see* Essential Information for North Sumatra, *below.*

North Sumatra

Traveling in Sumatra is for the adventurous and tolerant; those who need exact schedules, fixed prices, luxury, and planned itineraries will probably not enjoy the island. The structured and organized tourist infrastructure of Singapore, as well as the high level of hygiene, does not exist on Sun.atra. The Indo-nesians are freewheeling entrepreneurs, but all the basic tour-ist amenities are available, as are local people to help direct you to what you want. Sumatrans are friendly and welcoming, and many speak a few words of English. Taxis and a comprehensive bus system link the towns, and the domestic airlines connect the provincial capitals.

Essential Information

Tourist Information The best place to pick up tourist information is at Singapore's **Indonesian Tourist Promotion Office** (#15-07 Ocean Bldg., 10 Collyer Quay, Singapore 0104, tel. 534–2837).

Passports and Visas Passports but no visas are required for citizens of Great Britain, Canada, or the United States wishing to enter Indonesia for less than one month.

Staying Healthy You may want to take antimalaria pills if you plan to stay in out-of-the-way places. Typhoid shots are strongly recommended, and yellow fever and cholera shots are also advised.

When to Go The most popular time to visit Lake Toba is June. Despite being near the equator, the lake's high altitude keeps it cool throughout the year. The wet season is November–February.

Currency At press time, there were 2,000 rupiahs (Rps) to the US$1.

Getting to North Sumatra **Garuda Indonesian Airways** and **Singapore Airlines** have daily hour-long flights from Singapore to Medan. The least expensive way of reaching Medan is by hydrofoil from Singapore to Bataam and by plane to Medan. Domestic airlines are considerably cheaper than international airlines, and all major towns in Indonesia are connected by air routes.

The MS *Gadis Langkasura* ferry makes two trips a week to Penang, Malaysia, and Medan (Belawan Harbour). Sleeping berths are shared by four people, and economy passengers have reclining seats. Schedules continually change, so check with the Indonesian Tourist Promotion Office in Singapore before you commit yourself to this route. Cost: M$65 for a berth; M$55 for an economy seat. Check with the Indonesian Tourist Promotion Board for schedules.

Getting Around North Sumatra Distance traveling in Sumatra will be a combination of airplane, bus, and shared or private taxi. Buses range from unpredictably air-conditioned buses and express buses to crowded, local buses. Driving your own rented car is not advised; the risk of an accident is too great. Taxis do not use meters; fare negotiation is required before you enter the taxi. For a shared taxi, try **Indah Taxi** (Brig-jen Katamso #60, tel. 51-00–36). Private taxis can be found at hotels, bus stations, and airports.

Exploring North Sumatra

Numbers in the margin correspond to points of interest on the North Sumatra map.

A visit to Brastagi and Lake Toba requires two nights. Add another night if you visit the orangutans in Gunung Leuser National Park, and at least two more if you travel to Nias Island.

Medan ❶ If you arrive in **Medan** by plane, the only way into town is by taxi. A fixed rate of 4,800 Rps applies. A small tourist office to the right of the customs shed will supply a map of Medan, change money, and arrange transportation.

Medan, the capital of North Sumatra and the third-largest city in Indonesia, has a population of 2 million people jostling in a city designed for 500,000 people. The streets are bedlam—cars, taxis, bemos, motor scooters, bicycles, and pedestrians going in all directions on streets that have started to be re-

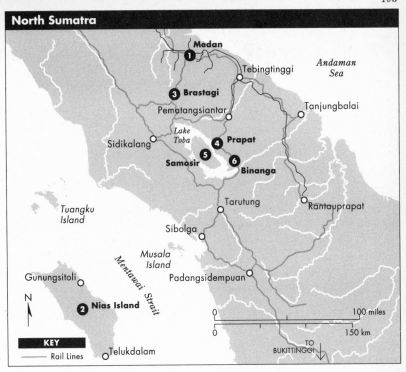

North Sumatra

paired but have never quite been finished. The two major sights are the large, multidome **Mesjid Raye Mosque,** built in 1906 and one of Indonesia's largest, and the Sultan's Palace, the **Isetana Sultan Deli.** Special permission from the tourist office is required to visit the inside of the palace.

The easiest way to visit the **Orangutan Rehabilitation Station** is to hire a taxi and guide for about US$75 for the 2 ½-hour drive. Leave Medan by about 11 AM to reach the **Gunung Leuser National Park** by 2 PM. You will then have a 30-minute walk in tropical heat up to the ranger's hut. A further 15-minute hike up the mountain takes you to the feeding platform where rangers, at 3:30 PM, spend 35 minutes feeding and inspecting the orangutans, preparing them for life in the wild. You need to be relatively fit to make the 45-minute hike, which involves rugged terrain and crossing a creek by raft, but the experience is well worth the effort.

Nias Island ❷ Fly to **Nias Island,** from Medan on Merpati Airlines to Gunungsitoli in the northern part of the island, thus requiring a seven-hour ride on a high-speed ferry down the coast to Telukdalam in the southern area that harbors most of the traditional villages. Alternatively, take a 10-hour ferry from Sibolga; Sibolga may be reached by bus or private taxi via Prapat. In little hilltop villages with stone-paved streets that are lined with unique stilted houses, you will see stone obelisks, huge stone benches, tables, chests, and massive drums, all vestiges of a magnificent megalithic culture that thrived on this once remote island well into the 20th century.

Brastagi
❸
Brastagi, 68 kilometers (41 miles) from Medan, is a refreshing hill station 1,400 meters above sea level that maintains an Old World air from when it was used by Dutch planters to escape the heat. You can stay in Brastagi's charming colonial hotel. Several groups of the Karo Bataks have their villages in the highlands, and one worth a visit is **Lingga,** 15 kilometers (9 miles) from Brastagi. Here you can see the 250- to 300-year-old multifamily tribal houses, which are still used today. Karo Bataks, as well as the Toba Bataks, are descendants from proto-Malay tribes who originally inhabited the border areas of what is now Burma and Thailand. They chose this mountainous region for its isolation, and their patrilineal society remains virtually intact.

Prapat
❹
From Brastagi it is an easy two-hour drive (by bus or taxi) to **Prapat.** The last 30 minutes of the journey are the most dramatic. The road winds through tropical vegetation to a pass, where Lake Toba suddenly is visible spread out below.

Lake Toba (Donau Toba), one of the largest lakes in Southeast Asia and one of the highest in the world, sits 2,953 feet above sea level, surrounded by steep slopes that plunge headlong into the water to depths of 1,476 feet. Prapat is the major resort town on the lake, but almost every visitor takes either a day trip or an overnight stay to Samosir, the 4,000-square-mile hilly island in the middle of the lake and home to the Toba Bataks.

Samosir
❺
A public ferry runs from Prapat's market square to Tomok (in **Samosir**), but the most popular way to get to Samosir is by the boat that boards passengers from the shore near the Hotel Parapat, for a round-trip fare of 2,000 Rps. Other boats go to Tuk Tuk, Ambarita, and Simanindo, and fares for these trips are slightly higher. You may also charter a powerboat for a three-hour trip to Tomok, Tuk Tuk, Ambarita, and Simanindo, which will cost about 35,000 Rps. For travel around Samosir, minibus taxis make irregular trips and there are motorbikes for rent for about 15,000 Rps an hour.

The main tourist destination on Samosir is **Tomok,** where you'll find the tombs of King Sidabutar who ruled in the 1800s, his son, his grandson, and several warriors of rank. Nearby are several Batak houses with curving roofs and intricately carved beams and panels. To reach these cultural attractions, walk 500 yards up from the ferry dock past stalls selling souvenirs, artifacts, and Batik cloth. Keep in mind the actual purchase price is 30%–40% of the initial asking price.

Tuk Tuk, reached either by road (a 30-minute walk) or by ferry, is the hotel village of the island. Next is **Ambarita,** the village where, in the past, miscreants had their heads lopped off. You can still see the courtyard where the king held council. Ancient, weathered stone chairs and tables form a ring in front of the chief's traditional house.

At the northern tip of the island is the village of **Simanindo,** site of a fine old traditional house, once the home of a Batak king. The village has been declared an open-air museum, and the one house not to miss is the Long House (Rumak Bolon) with its fine carvings and the sculpted depiction of the god Gajah Dompak. His job was to frighten off evil spirits, and by the look of him, he should have been good at it.

Binanga   Before you leave Prapat, consider a short excursion to **Binanga**
❻   (sometimes known as Lumban Binanga), approximately 15 kilometers (9 miles) from Prapat on the road to Bukittinggi. Park
at the side of the road (you'll see a sign) and walk down the hill
past some new houses and terraced paddy fields to a cluster of
five traditional Batak houses that are 150 to 200 years old. Few
tourists come here, so Binanga has much less commercial bustle than the villages on Samosir.

Dining and Lodging

The following is a sampling of hotels in North Sumatra. Most
restaurants of consequence are located in hotels.

Category	Cost*
Very Expensive	over 100,000 Rps (US$50)
Expensive	60,000–100,000 Rps (US$30–US$50)
Moderate	30,000–60,000 Rps (US$15–US$30)
Inexpensive	15,000–30,000 Rps (US$7.50–US$15)
Budget	under 15,000 Rps (US$7.50)

*All prices are for a standard double room with bath, exclud-
ing 10% service charge and 5% government tax.*

Brastagi   **Bukit Kubu Hotel.** This wonderful old colonial-style hotel is the
Moderate–   area's best. Ask for a double suite with a view of the mountains
Expensive   (the price is only US$5 more than the standard rooms). Lunch
★   is served on a breezy terrace; dinner inside in the surprisingly
formal dining room. Starched linen and billowing lace curtains
are reminiscent of the 1930s, when Dutch planters came here to
relax. Today, the hotel is popular with wealthy folk from Medan
who come for weekends in the cool mountain air. *Jalan
Sempurna 2, Brastagi, North Sumatra, tel. 0628/20832. Booking office: Jalan Jenderal Sudirman 36, Medan, tel. 061/
519636. 76 rooms. Facilities: laundry, gift shop. AE, V.*

Medan   **Tiara Medan Hotel.** This clean, smart hotel, with a fresh-look-
Very Expensive   ing dining room offering standard Chinese, European, and Indonesian fare for lunch and the more formal Amberita
Restaurant for dinner, is Medan's best hotel. Guest rooms are
well maintained, spacious, and air-conditioned. The hotel offers a conference center for delegates and recreational facilities. *Jalan Cut Mutia, Medan, tel. 061/516000, fax 061/510177.
204 rooms. Facilities: 2 restaurants, lounge bar with occasional evening entertainment, 24-hr room service, health club, tennis and squash courts, outdoor pool, newsstand, travel desk,
conference center. AE, DC, V.*

Budget   **Hotel Melati.** This is a good budget hotel with well-swept
rooms, none of which has a private bathroom. It is located near
the Garuda Plaza, where one can go for coffee and air-conditioning. *Jalan Amalun 6, Medan, no phone. 26 rooms without
bath. Facilities: shared toilets and cold-water showers, lounge
for coffee. No credit cards.*

Prapat   **Hotel Patra Jasa.** About 5 kilometers (3 miles) from Prapat on a
Very Expensive   bluff overlooking the lake, this hotel is the best retreat in the
area. For peace and quiet, nothing can beat it, but the location
makes every trip into Prapat an excursion, and its facilities are

somewhat limited. Guest rooms are located in pavilions surrounding the main lodge, about 10 rooms in each. Hot water is
available most of the time. *Jalan Siuhan, Peninsula Prapat,
Prapat, tel. 0664/41796. 45 rooms. Facilities: restaurant serving Chinese, European, and Indonesian food, outdoor pool,
tennis, golf. AE, V.*

Expensive **Natour Hotel Parapat.** The best rooms here are in the bungalows facing Lake Toba. They are comfortably large, worn, but
reasonably well furnished and have the benefit of lounge and
patio. All the bungalows are scattered on a terraced slope covered with flowerbeds. Recent upgrading of the main lounges
and dining room has made this the best hotel in Prapat. *Jalan
Marihat 1, Prapat, tel. 0664/41012. 85 rooms. Facilities: dining room serving Chinese, European, and Indonesian food,
bar, room service, hot water in the mornings and evenings, private lakefront. AE, V.*

Budget **Risis Hotel.** For a budget hotel that is clean and friendly, this
small whitewashed building on the street that leads into the
market square is the best. Some rooms come with a private
bath, all have bare walls and floors and minimal furniture.
*Jalan Haranggaol 39, Prapat, tel. 0664/41392. 20 rooms. Facil-
ities: limited breakfast. No credit cards.*

Samosir **Carolina Cottage.** Accommodations here are in Batak houses
Inexpensive– perched on the edge of the lake. All have spectacular views, but
Moderate only a few have hot running water. The service is friendly and
★ helpful. The best rooms, in cottages on stilts above the lake, are
No. 40 and No. 41. Continental breakfasts, snacks, and dinners
are served. If you cannot obtain a room here, there is the
Silintong (tel. 0622/41345) or the Toba Beach Hotel (tel. 0622/
41275), both down the road and both bare-bones utilitarian hotels. *Tuk Tuk Siadong, Danau Toba, tel. 0625/41520. 23 rooms
with bath. No credit cards.*

Index

Fodor's Travel Guides

U.S. Guides

Alaska

Arizona

Boston

California

Cape Cod, Martha's Vineyard, Nantucket

The Carolinas & the Georgia Coast

Chicago

Disney World & the Orlando Area

Florida

Hawaii

Las Vegas, Reno, Tahoe

Los Angeles

Maine, Vermont, New Hampshire

Maui

Miami & the Keys

New England

New Orleans

New York City

Pacific North Coast

Philadelphia & the Pennsylvania Dutch Country

San Diego

San Francisco

Santa Fe, Taos, Albuquerque

Seattle & Vancouver

The South

The U.S. & British Virgin Islands

The Upper Great Lakes Region

USA

Vacations in New York State

Vacations on the Jersey Shore

Virginia & Maryland

Waikiki

Washington, D.C.

Foreign Guides

Acapulco, Ixtapa, Zihuatanejo

Australia & New Zealand

Austria

The Bahamas

Baja & Mexico's Pacific Coast Resorts

Barbados

Berlin

Bermuda

Brazil

Budapest

Budget Europe

Canada

Cancun, Cozumel, Yucatan Penisula

Caribbean

Central America

China

Costa Rica, Belize, Guatemala

Czechoslovakia

Eastern Europe

Egypt

Euro Disney

Europe

Europe's Great Cities

France

Germany

Great Britain

Greece

The Himalayan Countries

Hong Kong

India

Ireland

Israel

Italy

Italy's Great Cities

Japan

Kenya & Tanzania

Korea

London

Madrid & Barcelona

Mexico

Montreal & Quebec City

Morocco

The Netherlands Belgium & Luxembourg

New Zealand

Norway

Nova Scotia, Prince Edward Island & New Brunswick

Paris

Portugal

Rome

Russia & the Baltic Countries

Scandinavia

Scotland

Singapore

South America

Southeast Asia

South Pacific

Spain

Sweden

Switzerland

Thailand

Tokyo

Toronto

Turkey

Vienna & the Danube Valley

Yugoslavia

Special Series

Fodor's Affordables

Affordable Europe

Affordable France

Affordable Germany

Affordable Great
Britain

Affordable Italy

**Fodor's Bed &
Breakfast and
Country Inns Guides**

California

Mid-Atlantic Region

New England

The Pacific Northwest

The South

The West Coast

The Upper Great
Lakes Region

Canada's Great
Country Inns

Cottages, B&Bs and
Country Inns of
England and Wales

The Berkeley Guides

On the Loose in
California

On the Loose in
Eastern Europe

On the Loose in
Mexico

On the Loose in the
Pacific Northwest &
Alaska

**Fodor's Exploring
Guides**

Exploring California

Exploring Florida

Exploring France

Exploring Germany

Exploring Paris

Exploring Rome

Exploring Spain

Exploring Thailand

Fodor's Flashmaps

New York

Washington, D.C.

Fodor's Pocket Guides

Pocket Bahamas

Pocket Jamaica

Pocket London

Pocket New York
City

Pocket Paris

Pocket Puerto Rico

Pocket San Francisco

Pocket Washington,
D.C.

Fodor's Sports

Cycling

Hiking

Running

Sailing

The Insider's Guide
to the Best Canadian
Skiing

**Fodor's Three-In-Ones
(guidebook, language
cassette, and phrase
book)**

France

Germany

Italy

Mexico

Spain

**Fodor's
Special-Interest
Guides**

Cruises and Ports
of Call

Disney World & the
Orlando Area

Euro Disney

Healthy Escapes

London Companion

Skiing in the USA
& Canada

Sunday in New York

**Fodor's Touring
Guides**

Touring Europe

Touring USA:
Eastern Edition

Touring USA:
Western Edition

**Fodor's Vacation
Planners**

Great American
Vacations

National Parks of the
West

**The Wall Street
Journal Guides to
Business Travel**

Europe

International Cities

Pacific Rim

USA & Canada

WHEREVER YOU TRAVEL, *H*ELP IS NEVER FAR AWAY.

From planning your trip to providing travel assistance along the way, American Express® Travel Service Offices* are always there to help.

SINGAPORE

American Express Travel Service
#01-04/05, Winsland House
3 Killiney Road
65-235-5788

American Express Travel Service
304 Orchard Road
#01-06 Lucky Plaza
65-235-5789

American Express Travel Service
15 Beach Road
#01-02 Beach Centre
65-339-3695

PENINSULAR MALAYSIA

American Express Travel Service
Bangunan Mas, 5th floor
Jalan Sultan Ismail
Kuala Lumpur
60-3-261-4819

Mayflower Acme Tours
Angkasa Raya Building
Jalan Ampang, Kuala Lumpur
60-3-248-6700

Mayflower Acme Tours
A-7348 Jalan Beserah
Kuantan
60-9-501-866

Sarawak Travel Agencies
70 Padungan Road
Kuching
60-82-243-708

Discovery Tours
G28, Ground Floor
Wisma Sabah, Locked Bag 23
Kota Kinabula
60-88-221-244

Mayflower Acme Tours
Ton Chong Bldg.
274 Victoria St.
George Town
60-4-628-196

INDONESIA

PT Pacto Ltd.
Jalan Brigjen Katamso 35-D
Medan, North Sumatra
62-61-510-081